Advance Praise for

CREATING
WEALTH

We've seen the local food movement grow and spread, and the local energy movement too. But the local money idea is just as important; here's some common sense explanation of why and how!

— Bill McKibben, author *Deep Economy*

Creating Wealth is the most practical and comprehensive guide for creating community wealth. It helps cities envision and model richer alternatives; healthier, more equitable, sustainable futures. This timely book deserves a wide audience.

— Hazel Henderson, author *Ethical Markets: Growing The Green Economy* and the Green Transition Scoreboard®

Two masters have come together to create an instant classic. Few can hold a candle to Gwendolyn Hallsmith when it comes to a systems approach that enables communities to vision a different future. Bernard Lietaer as an originator of the Euro is without peer when it comes to both the theory and practice of expanding the possible by creating new currencies. Together, they share a commitment to renewing cities and creating a sustainable world for all endangered species — including our own. This is a book that provides framework, theory, examples galore and tools. Get it. Use it. For us at TimeBanking and for our law school course in System Change, this is required reading.

— Edgar S. Cahn, PhD, JD, Ashoka Fellow,
Distinguished Professor of Law,
originator, TimeBanking, Washington, DC

CREATING WEALTH

GROWING LOCAL ECONOMIES WITH LOCAL CURRENCIES

Gwendolyn Hallsmith & Bernard Lietaer

Preface by Dennis Meadows
Foreword by Hunter Lovins

NEW SOCIETY PUBLISHERS

Cover design by Diane McIntosh.
Cover Images: Piggy Bank — © iStock (3dsguru);
Calgary skyline — © iStock (SensorSpot); Border design — ©iStock (sunnyfrog)

Printed in Canada. First printing April 2011.

Paperback ISBN: 978-0-86571-667-4
eISBN: 978-1-55092-477-0

Inquiries regarding requests to reprint all or part of *Creating Wealth*
should be addressed to New Society Publishers at the address below.

To order directly from the publishers, please call toll-free (North America)
1-800-567-6772, or order online at www.newsociety.com

Any other inquiries can be directed by mail to:

New Society Publishers
P. O. Box 189, Gabriola Island, BC V0R 1X0, Canada
(250) 247-9737

New Society Publishers' mission is to publish books that contribute in fundamental ways
to building an ecologically sustainable and just society, and to do so with the least possible
impact on the environment, in a manner that models this vision. We are committed to
doing this not just through education, but through action. Our printed, bound books
are printed on Forest Stewardship Council-certified acid-free paper that is **100% post-
consumer recycled** (100% old growth forest-free), processed chlorine free, and printed
with vegetable-based, low-VOC inks, with covers produced using FSC-certified stock. New
Society also works to reduce its carbon footprint, and purchases carbon offsets based on
an annual audit to ensure a carbon neutral footprint. For further information, or to browse
our full list of books and purchase securely, visit our website at: www.newsociety.com

LIBRARY AND ARCHIVES CANADA CATALOGUING IN PUBLICATION

Hallsmith, Gwendolyn
Creating wealth : growing local economies with local currencies / Gwendolyn Hallsmith
& Bernard Lietaer.

Includes bibliographical references and index.
ISBN 978-0-86571-667-4

1. Wealth. 2. Cooperation. 3. Sustainable development. 4. City planning —
Economic aspects. I. Lietaer, Bernard A. II. Title.

HD75.H34 2011   338.9   C2011-902041-6

NEW SOCIETY PUBLISHERS
www.newsociety.com

MIX
Paper from
responsible sources
FSC
www.fsc.org   FSC™ C016245

As this book goes to print,
we stand at the dawn of a new era on Earth.

We hope that this work will help in some small way
to build the bridge to a brighter future
for all of Earth's children.

Denise—
Good luck
with your www ork!
Gwendolyn
Hallsmith

Contents

Preface

by Dennis Meadows

A century from now social analysts will look back with angry astonishment at the extent our generation accepted the economists' fantasy — happiness requires perpetual economic growth. This may have been true once; definitely now it is false. Indeed, the exponentially expanding use of energy and resources brought by pursuit of growth now erodes the foundations for the happiness, even threatens the survival, of our species.

The growing numbers of people who recognize this tend to seek technological changes — factor four improvements in resource use, shifts to renewable energy sources, sequestration of carbon dioxide, genetic modifications of plant strains, and others. These are helpful. However, none of these efforts will succeed without a fundamental change in our understanding of human wealth. And that will require profound changes in our systems of money.

Those who gain profit from the current global system obviously will vigorously resist any efforts to change it. And they will prevail until industrial society collapses. Current policies will be desperately pursued until they must be changed in response to crisis. But individuals, families, communities, perhaps even regions, can begin now proactively to make the necessary changes that will lead to true happiness and sustainable wealth.

I know of no other pair better qualified than Bernard Lietaer and Gwendolyn Hallsmith to offer the theoretical understanding and the practical experience required for useful insights on these issues. This book is an extremely important and very unique resource. It offers theoretical insights and practical actions for those who want to respond now to the most important global issue of our time.

DENNIS MEADOWS is co-author of *Limits to Growth* and *Beyond the Limits*.

FOREWORD

Natural Capitalism Plus

by Hunter Lovins

Creating Wealth is a book that the world has needed for a very long time.

Arguably, if the economists and accountants who have run the world's financial system off a cliff had read this book, we'd all have a great deal more wealth now, and the world would not be in the parlous straits in which we all now find ourselves.

Its authors know whereof they speak and have practiced wealth creation in communities around the world. Bernard, Gwen and I first worked together on a project called LASER — Local Action for Sustainable Economic Renewal. Gwen and I came up with the name for the project on a very long (and scary) drive to Belgrade, Yugoslavia from a workshop we'd delivered in Novi Sad, Serbia. The war in Kosovo had just ended, and Serbia was rebuilding their economy from the ruins. America's Development Foundation (ADF) had invited us to Novi Sad because the local community resource people needed training on how to foster local economic development in hard times. Gwen brought the expertise she'd developed in such challenging economies as Kazakhstan and the townships of South Africa. I brought economic development lessons from Afghanistan, Jamaica and the hollows of Appalachia.

We realized during the workshop that people around the world needed the ideas we were giving the Serbians. When people in a community work together on economic development, they need to understand and productively use several forms of capital. Natural capital — the environmental services provided by Mother Earth — is critical, but so are the forms of human and social capital, historic and cultural capital, built capital. And the means we use to make exchanges are also very important. ADF funded the development of an international workbook and resource guide so that people trying to jump-start their economy would know how to begin, and LASER was born.

Natural Capitalism offers the way for businesses to profit by working with nature instead of against it. *Creating Wealth* likewise provides the basis for communities to grow their local economies by investing in all the forms of capital that lead to sustainable wealth. Community capitalism builds community assets so that enterprises, organizations and individuals can prosper. *Natural Capitalism* is the business model of the 21st century economy, and *Creating Wealth* is the community economic development model that business and citizens need to be successful. The two go hand in hand — businesses can't succeed without community investment in infrastructure, education, health and the rule of law. Communities can't succeed without the entrepreneurial initiatives that provide us with the products and services we need.

Using the strategies described here, businesses can further expand their profitability as they implement environmental stewardship and employee well-being — even in tough times — by finding alternative means of exchange. The example of the WIR system in Switzerland shows us that complementary currencies make the economy more resilient and significantly reduce the built-in growth imperative that drives environmental destruction and economic dislocation.

Growth and profit are key elements of the economy. With this book, Bernard and Gwen demonstrate that far from being a neutral means of exchange, the financial system serves as an almost invisible driver of unnecessary and unhealthy growth — the ideology of the cancer cell. By expanding the diversity of exchanges, we can achieve the growth we need — growth in intelligence, health, natural beauty, the arts, spiritual development, recreation and peace — and eliminate the unproductive waste and destruction that now threatens life on earth.

Welcome to the future. You're going to like living there.

L. HUNTER LOVINS is President of the Natural Capitalism Inc. (www.nat cap inc.com). Ms. Lovins has lectured extensively in over 15 countries, including at the World Economic Forum at Davos, The International Symposium on Sustainable Development in Shanghai, the Global Economic Forum, and the World Summit on Sustainable Development. She has consulted for industries and governments worldwide, and has co-authored nine books, including the 1999 book *Natural Capitalism*.

Acknowledgments

Every book comes into being with many hands shaping its birth. Beyond the creative work, there are also all the trees that provide the paper, the minerals that provide the ink, and the energy needed to give it life and shape. We are grateful to all the bright minds that influenced our work, and all of Earth's abundance for making it possible.

Gwendolyn is particularly grateful to Bernard, who has taught her much about the world of money, and whose patience with her learning process has shaped her thinking and helped her find new ways to initiate new currency projects. Three new currencies are currently being created and used in Vermont, where she lives with her family. George Hallsmith, Gwendolyn's husband, is a tireless editor and provides so much support for all her work, it is hard to find words to express how much an integral part of this work he is. Her son, Dylan Hallsmith, is now studying International Politics at George Mason University, but his support and tolerance of a mother who leaves for weeks at a time to get the book written is deeply appreciated.

Perhaps more than anyone, Gwendolyn's parents and family are also worth mentioning. Wesley and Joan Hall set amazing examples of principled, intelligent people who worked hard for what they believe. Joan died in 2007, but Wesley continues to be very interested in and supportive of Gwendolyn's work (even if he does refer to all these complementary currencies as "funny money"). Her sisters, Gaylynn and Gretchen, are both artists and create beautiful new ideas and realities every day. They are an inspiration.

The staff at New Society Publishers have been great to work with — Chris and Judith have been faithful to this rather unusual book project, which started out with the premise that it would take over three years to write, simply because we wanted to bring some of the projects we were developing to fruition. They kept the faith that it would get written, and it did. In the meantime, several new currencies have been developed in both the United States and Europe as a result of our collaboration, so this is a book that has shown real results even before it went to print.

Betsy Nuse, the editor, has worked hard to get all the editing done quickly and painlessly. Her assistance with all the vagaries of style and clarity have been enormously helpful. The marketing team at New Society are also amazing—I was never so surprised to find that people could purchase advance copies on Amazon.com before we had even finished the editing.

Other editing assistance from Gina Ottoboni came at a critical time when my schedule was very demanding and I needed help pulling the last pieces together. Finally, I'm grateful to the Balaton Group and Dennis Meadows, who saw the importance of what we were talking about and scheduled the 2010 meeting in Iceland. That gave us a reason to travel there and meet with all the activists who were trying to put that country back on its feet. They also were an inspiration, and we wish them the best as the country struggles with real economic challenges.

INTRODUCTION

Cities and Economies

Creating wealth — the idea catches people by surprise. Our system tends to instill the idea that our collective wealth adds up to a finite bottom line of financial assets, and the question is mainly one of distribution, not of creation. The call for lower taxes, the resistance to higher minimum wages, the idea that wealth held at the highest levels "trickles down" all contain this hidden assumption — there is only so much wealth out there, and we all need to struggle to get our piece of a finite, limited pie. Yet history and everyday reality tell a different story: we live in a world of expanding pies, and while some things on the planet are finite (the land area available, the fertile soils, the fresh water and fossil fuels, to name a few) there is no limit to human ingenuity, creativity and imagination.

Our ingenuity and innovation have expanded the wealth of the human species by orders of magnitude, especially over the last century. We have collectively built a remarkable wealth creation machine, and yet its construction over time has made most of us — even the people who turn its wheels and keep it in working order — blind to how it works. This new marvel has resulted in a middle-class lifestyle in the developed parts of the world that makes some of the royalty and aristocracy of yesterday look hardscrabble by comparison.

If time travel were possible and we managed to go back before the industrial era to talk about computers, iPods, the Internet, cellphones, automobiles and airplanes, the people there would think we were wizards and witches, and they would probably burn us at the stake. Central heat and running water were not common until the mid 1900s. Tours of the ancient manorial houses and castles of Europe reveal that their relative levels of creature comforts were on par with the modern middle class in Europe, Asia, North and South America.

We create wealth. We do it as a society, not as individuals, despite what the dominant myth of rugged individualism in North America would have you believe. Farmers have a hard time bringing their produce to market without decent roads. Merchants depend on a reliable currency to sell their goods and services. Even some of the iconic capitalists of the early 20th century — the Rockefellers, Carnegies and Mellons — depended on taxpayer-funded infrastructure to amass the vast fortunes that still form the foundation of companies like Exxon/Mobil, US Steel and Alcan. Even today, Bill Gates would be just another hacker without the laws our governments have passed protecting intellectual property.

Wealth's Foundation

One of the primary mechanisms for the creation of wealth is our banking and monetary system. We all put our money into the banks — the black box of the economy — and we assume the money will be there when we go to withdraw it. At least part of our mind probably believes that the money is there. We receive statements every month that say it's there, and we earn interest on the deposits.

Yet like the myth of the self-made millionaire, the presence of our money in the bank is an illusion. Banks use the deposits they have to loan money out to individuals and businesses — this is how they earn the interest they pay on our deposits, after all. The fractional reserve system, the legal structure governing how banks operate, requires that banks only maintain in the order of 10% of the money we have placed on deposit as a reserve. In other words, for every dollar we deposit, the bank can create an additional $9 in loans to businesses. They have the power to create financial wealth by issuing new money.

So, how is *real* wealth created? It is not the slips of paper we call cash. History has shown time and again that paper (and now electronic) representations of wealth are only as good as our collective confidence in their value. In this book, we will show how the roots of real wealth lie in our shared values, understanding and institutional structures, but also in the different forms of capital we generate and regenerate as a community. The word *capital* carries an implicit meaning that speaks to a regenerative capacity — it is, as we will explain in Chapter 3, an asset that can produce other assets. Of course, the foundation of all our wealth is the ecological integrity of the planet we call home...it is the source of all the regenerative capacities we need the most — land, air, water, food, materials and energy.

The singular form of money we have created through our laws and institutional arrangements has been a cornerstone of financial wealth through the 19th and 20th centuries. But the demands of the 21st century and the imperatives of the global challenges of climate change, resource scarcity and unprecedented growth in human populations call us to a more comprehensive understanding of wealth and more democratic and resilient wealth creation processes and mechanisms. Most of these alternatives can be initiated at the local level by cities and other organizations. City leaders can play a role in the education, funding and structures required to give us all a voice in the creation of sustainable wealth.

Overview of the Book

The original title of this book was *Intentional Cities, Intentional Economies* — to emphasize the link between the actions cities take and the health of their local economies. Cities don't often recognize this link — or realize that they have the capacity to improve their economies. They can do this by bringing the community together around a shared vision, setting goals and identifying strategies to make their local economy more self-reliant, more vibrant. They can help their citizens achieve real and lasting wealth. In this way, cities become more *intentional*, meaning that they are moving in a direction they choose rather than being buffeted by the winds of change. When they focus on the ways they create wealth, they also choose the focus, the intention, they want to give to their economies.

Part I of the book describes the process by which wealth is created and explains the role of the existing financial system in this process. Part II describes a variety of different forms of local currencies, circulating in parallel with the official currency, that address specific problems that cities and communities face. Part III is designed as a case study and "how to" manual — it describes how several cities have managed to engage their populations in long-term sustainability planning and how these efforts have either supported local currencies or helped create them, as well as some lessons learned about when it might not be possible to succeed.

We hope you find the book inspiring and that it gives you enough information to move forward. Our compendium of community level currencies is not exhaustive — there are many hundreds we have not described. But the structures and mechanisms we include are all replicable in other domains — they are only limited by your imagination and the courage you want to take as a leader. Introducing new ideas is never easy, and we will see that introducing new ideas about money has its own unique challenges. More on this in the book's conclusion — until then, enjoy!

— Gwendolyn and Bernard
Reykjavik, Iceland

PART I

LOCAL ECONOMICS

CHAPTER 1

What is Wealth?

Wealth consists not in having great possessions,
but in having few wants.

EPICTETUS

The appeal of big prize lottery tickets comes in part from the fantasy the tickets allow. We imagine all the things we could do, charities, projects, real change that we could help make happen. There is no denying the appeal of vast sums of money. In our dreams, money solves all our problems, gives us resources to meet needs we never knew we had. But is it wealth?

You might have picked up this book because you thought it would tell you something about how you can increase your own personal wealth — and it will. But *Creating Wealth* is not another get-rich-quick scheme — this book will help you find and create wealth in places you might not expect. It also might show you how wealthy you already are.

Redefining Wealth

Wealth. It's something we all want. Wealthy is rich, after all — but rich in what? In possessions, money, income? This depends on how you define the word. Its original meaning, from the Old English *weal* (as in commonweal), was simply prosperity or well-being."[1] What a notion! How far from the meaning many of us have come to associate with the word.

Wealth is more than the accumulation of money and resources, and it can be generated in ways other than through conventional financial means. In order to truly capture the wealth of our societies, our cultures and our environments, we have to pay heed to that older notion of wealth as well-being. We might think that winning the lottery will make us wealthy and that wealth will make us happy, but we also know that it doesn't always work that way. While it's true that poverty does make for unhappiness, lots of money doesn't necessarily buy happiness.

We may have seen cases where someone who has had very low income wins the lottery or obtains a big court settlement — and yet the money often doesn't manage to improve their lives very much. In many such cases, things get worse as the stress of possessing money and all its new demands take their toll — how to keep it, suddenly meeting relatives and friends you never knew you had, con artists and an army of "investment advisors."

How do we obtain well-being, if acquiring more money doesn't do it? When are we happy? We know the answer to this question — we have a sense of well-being when all of our needs are met. Not just the basic needs of food, clothing and shelter. But also the need to be a creative participant in our community, to have a voice in our own destiny, to pursue our own spiritual development unhindered by social sanction, to have time to rest, play and just be with our families. Our needs are multi-faceted, and yet with the dominant emphasis on the consumer economy, the major economic actors — businesses and corporations — are always advertising to convince us to buy our way to fulfillment.

> We don't need money. We need the things that money can buy.

Overweight? Buy a diet plan and an exercise machine. Unhappy? There are lots of self-improvement programs you can buy. Spiritually lost? Buy a book, a videotape, join a successful megachurch or take a vacation at a resort. Our need for self-expression is increasingly met through the clothes we wear, the cars we drive. Arts and music are left to the professionals who have their own goods and services available for sale. And yet after all this we find that the consumer solutions don't work — the temporary gratification we get from new products only deepens the underlying need. But if we can't buy our way to happiness, there has to be another way.

We need to redefine wealth as the first step in charting a course towards *sustainable* wealth. So what is meant by that? Remember the notion of commonweal (public well-being)? Developing real wealth implies making choices that enable all members of the community to attain well-being. Sustainable wealth means projecting that notion into the future, much as the World Commission on Environment and Development did when it defined sustainable development as "meeting the needs of the present without compromising the ability of future generations to meet their own needs."[2] If we had sustainable wealth, we would have a community with *well-being*—a community whose needs were met without borrowing its wealth from future generations.

A Systems Perspective

What are our needs, and how are they satisfied? It is possible to do an empirical evaluation simply by looking around at the different institutions, programs, goods and services that are offered in society. Not that all of them meet real needs—some are obviously there because a *want* or an artificial need has been created, but taking an inventory of the assets we have—assets being defined as need satisfiers—gives us a good starting point.

 Human and Social Development needs: health and well-being

 Empowerment needs: equity, conflict resolution, self-determination

 Economic needs: income, meaningful work

 Material needs: housing, communication systems, transportation, energy, waste management, food

 Environmental needs: air, water, biodiversity, pollination, stable climate

FIGURE 1.1. Human Needs and Community Systems

Before we can be a contributing part of any community, we have a need for *human development*. We need education, healthcare, self-esteem, skills, recreational opportunities. There are assets in our communities that meet these needs — schools, universities, child care programs, wellness and medical services, hospitals, recreation programs and facilities. When the systems are in place to help us all be healthy, productive and happy people, we can also say that our community has sufficient human capital. *Human capital* can be defined as the capacity communities have to further our development as human beings, along with the aggregate skills, knowledge and abilities people in the community have and can continue to maintain.

We also have *social needs* — the needs that can only be fulfilled by being part of a community. We need to have a sense of connectedness, a sense of community. We need to feel safe, to express ourselves and enjoy the beauty of our surroundings. We need a sense of meaning and purpose, and meaning is invariably generated only through relationships (relationships to our children, our family, our country, or to our idea of the divine). These human and social needs have given rise over the centuries to many of the religions and spiritual traditions. We need supportive relationships, networks of friends and a sense that we're contributing to the community. When these needs are satisfied, we can say that we have many social assets. When we have systems in place that insure we can continue to meet our social and cultural needs as a community, we can say that we have sufficient *social and cultural capital*.

To make decisions, resolve conflict and to insure that we all have a level of equity, we all have a need for *empowerment*. The institutions we have established to govern ourselves, the programs in the community that help people resolve disputes and the laws and regulations we have to provide a just and peaceful society are the assets we have in this area. The *institutional capital* in our community is the legal framework and the traditions, structures and other foundations that enable our societies to continue to recreate the institutions they need.

When people think of needs, the first things that often come to mind are the basic needs of food, clothing and shelter. These *material needs* are obviously important, and the buildings, manufactured products, technology and infrastructure we develop in our communities are the assets we have to satisfy these needs. When we have good affordable housing, safe and healthy drinking water, effective systems for recycling and re-using waste, renewable energy systems, healthy local food production, communication systems that link us up with each other and the rest of the world, we have the *built and technological capital* we need to prosper.

Our material needs go beyond what we make ourselves, obviously, and so we can also speak of the *environmental needs* we have. We need clean air to breathe, diverse ecosystems that support a wide variety of plant and animal life, a stable climate, assimilative capacity for our waste products, water to support other forms of life as well as for us to wash, drink and enjoy. We need healthy soils, pollinators; all of these things are the *environmental assets* that serve as our basic life-support system. When the ecosystem is healthy and productive, the core regenerative capacity of the ecosystem is the *natural capital* that we need for sustainable communities.

We've described several kinds of assets and capital that satisfy the needs we have, and still there has been no mention yet of the financial assets and capital we typically associate with the words *money* and *investment*. That's partly because money is really more of a means to an end than a need in itself. We don't really need money. We need the things that money can buy. We don't need financial capital for its own sake if we can obtain the things it buys. The exchange capacity of money is now, and hopefully in the future, one of the key reasons we need it. Money helps us exchange things that are of value to us — like our time and labor — for things that are of value to someone else.

Money, however, is not the only medium of exchange. After all, people have been exchanging goods and services with each other for millennia without using money. You help your neighbor put on a new roof. He fills your cavities and gives you a new crown. You drive your friend's kids to school. She baby-sits your kids. In both these examples, no money changes hands, but goods and services do. The value of this type of exchange is another asset and a form of capital — *potential exchange capital*.

Our community systems have developed over centuries, driven by our needs and the necessity of satisfying them. When we speak of a wealthy community, we mean one that has the capacity to meet a wide variety of human needs, one that had invested in all these forms of capital: social, cultural, human, institutional, built, technological, natural,

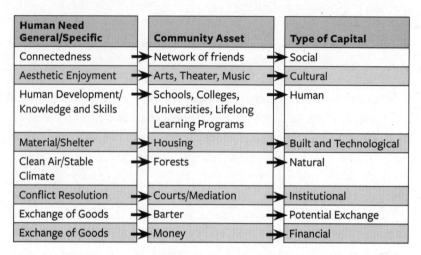

Human Need General/Specific	Community Asset	Type of Capital
Connectedness	➤ Network of friends	➤ Social
Aesthetic Enjoyment	➤ Arts, Theater, Music	➤ Cultural
Human Development/ Knowledge and Skills	➤ Schools, Colleges, Universities, Lifelong Learning Programs	➤ Human
Material/Shelter	➤ Housing	➤ Built and Technological
Clean Air/Stable Climate	➤ Forests	➤ Natural
Conflict Resolution	➤ Courts/Mediation	➤ Institutional
Exchange of Goods	➤ Barter	➤ Potential Exchange
Exchange of Goods	➤ Money	➤ Financial

FIGURE 1.2. How Needs, Assets and Capital Relate to Each Other

financial and potential exchange. Creating and maintaining these diverse forms of capital over time is the sustainability challenge.

More than half of humanity now lives in cities, and this trend is expected to continue for at least another decade. So our community wealth is often the wealth that can be found in our cities. Cities are monuments to collective human endeavor over thousands of years. They form the physical, spatial and even the cognitive structures that meet so many of our needs. Realizing this, the bulk of the concrete examples of wealth creation we discuss will focus on cities.

The Wealth of Cities

To understand alternative paths to individual, community and economic well-being in an urban context, we need to look at how cities work, and we need city leadership to address the critical issues of a sustainable economy. In *Cities and the Wealth of Nations*, Jane Jacobs identified urban regions as the most important driver of economic growth throughout history. She documented both how cities and regions had the economic clout to import goods from other areas and also how they devised new ways to replace these imports with locally produced goods and services. This import replacement was the key source of urban economic expansion.[3]

Since the Earth Summit in Rio de Janeiro in 1992, cities all over the world have played a leading role in the efforts to stabilize global climate and address environmental destruction. There have been several different movements — sustainable cities, healthy cities, ecocities, resilient cities and most recently transition towns — and several different new organizations organized to support cities' efforts. ICLEI was one of the first; it was originally the International Council for Local Environmental Initiatives, but has been renamed ICLEI: Local Governments for Sustainability.[4]

The scope and depth of this movement is confirmed by the proliferation of other organizations that have emerged over the past two decades. This includes, for instance, the Institute for Sustainable Communities, the World Health Organization's Healthy Cities program, Healthy Cities International, Ecocities International, the Center for Resilient Cities, the Cities PLUS Network, Global Community Initiatives and the largest one of all — United Cities and Local Governments (UCLG) — a new international congress of cities established in 2004 when several global coalitions of cities (The International Union of Local Authorities, Metropolis and the World Federation of United Cities) merged into one organization.[5] UCLG's Millennium Cities Campaign embraces the United Nations Millennium Development Goals, which put a sustainable environment and a sustainable local economy on the same page. Cities are increasingly aware that the solutions to climate change and environmental problems are embedded in the economies we have created. These cities are positioned to be key catalysts for large-scale change.

Cities take action on several levels, ranging from broad policy changes like rezoning an area of the city from commercial to industrial to even small actions like buying paper towels for public restrooms. The policies take different forms — long-term planning documents with a vision statement, goals, targets and strategies, operating budgets and capital plans, ordinances and regulations, annual goals and policies to guide operations such as personnel and purchasing policies. The long-term plans guide ordinance changes and budgets, and in turn, the budgets, capital plans and annual goals shape the implementation activities that occur every year. Other policies provide direction for day to day operations.

So, for example, a new city councilor is elected who promised during her campaign to reduce the carbon emissions and fossil fuel use of the city. During her first day in office, she is presented with a vehicle purchase by the police department of a gas-guzzling car for the new fleet. If she tries to stop the purchase, she might immediately be frustrated by resistance from the police chief and city manager describing the fact that the vehicle was in the capital plan and part of a long-term replacement policy, possibly with contracts with local car dealers that can't be broken. The new city councilor's objections will probably be overruled by the councilors who have been serving for many years, and the vehicle purchase will go forward. The newest council member might protest "...but citizens showed in this election they wanted to reduce carbon emissions and fossil fuel use." Patient smiles and knowing looks exchanged between the veterans on staff and the council will tell her that idealism will be tolerated but that change at this level — daily implementation — is not that easy.

Campaign promises, regular local elections, referenda and bond votes form a steady pulse of new information and citizen input into city government, but significant changes in direction take more of a concerted effort. Freshly minted city councilors are often blind to the processes that guide large-scale implementation, and it's all too easy to get pulled into the "business as usual" pattern of behavior, especially when you consider all the systemic forces that work to keep things the way they are.

Cities are complex engines powered by union contracts, standing purchase contracts with suppliers, experienced professional staff and material and energy flows which have their own visible and invisible infrastructure. Major alterations to the infrastructure take careful planning — you would not cut sewer pipes to stop the flow of waste to the treatment plant if you wanted to reduce a city's waste impact, regardless of how easy it might seem at the time. In that case, it's obvious that the unintended consequences of action would far outweigh the short-term results. It's less obvious, but no less true, in other areas (even, for example, with a gas-guzzling vehicle that the police department wants).

A long-term vision guided by people's values — what they care deeply about — is a prerequisite for mobilizing collective action. Once a city has a long-term vision, however, things do not magically change. It still will be hard to redirect the purchase of a vehicle for the fleet unless the long-term vision is translated into the short-term policies and programs which guide implementation. A larger vision for a walkable city with friendly neighborhoods and less suburban sprawl still requires changes in the land use ordinances before there will be any measurable change in density. A larger vision for clean air and reduced climate impacts will have to be translated into a number of policies — ranging from a purchasing policy that requires alternatives to energy-intensive items to capital planning for renewable energy production.

Today, very few cities have the integrated long-term plans and policies necessary to pursue the types of implementation activities that will move a community in a more sustainable direction. Often the policy context is fragmented, short-term and internally contradictory. The city might have a master plan or a comprehensive plan that addresses infrastructure, land use and economic development over the next three to five years. If city staff and/or the city council are oriented toward integration, the capital plan might actually reflect the goals of the master plan, but all too often a city's capital plan is a long list of projects that reflect departmental or council imperatives in isolation from each other, without a sense of how they relate to overarching long-term goals such as climate stabilization and poverty eradication. Cities almost never address some of the important underlying drivers for the policy context — a sense of shared values, social and human development issues and governance structures.

The action needed to achieve long-term sustainability goes beyond actions taken by city government, and city government actions can be ineffective if there aren't concurrent and commensurate changes taking place in the larger community. A multi-stakeholder process gives individuals, organizations and other major institutions in the city a role and a voice in the preparation of the plan so that later they will also work within their own context to find ways to implement it. In this way, the city and all its independent moving parts will start to work toward the same ends. Here again, however, this synchronized action doesn't happen on its own — it takes direction and organization from the city and the stakeholders.

Integration and long-term time horizons define sustainability planning, and are more important for achieving a city's goals than attention to single issues such as climate change, health or local economic development. While these issues are important, action to address them cannot be successful if it occurs in a silo. An integrated approach makes connections across issue areas, across socio-economic boundaries and across city departments.

It also helps insure that the pursuit of one objective won't be at the expense of another. Environmental policies that marginalize or impoverish a group of people or area in the city (or in another part of the world) won't succeed in the long run. Housing plans that ignore their impact on important open space, wetlands and agricultural land will hurt the city over the long term. Economic development practices that rely on an unsustainable exploitation of natural resources or human potential will also ultimately have the opposite effect — they will further impoverish the community rather than creating real wealth.

If you ask some local mayors or city councilors, however, what influence they have on the economy, they are likely to give you a blank look. Some may have gone as far as to build industrial infrastructure in the hopes of attracting manufacturing firms, with their 19th and 20th century highly paid jobs, ignoring global trends that have moved most manufacturing to other parts of the world. Others place their hope in the marketing efforts of the local Chamber of Commerce that diligently attends trade shows and places ads to market the locality as business-friendly.

Some of the more progressive city governments have instituted revolving loan funds to serve as a lender of last resort to local businesses with cash flow or growth issues. They build incubator space, offer business planning services, maybe even identify sources of venture capital for start-ups. Many governments are aware of the importance of locally owned businesses, but are still frightened away from taking a stand when large firms threaten to come in and outcompete smaller local ventures. Most local government think that all jobs are equal and that any and all new tax bases are sacrosanct. The economy is the master, and local communities are the servants who bend over backwards to accommodate investors, even in the face of questionable business practices.

Redefining wealth and refocusing local initiatives on meeting human needs can help local leaders see the economy as being at the service of their community, not the other way around. There are many forms of capital that demand investment for a local community to thrive, not just financial capital. Social capital, human capital, natural capital, institutional capital, technological capital, potential exchange capital, built capital and cultural capital all need to be understood and strengthened — and this multidimensional effort is absolutely the domain of local communities.

The Myth (and Potential) of Individual Wealth

So far, we've touched on three things that define what we mean by wealth:

1. The obvious idea of possessing a lot of money
2. The presence of well-being through the satisfaction of a broad spectrum of human needs
3. The community systems we have developed to provide for many of our needs

True wealth might be defined as a sum of all three of these. Yet it is possible to feel wealthy with only the latter two, and it is possible to be impoverished if all you have is a lot of money, but no way to meet any of your critical needs and no community systems to support it.

The North American mythology of rugged individualism tends to make us blind to the fact that real wealth can only exist in community. "Self-made millionaires" sometimes happily forget the fact that the context for their enrichment comes out of public infrastructure, institutional arrangements and participation by many other people in their enterprise. They are the first ones to call for lower taxes — the US Chamber of Commerce spends more on lobbying than any other lobbying group in Washington. They often don't seem to recognize that without the rule of law, without water and sewer services to industrial areas, without policies that enable their businesses to operate, they would not survive, let alone make a profit.

If most people are blind to the structures of cities and communities that enable businesses and organizations to operate successfully, we are also blind to the structure of the other important ingredient of individual wealth — money. Most people do not understand the current monetary system, hidden as it is from public view. If they did, they might have second thoughts about whether or not to blindly trust their financial security, or insecurity, exclusively to this particular system.

We hope in this book to open your eyes about both the role of community in wealth creation and also the role of money and other means of exchange. To do this, we need to help you remove the blindfold you've been wearing (through no fault of your own) — the monetary system has been obscured by the forces that profit from it. After all, before you can create wealth and build sustainable, local economies, you need to understand wealth — what it is and what it is based on. The good news is that you too have the power to create wealth, real wealth, for yourself, your children and your community. But before you buy more lottery tickets, read on to see how effective local action can accomplish the task with a lot less risk.

CHAPTER 2

Crash and Burn Economics

*Almost all systems of economic thought are premised on the idea
of continued economic growth, which would be fine and dandy
if we lived on an infinite planet, but there's this small, niggling,
inconvenient fact that the planet is, in fact, finite, and that, unlike
economic theory, it is governed by physical and biological reality.*

GEORGE MONBIOT

The Roller Coaster Economy

We all know the positive side of our economic history. Our current financial system has enabled an industrial age which has proved to be the most impressive wealth creation machine in human history, at least for those countries that adopted industrialization early on.

However, the financial markets also have an unfortunate tendency to hurtle forward like a runaway train, careening into valleys of unpredictable recession, then chugging up hills of new opportunity, only to derail at the slightest bend in the track—an Asian market blows up, the Russian ruble crashes, subprime mortgages trigger a global banking meltdown, etc. The World Bank has identified no less than 96 major banking crises and 178 monetary crises over the past 25 years.[1]

US dollars, European euros and Japanese yen stoke the train's engines, shoveled in to support financial interests in every corner of the globe. To keep the system going, we subsidize ravenous consumer consumption that devours rainforests, guzzles fossil fuels and tops it off with melted ice caps for dessert. Finally, in the shadow side of our economy we find also all the shadows of humanity itself: the operation cloaks international syndicates trading in violence, weapons, war, terror, illegal drugs, slaves and prostitution.

In short, for better *and* for worse, the flawed system we have has driven the evolution of the human species on this planet to the state we have achieved today.

Our financial system influences everyone on the planet — from parents, farmers, shopkeepers and students, to all the corporate and political leaders around the world. Most people accept it on faith, and yet some inconvenient questions need to be asked: Why do the avowed principles of most national and state constitutions — like peace, democracy, a healthy environment and healthy people — diverge so far from practices we accept as business as usual? Why does the system break down as often as it does? How do rational people with no ill intent to humanity or to Earth's environment perpetuate a system that produces violence, pollution and corruption as its byproduct?

Despite the centrality of financial systems to our daily lives, most of us don't understand the fundamentals of that system. And how could we? It is as hidden and complex as the workings of a secret society. We have been told that the *principia economica* behave like Newton's natural laws, rather than being controlled by the decisions we make. This faith in the science of economics has been challenged repeatedly by "unforeseen crises." Aren't sciences supposed to be able to predict the future?

Faulty economic assumptions can have significant ramifications. For example, many lead economists dismiss environmental pollution as an "externality," a factor not adequately priced or otherwise accounted for in the existing system. In other words, when the theoretical system does not account for it, the problem itself is a bit of an anomaly. If the very basis for all economic activity — the natural resources and ecosystem services we depend on for life — is being irreparably harmed, and yet this is described as if it were a minor accounting mistake, there is a serious problem with the underlying theory, not with the facts. If we could bring the hidden drivers of the system that are embedded in these theories into the open and redesign them for health and real prosperity, it might help turn the ship around.

Why does the economy appear to be so erratic? Even if 90% of the time some economic models have predictive value, they turn out to be of little help during the 10% of the cases when structural change is involved, which is unfortunately the situation we find ourselves in today. After all our history, why don't we have a better idea about how to manage things so there aren't wild fluctuations and sudden changes where some are impoverished while others reap huge profits? Even bankers, CEOs and CFOs who make the real decisions are often blind to the underlying systemic forces that present them with an increasingly narrow range of choices.

What are the assumptions, frameworks, social decisions and projections driving the economic juggernaut? If they are faulty, then are there alternatives? What steps can we take to bring all of these invisible forces into the open so that people in every community can make conscious decisions about their own destiny, rather than blindly accepting a culture that seems to lead to its own destruction? Now, please hold onto your hats — some of these ideas have the potential to change the way you see the world. You may even discover why Henry Ford, one of the fathers of modern manufacturing, said: "The people must be helped to think naturally about money. They must be told what it is, and what makes it money, and what are the possible tricks of the present system which put nations and peoples under control of the few."[2]

False Assumption #1:
The Economy is Beyond Our Control

In a country that has taken so much pride in its democratic traditions, the wholesale capitulation of basic rights to the doctrine of laissez faire, survival of the fittest, free market ideology is hard to explain. Yet we've lived through an era where the gap between the rich and the poor has widened by orders of magnitude. The social contract has changed dramatically in our lifetime; there was a time when the government was seen as having a legitimate role in reducing inequality and promoting social justice. The last 20 years have seen a widespread challenge to the legitimacy of government action of any sort. But there is hope, even in this shift. If it was changed once, it can be changed again. Why not make it better than it has ever been?

There have been several times in US history where large economic changes have happened as a result of democratic intervention — the anti-trust laws of the early 1900s, labor union laws, the New Deal under Roosevelt. We need to consider what institutional changes are needed to eradicate poverty if we really want to create a more sustainable world.

False Assumption #2:
Money is a Neutral Means of Exchange

Most people do not know any more about money than what they need to count what's in their pocket, balance their checkbooks and pay their taxes. They know there is never enough of it for everything they want and need, but they never stop to ask why. Do they work hard enough? Sometimes people with two and three jobs can't make ends meet for their families. Didn't they study hard enough in school? If intelligence is a prerequisite for high pay, then why do so many of our teachers qualify for subsidized housing in the communities where they live?

Money is not neutral with respect to affluence and poverty. Our national monetary system is based on debt — every dollar that is created is someone's debt, be it the government's, corporation's or individual's. Every dollar comes therefore with a built-in expectation that it will earn interest. The interest it earns goes to the bank and the people who buy the bonds. This automatically concentrates wealth in the system. At the same time, the debt basis for money also exerts continuous pressure on individuals and corporations to grow forever at any cost, to stay ahead of the interest payments on the basic unit of exchange.

Money is not neutral with respect to community economic development. The existence of a national monetary system in a country with regional economies as diverse as the Midwest industrial belt, the prairie breadbasket and the Hollywood creative economy is guaranteed to undermine the economic health of at least some individual communities. If Mexico is doing better than Costa Rica, the value of their currency will reflect this, and Mexican citizens will be able to buy more Costa Rican products with their pesos. When this happens, more products in Costa Rica are sold, and their economy will improve. If Hollywood is doing better than Detroit, however, they are bound to a currency with the same value, so no similar balancing act takes place. Jane Jacobs, the author of *Cities and the Wealth of Nations,* compared this to everyone at a soccer game — the players, spectators and referees — using the same set of lungs.

Money is not neutral with respect to competition and cooperation. Our current money creation process, with interest built in, systematically promotes competition among its users, largely due to the need to pay interest on the bank-debt money that drives the system. The story of the Eleventh Round below, taken from *The Future of Money,*[3] illustrates this problem as a parable.

THE ELEVENTH ROUND

Once upon a time, there was a small village where people knew nothing about money or interest. Each market day, people would bring their chickens, eggs, hams and breads to the marketplace and enter into the time-honored ritual of negotiations and exchange for what they needed with one another. At harvests, or whenever someone's barn needed repairs after a storm, the villagers simply exercised another age-old tradition of helping one another, knowing that if they themselves had a problem one day, others would surely come to their aid in turn.

One market day, a stranger with shiny black shoes and an elegant white hat came by and observed the whole process with a sardonic smile. When he saw one farmer running around to corral six chickens wanted in exchange for a big ham, the stranger could not refrain from laughing. "Poor people," he said, "so primitive."

Overhearing this, the farmer's wife challenged him. "Do you think you can do a better job handling chickens?"

The stranger responded: "Chickens, no. But there is a much better way to eliminate all the hassles. Bring me one large cowhide and gather the families. I'll explain the better way."

As requested, the families gathered, and the stranger took the cowhide, cut perfect leather rounds in it and put an elaborate and graceful little stamp on each round. He then gave ten rounds to each family, stating that each round represented the value of one chicken. "Now you can trade and bargain with the rounds instead of those unwieldy chickens." It seemed to make sense and everybody was quite impressed with the stranger.

"One more thing," the stranger added. "In one year's time, I will return and I want each of you to bring me back an extra round, an eleventh round.

That eleventh round is a token of appreciation for the technological improvement I just made possible in your lives."

"But where will that round come from?" asked the wife.

"You'll see," said the stranger, with a knowing look.

Assuming that the population and its annual production remained exactly the same during that next year, what do you think happened? Remember, that eleventh round token was never created, meaning that it didn't materialize out of thin air. As the stranger had suggested, it was far more convenient to exchange rounds instead of the chickens on market days. But this convenience had a hidden cost beyond the demanded eleventh round—that of generating a systemic undertow of competition among all the participants. The equivalent of one out of each eleven families would have to lose all of its rounds, even if everybody managed their affairs well, in order to provide the eleventh round to the stranger.

The following year, when a storm threatened some of the farmers, there was a greater reluctance to assist neighbors. The families were now in a wrestling match for that eleventh round, the round that had not been created, which actively discouraged the spontaneous cooperation that had long been the tradition in the village.

This story is a simplified description of how our money system pits every user against all its other users. It is simplified mainly because it assumes that there is no growth in the population, in the production and the money during this story. In reality, all three of these variables grow over time, obscuring the underlying process. However, it is nevertheless systemically correct that anybody who pays interest uses someone else's principal to do so. Even within a single family, money issues are the most frequent reason for a family breakdown. When everything becomes monetized and fosters the same competition driving the currency, aren't we losing something important?

The Building Blocks of the Economy: How Assumptions Create Reality

There are plenty of theories in the economic pantheon that are worthy of criticism; Herman Daly and John Cobb characterize the error of faulty economic assumptions as the "fallacy of misplaced concreteness" in their book *For the Common Good*.[4] They argue that most economists work primarily with abstractions and are sometimes tempted to adjust reality to their abstractions rather than developing more robust explanations when reality and theory are in conflict. This applies to economic thinking about prices, the "free" market, the economic behavior of human beings, resources and just about every basic tenet of the science of economics.

Assumptions have also guided the construction of frameworks and institutions to facilitate the economic activities needed for modern human commerce. These in turn have shaped our lives, everything from the products we use to the rapid urbanization of the planet. If we can identify these hidden assumptions and use the tools available today to reshape the monetary institutions, we are on the road to changing our cities and the quality of our lives.

The Banking System

Most people are not aware of the role that bank financing plays in the creation of money, or the fact that the creation of money is done by private banks, and that the system is not working well. After all, there are all sorts of government logos, symbols and statements on the dollars we use. Furthermore, the dollar printing presses are located in the United States Mint, and the US Department of Treasury stores and distributes them for our use. However, contrary to what all this suggests, that doesn't mean that the government creates money.

You can have as many dollar bills that you want, on the condition that your bank can debit your account (today in electronic form) for the same amount. Your bank similarly requests dollar bills as needed, and gets its own account debited as well. Dollar bills represent only a very small percentage of the amount of dollars in circulation. The vast majority of the money that changes hands in the world is on computers and ledgers, not in actual notes and coins. Even on a personal level, very few of our typical transactions use cash — we use checks, credit cards, debit cards and direct transfers from our bank accounts to others.

So how does the government obtain the money it needs? Like you and me, through income (in the government's case through taxes) and by borrowing. Money is created for the government by the banking system when it incurs debt by issuing bonds at the state and local level, and treasury securities at the federal level — which are loans that are made by the banking system and then sold on the international market, with the principal and interest repayment guaranteed by our tax system.

THE US GOVERNMENTAL DEBT MAZE

The US federal government also has an array of what it calls *non-marketable securities* that aren't traded on the market like US Savings Bonds: *intergovernmental debts* (when the federal government borrows from savings accounts like Social Security) and *Certificates of Indebtedness* the Treasury issues that don't pay interest. All of these still represent government debt.

Bonds are the long-term debt incurred by all levels of government for long-term investment in things like roads, wastewater treatment systems, water pipes, prisons, libraries and schools. At the federal level, the long-term debt takes also the form of *treasury notes* (a one to ten year debt), *treasury bonds* (20 to 30 year debts) and something called a *Treasury Inflation-Protected Security* (or TIPS) which are issued for 5, 10 and 20 year debt. At the state and local level bonds legislatures and city councils vote on bonds, and then they are bought by banks and other investors. Typically the low interest paid on the municipal bonds is tax-exempt, so investors can earn income from the interest paid (with state and local taxes) without paying taxes on it.

Short-term debt is also incurred by the government, usually to address the need for cash flow, just as a business might have a credit line for times when income is less than expenses. At the federal level, short-term debt is loaned by the banks in the form of *treasury bills*, which all mature in less than one year. At the state and local level, short-term debt comes in the form of tax anticipation notes and bond anticipation notes, which are loans from the banks, usually at a low rate that is linked to the rates on the treasury bills at the federal level. So when a city issues a bond for a school but they don't have the money in hand yet (it takes time to sell the bonds to the banks), they can go to a bank for a *bond anticipation note*. When a city needs to pay its bills but all its taxes aren't collected yet, they go to the bank for a *tax anticipation note*.

In short, the government triggers the creation of the money it needs by going into debt. The debt incurred by government is first and foremost to the banking system. The banks do not always have to be US banks — foreign banks and governments also buy US government debt. But despite concerns that China, the oil countries and other foreign interests own a lot of US debt, the majority of the debt is still owed to private banks — private businesses that are set up to make a profit on the process of managing money. All of this interest paid on the debt is the equivalent of an invisible tax, because all the interest does ultimately come from the taxes we pay, even though we don't get to vote on the interest rates.

Internationally, six central banks — including the Federal Reserve in the United States — are owned by the private banks although most countries do have publicly owned central banks.[5] It makes no difference, really, whether the central banks are owned by the public or by private banks; their function is still the same. Their main function is to keep the system working. They were established to help avoid banking panics and runs on banks, and to maintain the standing of the US currency in the world. They also play the role of "lender of last resort:" if banks and financial markets aren't willing to buy government bonds, the Federal Reserve will do so. Finally, most central banks have expanded their mission over the years to regulate private banks. However, experience has proven that their interventions don't always work the way they hope it will.

Government is not the only one to trigger the creation of money by the banking system in this way. Individuals and businesses also do the same when they take loans from banks for their homes and businesses. So when we go to bankers for a loan, they are not opening their vault and taking money out to give us, they are creating new money based on the *fractional reserve system*. When we take that money and put it into another bank — that other bank counts that money toward its reserves, on the basis it can in turn create more new money. It's not a bad business model. The single most profitable business in the US by SEC code, is the central bank, the Federal Reserve.[6] But most people simply don't know that the Federal Reserve is barely more "federal" than Federal Express.

Money is a lot of things: textbooks describe it as a means of exchange; it is a unit of account, a store of value and a vehicle for international trade. We have combined all these functions into one instrument, and this instrument is controlled by private banks that need to earn interest on the issuance of the money to make their profits. Because all of the money we currently use comes from this system, for the rest of the book, we will refer to this type of money as *bank-debt money*.

The "Free Market" System

Evidence of both markets and money predate recorded history. Money was used to facilitate market exchanges, as proven by the many forms of small tokens (whose most logical use would be as a medium of exchange to value an exchange of goods) that have turned up in archaeological digs around the world. Arguably, markets represent a characteristic feature of human existence — we are partly defined by the fact that we share goods and services. No person is independent of society; the trading and sharing we do provide for our needs in a way apparently unique to our species.

The problem arises when we move the market to the center of human existence, instead of it being a mechanism with its appropriate place in a more diverse set of human institutions. Amory Lovins captured the central issue facing our economic thinking when he said "...markets make a good servant, a poor master and a worse religion."[7] The giant global experiments with planned vs. market economies have demonstrated that the market is a very efficient and effective way to allocate goods and services, but when we ignore its failures in other areas and use it as a universal panacea for all our problems — from saving endangered species to fostering support of the arts — we are making it our master and our religion.

Even contemporary environmental economists are not bucking this trend. Their antidote to the warped regulatory system is to start to place financial values on the environmental services offered by the planet. How much would it cost to replace the pollination services bees offer when they are extinct? How much would it cost to replicate the global water cycle to produce healthy water? Can we buy our way to climate stability, and if not, what would it cost to restore our climate to health? The "objectivity" of the market is still seen as a final arbiter for the need to make real value judgments in a pluralistic society. But the market is not objective — it is a contrivance as human and value-laden as any other institution.

A three-day introduction to Environmental Economics conducted in Bulgaria in 1993 illustrates the values hidden in our market mechanisms.[8] The methodological emphasis was on cost-benefit and cost-effectiveness analysis to help regulators determine the most appropriate technologies to introduce to address problems. Participants also learned something about risk assessment, so government could be sure that the issues they faced were, in fact, the greatest risks to human and environmental health. After learning the new tools for environmental management, Bulgarian regulators had a gestalt experience: one of their teams determined that the best way to handle the case study they were given, in which a factory in a city was belching waste that killed people rather quickly, was to relocate all the native Bulgarians that lived there to a cleaner part of the country and move in Vietnamese workers, who had a perceived lower value in their society. Needless to say, the goal of the workshop was not to teach this lesson, yet it's not surprising that the fundamental assumptions being used about the price of life could lead to this outcome.

When the US Bureau of Labor Statistics found in 2007 that corporate CEOs earn 885 times what minimum wage employees earn (Do they do 885 times more work? Are they 885 times more clever?) and 364 times more than the wages of an average employee, can we hear echoes of aristocrats and feudal serfs, even as we've begun the 21st century?[9] Because of these inherent inequities in major economic institutions, the market is not an invisible hand driven by the rational decision making of autonomous individuals. It prevents the vast majority from obtaining anything that resembles the decent life, liberty or a chance at happiness that the USA's founders promised.

Equity and self-determination are basic human needs. Any society will be more stable — less likely to be disrupted by unrest, revolution or other conflict — if all of its institutions provide people a voice in their own destiny and insure a level of fairness in all relationships. This is no less true of economic institutions than governance institutions.

The Financial Market as a System

The term *financial system* is used so frequently that we often lose sight of its meaning. Systems have certain characteristics, and by understanding more about how systems work we gain valuable insights into how to improve our local financial system. Each local economy is a bit like a different kind of car. Each make and model has its own unique features — a convertible roof, cruise control, one burns diesel while another uses high test gasoline; there are hybrids, electric cars, trucks and vans. But they all have a transmission, wheels, a steering system, gauges that give you an idea of the fuel level, warning lights. So by understanding what all cars have in common, you also can understand more about your particular vehicle.

To start at the most basic level, the definition of a system is, according to the Merriam-Webster dictionary: "a regularly interacting or interdependent group of items forming a unified whole."[10] In a car, these are all the components, and the unified whole that is formed is greater than the sum of individual parts. If you lined up the wheels, the engine, the axles, the steering wheel, the windshield, the seats, the body, the mirrors and the gauges along the floor of your garage, it would just be a large pile of stuff. But once all the parts are working together, the car can roll out of the driveway and down the street.

A system is a unified whole with interacting parts, and the parts have characteristics that all systems share. One part is that system's *flow* — something that moves through the system and interacts with other parts (like gasoline moving through the engine and making the pistons move up and down). Another part is a system *stock* — a place in the system where the flow might tend to accumulate (the gas tank). When we describe the interacting parts of systems, we assume that one variable in a system has an effect on other variables. The word for this effect is *feedback*, and interactions can produce either positive feedback or negative feedback. Positive feedback is when a change in one variable produces a change in another variable in the *same* direction (more gas, more speed). Negative feedback is when a change in one variable produces a change in another variable in the *opposite* direction (more brake, less speed).

Positive and negative feedback among different variables in a system can produce a number of different results. In our car example, the goal of the system is equilibrium — the driver of the car wants to travel at the speed limit, so there is a combination of positive and negative feedback that produces a relatively consistent result. The same is true in our bodies, where our body temperature is maintained at a relatively constant level of 98.6°F through the positive feedback of metabolism combined with the negative feedback of perspiration.

When there is only positive feedback in a system, or when the sum of all the feedback in the system is positive (just like basic math, where two negatives can equal a positive), the system produces a reinforcing result, where things get worse and worse or better and better, depending on the variables. There are many examples of this: compounding interest in a bank account, population growth or some important processes in climate change are just a few of the obvious ones. In the bank, more money means more interest is paid, which means there is more money, and so on — positive feedback plus more positive feedback. With population, more parents produce more offspring, who in turn become parents. With climate change, more warmth means less white ice at the poles to reflect the sunlight, which makes the temperatures there warmer, which in turn leads to less ice. In this example, more CO_2 makes more warming (positive feedback), more warming means less ice (negative feedback), less ice means more warming (negative feedback), and the net result is positive, creating a vicious cycle.

These two patterns — a combination of positive and negative feedback that results in equilibrium or in reinforcing increase or decrease — are called *archetypes*, which means a pattern of behavior over time that can be seen in a variety of different systems. There are many system archetypes, and understanding how patterns of behavior in systems can be changed is a key to understanding the economy as well.[11]

The economy's behavior over time exhibits the characteristics of an archetypal system with cycles of expansion and contraction driven by positive and negative feedback from different variables. At a very simple level, one kind of economy — the boom and bust natural resource economy of gold rushes and fossil fuels — can be seen as an archetype called limits to growth. In this archetypal pattern of behavior, positive feedback on the right side of Figure 1 below leads to exponential economic growth (the result of reinforcing feedback), which finally hits the wall of finite resources on the left, which then leads to exponential decline

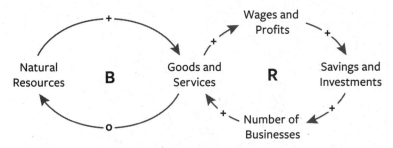

FIGURE 2.1. The Limits to Growth Archetype

as the positive feedback of the right reinforcing loop collapses in reverse on itself.

Please remember: positive feedback does not mean more, or an increase — it means that both variables move in the same direction.[12]

Obviously, the global economy is more complex than this illustration, although on an aggregate level, this particular pattern of reinforcing feedback and balancing constraints is true. We live in a relatively finite world, where the only external input comes from the sun (ignoring meteorites and the contributions to science from the moon rocks collected 30 years ago), and yet we have structured our economy as if we had access to 10 — 20 similar planets. The subject of the archetype was explored extensively in the book *The Limits to Growth* by Dennis and Donella Meadows, Jorgen Randers and William Behrens in 1972 and then revisited by the authors in a new book called *Limits to Growth: The 30-Year Update* published in 2004.[13] *Creating Wealth* focuses more on the invisible structures of the economy (that drive the exponential increase and decline on the right side of the diagram) than the very visible limits we have been reaching on the left.

To consider the economy as a system, it is important to look at the flows through the system, the stocks where things accumulate in the system, as well as the variables and feedback patterns that drive change in the system. Money is a critically important flow through the economic system, and the ways in which it accumulates and provides feedback to all of the other variables can also be illustrated using the language of system dynamics.

When a bank issues a loan to a business or a mortgage to a homeowner, they repay the loan at higher rates of interest than the bank offers on its deposits, one of the basic equations of the current banking business model. A system diagram of this interaction would be as follows:

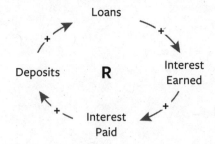

FIGURE 2.2. The Current Banking Business Model

In Figure 2, the more deposits a bank has, the more loans it can issue. The more loans it issues, the more interest it earns. The more interest it earns, the more interest it can pay on the deposits, which in turn will attract more deposits — a simple reinforcing loop with positive feedback. On this very simple level, banks are endless money machines. In much the same way, our individual accounts should make us incredibly wealthy with accumulated compounding interest over time. The same factors that reduce our compounding interest accounts — like the fact that to live we often need to make withdrawals to purchase goods and services — also mitigate the bank's profits. Not all loans are repaid. The demand for loans fluctuates. The banks themselves need to be attentive to the interest rates of the central bank and the bond markets. The amount of money on deposit changes with the economy, as people are either saving or spending more.

The net effect of the money machines we have created when we authorized banks to have a monopoly on the creation of money is that over time, the real value of this bank-debt money declines. There is a built-in expectation that money needs to earn interest. When every dollar in circulation came into existence with the issuance of debt — either private debt from mortgages and business loans or pubic debt with bonds and public borrowing — those dollars had better be working as hard as they can to produce a return. This return comes in the form of interest payments on deposits or returns on investments made in productive enterprises.

If instead of putting my money in the bank or investing it in the stock and bond markets, I put it in a can under my bed at home, the money in that can will be worth less five years from now than it is right now. On a larger scale, the declining value of money is factored into business accounting through the use of a *discount rate* which includes the interest rate used to discount future cash flows.

Now look at it from the company side. The company gets a loan from the bank for its business, and has to repay it over time with interest. The cost of the loan is one of the company's costs of production, along with resource costs, labor costs and other operating costs. In Figure 3, several key functions within a business organization are identified, with finance being pivotal to both the beginning of a business and its ongoing profitability.

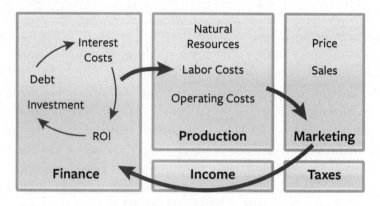

FIGURE 2.3. The Corporate Process

The financing of a business is usually a mix of debt and investment. The more investment that is available, the less debt needed, but there are often perverse incentives built into our tax and accounting systems that make debt more desirable than it would be otherwise. So even if it isn't absolutely necessary, businesses will often have debt on their books. Debt comes with interest payments, so the interest — the cost of the money — is deducted prior to determining whether or not the business is profitable. This is illustrated by smaller black feedback loops in Figure 4.

The total financing available will drive the production capacity, which in turn is a combination of the natural resources needed, the labor costs and other operating costs. Once there is a product, it is sold for a particular price, and the income from sales (after taxes and other costs of production) are deducted. This is what determines the *return on investment* (ROI in the diagram). ROI is the profit that is distributed to the investors in the business, and the cycle starts over again — the more profit, the more reinvestment is possible, the more production capacity and (assuming there is demand for the product) the more sales.

The external factors that influence the outcome of any business venture are the demand for the product, competition for sales of the same or similar products, the costs of production, tax rates and the cost of money. Most of these cost factors are directly related to the product, and need to be considered in the overall business plan when determining if the venture will be profitable.

Money is the one systemic cost which influences both the profit margin on a particular product and also how profit is calculated and the total value of the returns. On a systemic level, the cost of money is a big part of the reason that it is not sufficient merely to make a profit. Companies need to make a profit that continues to increase *at an increasing rate* when the costs of capital and the value of money throughout the system are in a constant state of inflationary devaluation. Figure 4 illustrates the reinforcing nature of this dynamic.

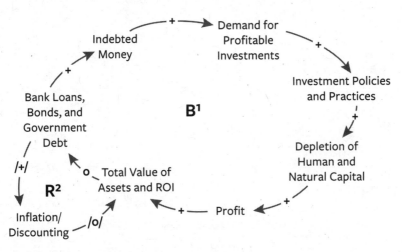

FIGURE 2.4. How Bank Money Interacts with the Corporate Process

Of course, resources and labor are not unlimited, and so this reinforcing system will eventually hit the wall described earlier in Figure 1. Peak oil, resource depletion, scarce fresh water, climate change, exponential population growth, the widening gap between the rich and the poor — all of these are symptoms that indicate we are approaching these outer limits to growth. When there are scarcities of key resources — oil, water, pollination, food — costs go up. When people's health deteriorates because of poor nutrition, lack of safe water, poor health services — costs go up. The profit derived from a depletion of human and natural capital is necessarily a short-term gain at the cost of long-term well-being. It's like spending the principal in your bank account — it might get you another meal on a hungry day, but there will be no more money in the bank tomorrow.

If costs go up as the limits to growth are reached, then yet another delayed loop which provides additional reinforcing feedback to a cycle that was already growing exponentially is added in. Higher costs mean that profit and return on investment will be lower. This in turn will drive the need for more debt, more inflation and more pressure on already limited resources.

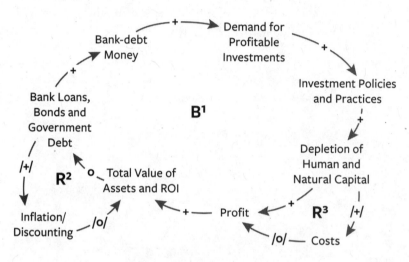

FIGURE 2.5. Adding Higher Costs

In our current era, where high priced oil and overleveraged assets triggered an economic collapse which forced the US government to provide huge "bailout" loans to banks (created with government bonds and debt) and then other huge "stimulus" grants to state and local governments and businesses (also created with government bonds and debt), this system dynamics hypothesis seems to hold true. As long as the fundamental assumptions and conditions don't change, this is a trap — a systemic spiral that threatens not only the health of our money system, but also our well-being and the life-support systems Earth provides.

This hypothesis isn't just theoretical — it is proven by the graph in Figure 6. Anytime you observe an exponential growth curve like this, you know that there is a reinforcing system of positive feedback behind it.

The total US credit market, i.e., borrowing by governments, corporations and individuals, is as close to a statistical fit of an exponential

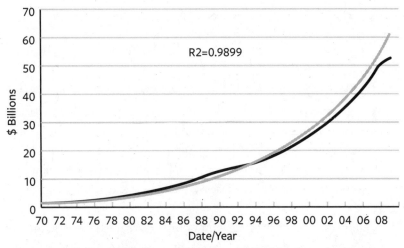

FIGURE 2.6. The Exponential Curve of Money Creation in the US. The light line represents a perfect exponential growth curve. The dark line represents the growth in Total US Credit Market Debt. The R2 figure represents how closely the trend tracks to perfect exponential patterns – 98%. Source: *Flow of Fund Accounts of the United States*. Federal Reserve Statistical Release #Z.1, September 17, 2010. [online]. [cited October 23, 2010]. federalreserve.gov/releases/z1/current/

curve as is scientifically possible. (For those with an econometric background, the R2 value of .9889 means that it is almost a perfect fit.)[14]

Exponential growth in money supply can only end up with an inflationary blowout. We should remember the warning of one of the foremost economists of the 20th century, John Maynard Keynes: "By a continuing process of inflation, government can confiscate, secretly and unobserved, an important part of the wealth of their citizens."[15]

Systems Change

What are the fundamental assumptions and conditions needed to intervene in this destructive cycle? Where are the leverage points, those interventions where a relatively small amount of effort can achieve much larger results? Often, a systems diagram can help identify promising possibilities. In this vicious cycle, there are two important drivers — the bank-debt source of our monetary system and the economic policies we have enacted to facilitate the process of human and natural capital depletion for the sake of the ever higher profits that the system demands.

These are the two variables where policy interventions could have an important impact on the destructive force of the system.

Economic Policy Change

The legal structures and policies we have enacted and the public investments we have made to enable companies to be as profitable as possible number in the thousands. In much the same way as cities cannot transform the monetary system on their own, they do not have the ability to change the dominant policy context. There are a few policies worth mentioning, however, which deserve particular attention as we move into a new era.

Looking back over the long arch of history, there are several important changes we encounter in the 21st century which are significantly different than prior centuries. Up until the late 20th century, human beings lived in a world where nature was abundant and human beings were, by comparison, scarce. The natural world was awesome and scary — the raw power of storms, earthquakes, floods, volcanoes, droughts, plagues — all kinds of natural disasters gave humans a clear sense of their inferiority on the scale of things. It's no wonder that *conquering* nature was a goal (at least for Western civilization — more successful and less violent relationships with nature had been cultivated in the East and among North American First Nations) when we were regularly defeated by these overwhelming forces.

But nature was also abundant. There were lots of fish in the sea, and fresh water flowed in pristine streams down mountains where the air was clear and crisp. Agriculture had its ups and downs, but the 20th century dawned in the United States with over 80% of our population living on farms and growing their own food. The wood from forests had already gone to warships in Britain, but in the US trees were plentiful, and the steel industry had taken the pressure off the trees that had been used for ships.

Today, in the 21st century, we are facing a different world. Nature is increasingly scarce, and humans are increasingly abundant. The policies that were enacted in an era of abundant nature need to be changed. In that era, the prices of natural resource extraction were at zero cost to a company, and were often even subsidized by government. Machines created by these resources did the work of more and more people, and emissions into the air, water and soil were allowed without regulatory limits or fines. Arguably, even the mathematics of the banking system itself, which seems to rely on an infinite capacity of the world to continue to grow and produce profits, needs to be rethought in a new era of obvious limits. The paradigm of infinite growth has allowed and even fostered the increasing concentration and centralization of wealth through the tacit assumption that there's more than enough for everyone: a rising tide floats all boats. Yet on the natural resource side of the equation, the tide is not rising, it's receding, and some oversized yachts are crushing the canoes in their wake.

The enabling policies which need to be addressed to change the system fall into two main categories: Earth and corporations. The Earth policies are all those which form and regulate our relationship to the natural world. The corporate policies are those which structure the key institutions we have created to foster collective action and wealth creation. This is a tall order, obviously, and full details are beyond the scope of this book. But the ethic that is needed to shape these policies on any level (local, state and national) can be described here briefly.

Earth Policies

The values and ethics that govern our relationship to Earth need to embody a deep and abiding sense of respect and care for all life. Just as the 20th century saw the realization of the Human Rights movement's demands for equality, the 21st century needs to recognize the critical importance of biodiversity and abandon those practices which erode the wealth of species we need to survive into the 22nd century. Our policies need to make all destructive practices prohibitively expensive and morally impermissible. These include, but are not limited to, monoculture crops, genetic engineering, destruction of habitat, emission and disposal of wastes beyond Earth's assimilative capacity and extraction of non-renewable resources from Earth's crust.

The *precautionary principle* has been introduced into several legal systems as one way of turning back the tide and valuing the integrity of Earth's ecological systems above narrow corporate goals of production, consumption and profit. Most legal systems now place the burden of proof on parties who object to a new technology, development project or innovation to demonstrate that it does harm. The introduction of the precautionary principle shifts the burden of proof to the proponent of a new idea, so that they would need to demonstrate that it will not harm important biological, human or community systems before it was introduced.

Other policies need to be introduced that reward activities which enhance the ongoing capacity of ecosystems, human and community systems to continue to produce the assets that meet our needs. Tax breaks for ecosystem restoration, educational programs and organic food production are three possible examples, along with incentives for lowering consumption, reducing population, paying livable wages and investing in renewable, local, energy generation.

In summary, the policies we need eliminate harmful practices, curb the introduction of new practices that would do more harm than good and encourage practices that are life-enhancing and promote more harmony among all the different inhabitants of the Earth community.

Corporate Policies

To follow the model we've described for Earth policy changes, we need to identify and eliminate policies that are destroying the ecosystem, exploiting human beings or undermining democratic governance. We then need to curtail the introduction of new ideas and policies that would have harmful effects. Most importantly, we need to introduce policies that bring corporate life into harmony with the life-support systems on Earth, so that these two most powerful processes do not continue to work at cross-purposes.

The modern corporation emerged at the end of the feudal period in Western history, when the European powers were exploring other parts of the world and engaging in expanded colonization and international trade. The original corporate charters enabled individuals to band together in a common body to undertake enterprises that were beyond the capacity of even the wealthy aristocracy of the time. The idea of a corporation being its own entity, a legal person of sorts, goes hundreds of years back in time.

Yet this corporate personhood took on new dimensions in industrial America, as companies grew and people started to challenge the roles and resources they claimed. Courts have not always addressed the issue of whether corporations are *persons* in the same way as individuals are, but a large and growing body of law does afford corporate plaintiffs and defendants many of the same rights and privileges. As recently as 2008, when the mercenary firm Blackwater sued the City of San Diego, California, to get the city to issue a certificate of occupancy for their training center when the firm had not followed the correct procedure for obtaining land use permits, the judge ruled in Blackwater's favor on the basis of the firm's constitutional right to due process.[16] Another more recent example of this is the ruling in 2010 on the rights of corporations to add almost unlimited money to the electoral process in the US. A Supreme Court case — Citizens United v. Federal Elections Commission — upheld a corporately funded nonprofit organization's First Amendment right to invest in and publicize a political documentary targeting then-presidential candidate Hilary Clinton.

One of the important differences between legal entities like corporations and real people is that real people have an innate ability (barring some kind of mental disorder) to recognize their interdependence with other people and with nature. Legal entities which are established to make a profit are organized instead around overly narrow goals and ignore the imperatives of an interdependent web of life and society. The bottom line for for-profit corporations in the United States is the profit that is returned to shareholders, a phenomenon also known as *shareholder primacy*, and this mandate requires that corporate leaders behave in sometimes completely inhuman and unnatural ways that ultimately undermine society's (and even the company's) longer-term interests in return for short-term gains.

Further, if policies incorporating the precautionary principle were implemented in concert with incentives for investment that enhanced human, social and ecological, we would succeed in curtailing further innovations that cause harm and introducing beneficial practices to repair the damage that's been done. Imagine US Sugar unveiling a long-term investment plan that would repair the damage that overdevelopment has caused in the Everglades because it's in their corporate interest. Or if Freeport-McMoRan Copper & Gold Inc., the owners of Climax Mine in Colorado, restored the mountains in the Freemont Pass area to their original pristine state, it would be a massive long-term investment for ecological systems restoration that would dwarf the original profits made from strip mining molybdenum in the 1900s.

On an operational level, policies such as life cycle accounting and employee ownership stock options would help the structure of corporate decision making change so that it is systematically more accountable to all the social and ecological systems which support it and to the employees that make it work. This would be one way to help change the narrow, short-term focus that undermines community life in favor of profit for distant investors.

Monetary Reform

Attempts to change the national money system in the US have a long history described in *The Lost Science of Money* by Stephen Zarlenga, the founder of the American Monetary Institute.[17] In our time, members of Congress such as Dennis Kucinich, a former presidential candidate, are also pushing for monetary reform at the national level. This would have an enormous impact on the public spending that can be done and on our effective tax rates. Estimates have been made that the invisible money tax we pay to cover the interest costs of the money we use adds several thousand dollars to the average tax bill each year.

There are alternatives to the private monopoly on money which banks have enjoyed since the creation of the Federal Reserve System in 1913. A public and democratic debate on the alternatives would certainly illuminate what for most USA citizens is unknown territory. There have been two times in US history, in fact, when this kind of private, debt-based money was not the main currency in use. During Colonial times, notes known now as *Colonial Scrip* were used for most transactions. These notes were issued by the Colonies based on the level of economic activity they anticipated. The system worked so well, in fact, that it undermined the profits and taxes collected by the British, and it was outlawed in 1764. Many scholars attribute both the Boston Tea Party and the American Revolution more to the British prohibition of Colonial Scrip than to any of the factors taught in grade school history class.

During the US Civil War, the costs of the war also made it imperative for the government to issue notes that weren't borrowed from private banks. These were known as *greenbacks*; they were subsequently discredited as the government returned to the gold standard and the banks regained control of the money creation process.

Another attempt to change the monetary system in the US, the Chicago Plan, was made in the wake of the Great Depression. This plan would have divided demand deposits from savings deposits and required a 100% reserve on demand deposits. Bank bonds would cover the reserve requirement, and the federal government would issue the currency and all moneys as needed. It was introduced in the House and Senate in 1934, but it never made it out of committee. People haven't forgotten the plan, and in our time economists such as Milton Friedman have been its advocates.

Any plan for monetary reform would need to consider three basic objectives:

1. Ending practices that have proven harmful to the common good
2. Curtailing further innovations that would add to the harm that's already been done
3. Adding new practices that bring our financial system into congruence with the human, social, and ecological systems that support life

The practices that have now proven harmful to the common good are the constellation of forces which foster and exacerbate the endless boom and bust business cycle whereby wealth is consolidated into fewer and fewer hands. Monopolistic control of money is at the root of this system. For this practice to end, we need to rethink our money system. We are not, however, recommending a solution that would reproduce the flaws of a monopolistic money system by simply replacing a bank monopoly with a government monopoly.

As with agriculture, a monoculture crop has the effect of making everything dependent on its health and well-being. If you grow only one crop, you are more susceptible to the ravages of insects and blight. The same is true of the monetary system we have adopted. Textbooks state that there are several functions that money serves — it is a means of exchange, a store of value, a unit of account. As history and current experience conclusively prove, all of these functions do not need to be covered by the same instrument. Our economy would be more resilient

> If supply and demand drive the *invisible hand* of the market, bank-debt money keeps the *invisible foot* on the accelerator of the growth imperative.

to big changes and would have fewer disruptions if there were more diversity in the ways in which we make exchanges, store value and keep our accounts.

The Vortex of Urbanization

While the economic roller coaster appears to go up and down — the business cycles, the fluctuations in the stock market — the roller coaster itself is heading inexorably into a centralized and concentrated vortex, like matter and energy being sucked into a black hole in space. The patterns of behavior visible in the economy produce similar forms in other human endeavors, most notably in the cities around the world.

On the physical level, the roller coaster is leading to urbanization on an unprecedented global scale. As stated earlier, the United Nations claims that for the first time in history, more than half the world's population lives in cities. Furthermore, many of these cities in turn are becoming megalopolises at a remarkable rate. Megacities of more than 10 million people were rare 20 years ago (there were only nine in 1985, most of them with familiar names — Paris, London, New York, Beijing, Istanbul, Moscow); now the world has 25 of them. Karachi, Dhaka, Manila, Jakarta, Lagos, Shenzhen and Cairo are some of the newer members of the megacity club. Some cities grow by over 10,000 people *per month* and are completely incapable of providing the necessary infrastructure and services fast enough to serve the new populations.[18] This explosion of urban population has left millions of people living in dangerous and unhealthy slums.

Cities growing at extraordinary rates have no choice but to abandon most rational ideas about urban planning — there is no way to describe the resulting urban environments except as gigantic experiments, accidents of human migration. Whole neighborhoods share one filthy portalet, if they're lucky. There are human settlements that live on and in landfills, their sole economy scavenging the waste of others for their livelihood. Homes made of found materials — cardboard, tin, plastic tarps — are the only shelter for over one billion of Earth's human inhabitants today. No running water, no sanitation, rampant disease, constant hunger, violence, crime and oppression are a way of life. If the current situation continues unabated until 2020, one out of every five human beings on Earth — over 2.5 billion people — will live in a slum.[19]

Cities, Democracy and Economic Change

For all their difficulties, cities are the level of government closest to the people, and they provide people with the largest number of critical services — everything from education to wastewater treatment. They are collectively the largest government on Earth, dwarfing state and national governments in public service budgets and employees. While in some parts of the world, city budgets come directly from national government, cities still need to be the ones providing the services; it is the only way to effectively and efficiently serve the majority of the population.

This makes cities the logical nexus for increased democratic practice in government and more democratic economic systems. New England cities and towns in the US, for example, have something that is closely akin to direct democracy, where their budgets, ordinances and other city actions need to be ratified by voters. In the Town Meeting form of government, the registered voters make up the city legislature every year and deliberate and vote on all city matters.

Cities need to deepen their mandate for real democratic and economic change. To do this, they need to involve their residents in government more effectively — four stories of how cities have done this are included in Chapter 13. Cities need to understand how each of their economies work and where there are opportunities for making economic improvements. They can do this by conducting an inventory of their assets and identifying where they have unmet needs and underutilized resources. Cities can also design and sponsor new ways of making exchanges and providing incentives to match their assets and resources with the needs of their residents. Examples of some of the ways local currencies have mobilized people and improved economic conditions are offered in Part II. To start projects and identify the kinds of currencies which might be most useful, city leaders can follow the directions offered in the Appendix.

Cities can and will change the world as they absorb and accommodate the majority of the world's population. The choice city leaders have to make is whether to let the forces of globalization and population mobilization overtake them, or whether to take the initiative to consciously and deliberately plan for a vital and dynamic local economy. The building blocks for taking this initiative are the subject of the next chapter.

CHAPTER 3

Community Capitalism

I believe totally in a Capitalist System,
I only wish that someone would try it.

FRANK LLOYD WRIGHT

If you look up the definition of capitalism in the dictionary, it will say something like this: "an economic system characterized by private or corporate ownership of capital goods, by investments that are determined by private decision, and by prices, production, and the distribution of goods that are determined mainly by competition in a free market."[1] In that context, the term *community capitalism* sounds a bit peculiar — are we going to talk about community expropriation of private property in this chapter? The answer is emphatically no. Yet there are many forms of capital which are not entirely in private ownership, or that benefit from services, infrastructure and other public capital, so this chapter will help you understand how a community manages all its forms of capital to create real wealth for its residents.

If you look at the community as an enterprise and its citizens as the owners, the capacity the community has to create real wealth and well-being can be characterized as the *community capital* used to produce that wealth. One definition of the word has been assets available for use in the production of further assets. The word's origin comes from *caput*, the head of a cow, from a time when pastoral civilizations counted the livestock they owned to determine their wealth. If assets are examples of the real wealth we have to meet our needs, then community capital represents the capacity to create this real wealth on an ongoing basis for the benefit of the community and its members.

This generative nature of capital is of particular interest for community leaders. Community capital — the generative capacity of a community — forms the foundation of the economy. A thousand boards are assets that might be enough to build a house, but managing a forest for sustainable yield and operating a sawmill will help insure that many more houses get built. The forest and the sawmill are the capital base. Their combined capacity to continue to produce lumber, along with the forest's capacity to produce oxygen, to absorb carbon dioxide, to provide habitat for wildlife and to serve as a critical part of the water cycle, will help insure a healthy and sustainable human community can continue to live nearby.

Competent capitalists know that in order to produce the items that make it possible to earn a profit and create wealth, they need to maintain their capital in good working order. This means continually reinvesting in upkeep and maintenance of the assets, keeping on top of the latest technology and minimizing the costs of production. The accounting and taxation systems that are prevalent in North America and Europe systematically account for the capital reinvestment needed — through depreciation schedules that estimate what investment is needed to maintain the capital's current value by compensating for the loss in value over time, as an asset is used up.

To begin a local community economic development program that will create long-term wealth, it is important to start to think like a community capitalist — to know all the local sources of real wealth and to have a plan for their ongoing care and maintenance. It is equally important to know their generative capacity over time — the conditions needed to insure that the community capital can continue to produce the assets the community needs. In the case of the forest, the conditions might be adequate rain and sunlight and a conservative management plan that attends to the life cycle regeneration of the trees and their ecosystem. In the case of the sawmill, it might be regular maintenance on the machinery along with a replacement schedule for the major equipment. The long-term capital plan will also include the conditions for the employees—training, wages, opportunities for growth and development. An additional consideration will be the impact of operations on the community—if the sawmill is routinely filling the surrounding environment with emissions and waste, this will obviously work against the neighborhood's quality of life.

Ten Types of Community Capital

What are the different types of community capital we need to achieve real wealth creation? The community systems and the asset inventory give us insight into the community capital we have, and the resulting productive, or generative, capacities are important enough to highlight when considering the strategy for our community enterprises. Looking at these different systems, the types of community capital they use to create assets follow.

Infrastructure

1. Natural Capital

Natural capital is the stock of environmental assets that produces more assets; for example, a healthy forest produces trees, habitat, carbon sequestration, erosion control, beauty, recreation and water purification if the natural capital base—its essential regenerative capacity—is maintained. Clearcutting the forest might produce some monetary income for a short period of time for a limited number of people, but it is spending down the region's capital, just as if you start to use the principal of the savings account that you have in the bank instead of taking the interest income to pay for your expenses. If spending capital goes on for too long, you won't have any money left. Strengthening our natural capital involves finding ways to protect and enhance those natural systems that provide the environmental services we need—air, water, climate, soil, food, waste assimilation, beauty, recreation, materials—without undermining their capacity to continue to provide the services in the future.

2. Built Capital

Built capital in a community includes the buildings, the physical infrastructure (e.g., roads, electric generation and transmission, pipes, wires, cables, water and wastewater treatment plants), housing, parks and recreational facilities, commercial and industrial facilities and other constructed elements of community life. Strengthening the built capital involves standard capital planning, as well as a thorough review of how the existing built capital is meeting the range of needs that have been identified. A very important and problematic aspect of the built capital, of course, is the land use patterns that result from its development. Sprawl, unserviced areas, squatter settlements...all these represent dysfunctional side effects of badly developed and poorly maintained built capital. The new approach is to build the infrastructure needed for community well-being and real wealth.

A Sustainable Energy Plan should also be part of the built capital plan. Revolutions in energy markets and technologies are happening because of the global ecological crisis and peak oil, so sustainable energy systems are becoming more cost-effective. This means that communities will benefit from a coherent, whole-system approach to energy that hasn't been required in the past.

3. Technological Capital

Technological capital includes the ways in which communities harness their intellectual resources to create tools, systems, machines, arts, skills and materials that are designed to improve our lives. Building on our capital in this area means supporting the education, creativity and access to materials that are required to create innovative technologies. For example, in a depressed township in South Africa, a young man who was educated in physics has developed an idea for a solar and bicycle powered battery charger — many of the people in the settlement use car batteries to power their homes' electrical needs. If he can gain access to the materials he needs to develop the new system, his good idea — which would generate income in an impoverished area, provide low-cost energy to the people in the community and reduce CO_2 emissions all at the same time — might succeed.

Social and Cultural Capital

4. Social Capital

The concept of social capital recognizes the economic importance of all the ways we are connected to each other: the relationships, networks and values we share and the cooperative systems we use for interacting.

The sum of social capital is the capacity for successful and effective collective action. When we're thinking in terms of how social capital produces additional social assets, we need to be mindful of all the ways that we can enhance the connectedness of our communities. When we're developing other strategies, we need to be careful not to do things that inadvertently rob our community of these connections. It's also important to avoid a situation where the social capital in one sector of the community works against the ability of other sectors to have connections with the community as a whole — the bonds between members of the local mafia could be called a form of social capital, yet its role in the community does not enhance other social assets.

5. Historic and Cultural Capital

Our community's historic and cultural capital are the historic resources we have that could be developed into tourist attractions, the cultural centers that celebrate our music, art, drama, dance and other creative endeavors, the programs in place to build and transmit our cultural understandings to others. To build and maintain historic and cultural capital involves a multifaceted approach that strengthens leadership qualities, enhances the built environment where cultural activities can happen, fosters creativity and talent, treasures historical records and information and promotes tolerance and respect for differences. The creative economy has now surpassed the traditional manufacturing sector in the United States, so the role of cultural capital is more important than ever.[2]

Human Development

6. Human Capital

Our human capital includes all the capabilities that people have to learn, to invent, to create, to work, to care for each other and to contribute to the community as a whole. To strengthen the human capital in our communities we need to develop strategies that increase capabilities on every level. People who live up to their potential enhance their lives and the life of their communities. Maintaining these capabilities also involves developing systems that enhance wellness, and that care for people who are sick, physically and mentally challenged, or, for example, too young or too old to care for themselves. It means building the caring capacity of our communities, so that people feel a sense of belonging and mutual support where family relationships and social networks are healthy for the individuals in them. This form of capital used to exist more frequently in rural and small town settings.

7. Institutional Capital

A standard definition of institutional capital is hard to find — to some it means the financial resources controlled by key institutions and to others it represents the institutional framework governing the economy. For the purposes of this book, we define institutional capital as the structures, organizations, legal and financial frameworks that enable a society and an economy to function. This includes the legal system and the rule of law, the insurance system that helps communities manage risk, the systems that establish different exchange mechanisms (national and complementary currencies), the regulatory structures that protect the natural environment, human rights and human health and well-being and all the institutional arrangements that provide a foundation for economic activity.

Economic Capital

When you think of economic capital, the financial capital needed to undertake any type of enterprise is probably what comes to mind. For our purposes however, we will distinguish between three types of economic capital: financial, entrepreneurial and potential exchange capital.

8. Financial Capital

The financial capital available for the creation of real wealth includes the loan resources available through the banking system and the savings and investment made by individuals and institutions. Strengthening and increasing this type of capital always seems like the obvious path to successful economic development, yet by understanding the other two forms of capital, it is possible to identify other critical resources that new ventures need to get started.

9. Entrepreneurial Capital

The entrepreneurial capital in your community includes those businesses and organizations that mobilize all the other types of capital to produce the assets that meet human needs. Entrepreneurial capital includes both the for-profit and nonprofit sector — the manufacturers, service industry, retail shops, hospitals, daycare centers, architects, engineers, planners, beauty parlors, restaurants, amusement parks, golf courses, hotels, schools, universities, nursing homes — in short, all of the employers who put us to work. The sum total represents a critical part of the productive capacity in any community, and without it the economy wouldn't exist.

10. Potential Exchange Capital

Besides the economic assets which are measured in bank-debt money (e.g., dollars, euros, pesos, yen), another form of capital that is often overlooked is capital that can be mobilized through complementary currency systems. This capital is important because it contributes to our well-being without being limited by the scarcity of bank-debt money. The word economy comes from the Greek words *oikos* and *nomos*, meaning management of a household. The functions of a household include but also go beyond those that are captured in the monetized exchanges. To truly understand our economy, we need to look beyond the value that is translated into monetary terms.

All of these forms of capital produce the critical flows of assets through the economic system. Capital is the foundation, the reproductive system, the greenhouse that grows a healthy economy. If you picture your community as an island, and measure all the flows of money, resources, goods and services in and out of the community, it's easier to understand how this works. If the island maintains its natural capital, so that the soils stay productive, the water remains abundant and clean, and the plants and animals are all healthy, then it can produce food for the people that live there, with possibly some extra agricultural goods or products — jams, wool, sweaters, lumber, furniture — to sell to the mainland.

If the money from the mainland is saved in local banks (financial capital), then there are loans available to people who want to borrow to start a business. If the local schools teach people to foster their creativity and innovation and understand risks, then there might be some entrepreneurs who could figure out how to make better sweaters or furniture (entrepreneurial capital). They might charter a company (institutional capital) and work with local community leaders (social capital) to build a larger factory (built capital). A training program for the workers would help insure that there were people with the skills to make the products (human capital).

Each asset — the skills of the workers, the incorporation papers of the company, the entrepreneurial imagination — has a base of experience and collective support behind it that allows it to reproduce itself in new ways. This is the capital base. The way all the different forms of capital work together, and the flows of different assets through a community and among different communities, form what we've come to know as the economic system.

Exchange as Social Change

Could it be that one of the most profound things we could do to foster healthy economic activity would be to use an additional medium of exchange, instead of depending on bank-debt money for all our transactions? It seems too simple to be true.

In fact, connecting all the different needs in a community with assets available is one of the main goals of any currency. *Currency* — sharing the same root as the word current — makes things flow. So, consideration of how to start work on the local level designing and implementing currencies that can serve a community (as exchange mechanisms, stores of value and units of account) begins with an inventory of needs, assets and capital. This inventory would also identify those needs which are going unmet and areas where there are resources or assets which are underutilized. Unmet needs and underutilized resources are places in the system where flow is possible, but untapped. This potential exchange capital of any community is the basis for new kinds of economic flows and activity in a community. Mobilizing these flows is the essence of a community currency.

There are at least as many different types of exchange possible in any given community as there are underutilized forms of capital. Each set of assets fills different needs and uses different resources. Flows can move between the resource base, the productive process and the consumer without money — we have simply become used to using money as the medium. And we don't have to regress to barter — exchanges without any standardized medium — to correct this problem. We can simply introduce complementary currencies, designed to circulate in parallel with conventional money.

Tools Available Today

A *complementary currency* is an agreement to use something other than legal tender (i.e., national, or bank debt money) as a medium of exchange, with the purpose to link unmet needs with otherwise unused resources.[3] Complementary currencies exist on many levels and for many purposes — consider what has happened with frequent flyer miles issued by the airline industry around the world. Initially, frequent flyer miles were only a marketing gimmick for each individual airline; they could only be used to purchase airline tickets of that specific airline. Now, fourteen trillion airline miles have been issued by five major global airline alliances — more than all the dollars or Euros combined.[4] They can be earned without setting a foot in a plane (e.g., through the use of specific credit cards) and they have become redeemable not only for air travel, but for car rentals, long-distance phone services and an increasing range of products. For instance, ⅔ of all British Airways miles are now cashed in for something other than an airline ticket. In short, airline miles have become a corporate scrip with a specific commercial aim — customer loyalty. They mobilize the otherwise unused resource of an empty airline seat to achieve that aim.

Economists will correctly point out that matching needs and resources is the function of the market, even without complementary currencies. And if by the agency of some magic wand all humans on the planet suddenly had an optimal distribution of money, one could even imagine that there wouldn't be any unmet needs. The reality is clearly different. Therefore, the starting point for complementary currencies is to meet needs that remain unfulfilled after transactions facilitated with bank-debt money have taken place. Similarly, unused resources are those that haven't been used in economic transactions mediated by bank-debt money.

The economics of frequent flyer miles illustrates how this process works even in strictly commercial environments. A well managed frequent flyer mile system is the one that obtains something (customer loyalty) at the cost of an unused resource (an airline seat that would otherwise remain empty). Community currencies simply extrapolate these same concepts to a broader environment, where the benefits are chosen by the participants themselves.

An Ecology of Currencies

As needs and resources are identified, the possibility of an *ecology of currencies* emerges, where different economic goals could be achieved by different types of currency, complementary to each other — not so many as to make it impossibly complex and confusing, but just enough. This is particularly true in the US, where the taxation rules around complementary currencies often require there to be different systems for different purposes.

For example, in Montpelier, Vermont, the city started with a Time Bank system, which is a tax exempt form of community currency pioneered by Edgar Cahn, an attorney who has dedicated his life to social justice issues.[5] In a Time Bank, members exchange units of time, and all members' time is worth the same amount — an hour is an hour, whether you're a highly skilled computer technician or a babysitter. The Time Bank is particularly useful for a wide variety of social purposes such as anti-poverty, elder care, community organizing and alternative transportation. The fact that the value of the exchanges does not count toward income (unlike barter, which is taxable) means that people can raise their standard of living without putting at risk their government benefits like food stamps, subsidized housing, daycare and medical insurance. Time Banks will be discussed further in Part II.

Once the Time Bank was underway, the city started exploring other possible systems. The first was a commercial barter system, where companies can exchange goods and services with other companies for credits instead of money. Because this is a taxable form of currency, it cannot intermingle with the Time Bank units. If companies spend as much as they earn in commercial barter, however, the tax implications are generally negligible, since profit would have to be made on the transactions before tax would be imposed. (The US does not have a value-added tax.) The Vermont Sustainable Exchange is a new commercial barter system established in the Burlington area, so meetings were held between the Exchange and the Central Vermont Chamber of Commerce to recruit businesses in Central Vermont to the system. Commercial barter and other business purposes will be discussed further in Part III.

Going further, the Central Vermont Food Systems Council has designed a local food currency that would foster locally grown foods and support the local restaurants that use local food, farmers, restaurant workers and food processors. While similar to commercial barter, the food currency needed to cross the lines between businesses and employees, and businesses and customers. It needed to help farmers and restaurants keep good workers by providing extra income that would help relatively low paying jobs flourish in the local economy.

Taking a step back from these three relatively simple examples, the different flows through discrete parts of the local economy can be seen. The Time Bank fosters a social flow, where people are connecting with each other to provide a variety of different services on the basis of mutual respect and reciprocity. Commercial Barter works in the business sector to increase transactions which strengthen the buying power of local businesses and to give them an edge against larger, more vertically integrated global enterprises. This helps build local wealth and a higher level of resilience in the face of economic downturns. The Food Currency reinforces a critically important life-support system and raises the standard of living for all of the people working in the food service sector which are traditionally low-income jobs, at least in Vermont.

All living systems manage the flows of many different kinds of energy, nourishment, waste, information and reproduction. By restricting our economy's circulation to one type of money system we make it less resilient, at higher risk to shocks and other disturbances, and we lose a vast array of economic activity that could serve both humanity and the natural world more effectively. Creating an ecology of currencies that is more congruent with the ecological imperatives of Earth and the social and human needs of the human family can help bring the economic system back in line with the survival of our species.

Providing a new basis to increase the flow of assets throughout the local economic system in ways that meet real needs (while enhancing generative capacities) strengthens the foundation, the reproductive system, the greenhouse of the economy called capital. In this way, community and complementary currencies create new capital by fostering other forms of capital in the economy. A currency that encourages people to save energy, reduce fossil fuel use and lower emissions strengthens the natural capital of the climate regulation system and creates new capital for innovation in the energy sector. Using a local currency to link vocational trainees with houses that need renovation creates new capital in both the built environment and the human capital sectors. New capital can be created in most areas if we find new ways to unleash our creativity, interdependence and compassion outside and around the constraints national money imposes. Abundance and sufficiency are available to us, even in a finite world.

CHAPTER 4

The Possibility of Sufficiency and Abundance

No complaint is more common
than that of a scarcity of money.

ADAM SMITH, THE WEALTH OF NATIONS

We fear scarcity, the sense that there is never going to be enough for everyone. The sense of scarcity has driven human competition since the dawn of civilization—for water, for hunting territory, for women, for land. On Spaceship Earth, scarcity is a fact of life. Fossil fuels are increasingly scarce, along with sweet water, rainforests, precious metals and fine jewels. Other things will always be scarce—good pitching arms, original Rembrandts, Cliff Walk properties in Newport, operatic sopranos, true genius. When there are a lot of people who want very scarce things, the value of the scarce resource goes up relative to other resources—this is simple supply and demand economics.

Money is also scarce. There is never enough of it for everything people need. We all are so accustomed to money being scarce that it's hard to imagine a world where there is enough money for everyone. One of the important lessons all students learn in Economics 101 is that when money supply increases, inflation increases, so there's a good reason for money to be scarce—we don't want its value compromised by too much inflation. The specter of hyperinflation, when a national money system spirals out of control into ever higher denominations is a real fear associated with too much money in circulation. Zimbabwe was the first country in the 21st century to suffer from this with 231 million percent inflation.

But what if inflation is only the result of too much of a particular kind of money — this bank-debt money we accept without question? There are other units of exchange that aren't ravaged by inflationary trends. Is inflation the result of a lot of money in circulation, or is the type of money in circulation responsible for inflation? In fact, to retain its value, bank-debt money needs to be scarce.

Demurrage Currencies

At least twice in history, a form of money has existed where there was no incentive to accumulate it as a store of value because it didn't earn positive interest in bank accounts. Instead, it had the equivalent of a negative interest rate (known as demurrage) — the longer you held on to it, the more you would have to pay — similar to a parking fee on money. This gave people who were paid in this currency a strong incentive to spend it or to invest it — preferably in things that would continue to be valuable over the long term. The *velocity* of this type of money, in other words, was quite high. Since people didn't hoard it, it also was not scarce — there is strong evidence that its existence fostered long periods of prosperity in Dynastic Egypt and during the Central Middle Ages (10th–13th centuries) in Europe.

In the first example, from Egypt, people would receive shards of pottery with a date on them when they put their grain into the storehouse. The longer the grain was stored, the more the charge was for the guards and waste as the grain spoiled. Called *ostraka*,[1] these shards circulated alongside the precious metals rings and bars that were used for trade with foreigners. The Greeks, Egypt's main trading partners at that time, would mock the plain clay Egyptian currency. Yet the Egyptians thought the Greek obsession with metals was strange, "a piece of local vanity, patriotism, or advertisement, with no far-reaching importance."[2] They would accept Greek coins, but only for their metal content. The ancient Egyptians enjoyed an abundant and prosperous life. They lived in a fertile valley, producing grains, meat, wine and beer in quantities sufficient for all levels of society, and they were well-educated. They invested in quality public works and their irrigation systems were the envy of the world. When they built something to last, they built it to last forever — the pyramids and temples of this ancient culture survive today.

There is evidence that the money they used — this negative interest money made of plain clay shards — was at the root of the good life they enjoyed. The *ostraka* system, known as the corn standard system, was used for over 2,000 years until the Roman conquest of Egypt around 30 BC. When the Romans replaced the *ostraka* with their gold and silver, the long period of prosperity ended. From then on, positive interest charges accrued to Rome. Over time, this in turn changed Egypt into the equivalent of a developing country: poverty increased, as did the gap between the rich and the poor.

The second example of demurrage, or negative interest money, was special coinage used for local payments during the Central Middle Ages in Europe. These coins were produced by monasteries, bishops, provincial aristocracy and townships, and bore the resemblance of the current Bishop, Lord or King (*seignoriage* means fees earned through an authority's issuance of standardized currency, and it is derived from the Old French *seignior*, or lord).[3] During Carolingian times, the coins were changed when the rulers changed (a practice called *renovatio monetae*), and a recoinage tax would be assessed on the coins that were turned in. So the last person holding the coins would end up paying the tax. This provided a strong incentive to spend money rather than hoarding it for the future. However, instead of waiting for a lord to die, *renovatio monetae* evolved to a system where every five or six years coins would be reissued. The recoinage dates were not always predictable, and the abuse of this practice resulted in more frequent recalls, the first of which was in England when Harold I recoined only three years after Cnut had done so, and then Harthcnut did it again two years later. Archbishop Wichmann of Magdeburg revoked the money in his domain twice per year![4]

Like all taxes, the recoinage tax was not liked by the people, and yet without their knowing the existence of a negative interest currency led to a flourishing medieval society, especially during the period between 1000–1300 AD. Local coinage was not the only kind of money — as in Egypt, long-distance trade with other countries (usually for luxuries) required some kind of convertible coin, usually made of precious metal.

But local coins were an important medium — or even the dominant one — for local trading, and its periodic tax gave people an incentive to spend money on productive items rather than to save and hoard it. This increased velocity made the coins less scarce. As in Egypt, it also led to an era of building where things were made to last — the great cathedrals of Europe were all built during this period.

The era came to an end as centralized authority expanded, enabled and further strengthened by the introduction of gunpowder in the 1400s. As kingdoms grew, reissuing money became more and more cumbersome. This, combined with opposition to the practice (it was a tax, after all), as well as its abuses, led to its demise. Rulers like King Philip IV of France turned to debasement (reducing the metallic content in the precious metal coins) rather than demurrage for their taxes — an early trigger for inflation. This change, introduced in the 1290s, preceded the economic collapse that provided fertile ground for the plagues that ravaged Europe beginning in 1347 AD.

The point here is not to wax nostalgic for some lost golden eras, as there were plenty of other problems that people had to struggle with at those times. Rather, the purpose is to show that there are alternatives to a monopoly of the particular form of money we have in existence today. It is also an illustration of the possibility of separating two functions that money serves — the store of value and the means of exchange — as a way of creating more prosperity and more economic activity.

Cooperative and Competitive Currencies

Cooperation and competitiveness are two characteristics of the human condition that make civilization possible. We know that too much or little of either characteristic leads to its own set of problems. Too much competition and both sides lose when each compromise their own long-term integrity to score a point right now. Too much cooperation, and there is no room for the dialectic of innovation and critique that fosters continual improvement. There needs to be a balance between the two, and yet the balance is always hard to find.

There is no doubt that the economy of the United States in the 21st century could be called a competitive economy. Competition in free markets is held up as the only way to get low prices and all the benefits of a well-oiled economic system. Schools are competitive, as students vie with each other to get the best grades and to be accepted in exclusive colleges. Sports are competitive, and even families living on the same street have been known to do what it takes to "keep up with the Joneses." Competition provides the energy most US citizens thrive on, at least on the airwaves and in public discourse.

Things are a little different north of the 49th parallel. Although Canada shares many of the characteristics of the United States, its economy and culture is somewhat less competitive. This can be documented by the large number of cooperative enterprises in Canada per capita as compared to the United States, and the fact that Canadians successfully managed to create a national healthcare system, something the US is only now starting. Many other western industrialized countries exhibit more of a balance between competition and cooperation than the US, as demonstrated in public benefits, inexpensive education systems, high quality national healthcare and other policies that strengthen the common good, rather than being oriented toward the individual.

All currencies do not need to be scarce. For instance, a currency can be designed to be always in sufficiency, because it is created at the moment of exchange as a credit for the seller and as a debit for the buyer. Examples of this are *mutual credit currencies*, which form the basis of Time Banks, commercial barter systems, Local Exchange Trading Systems (LETS) and others. In the Onion River Exchange, Montpelier's Time Bank for example, if I need a ride to the airport and you are willing to give me a ride to the airport, we'll agree on an amount of Community Credits (the name of the currency units, which in this case are measured in time) to exchange for the service, and off we go. Community Credits are simply notations in a central computer system and there are no notes or coins exchanged at all. You don't need to have surplus to make transactions — it is acceptable to have negative balances in the system. The optimal balance, in fact, is zero, since that would mean you are giving as much to the system as you are receiving.

There is no inflation in such a system, and no worries about over-abundance triggering lower values. Let us emphasize that such a currency is sufficient for the purpose it serves. Cooperation is high — every transaction in the system is a result from an agreement. There are no price wars or people trying to secure a monopoly on a particular good or service. The quality of transactions is high, and the exchange's reputation spreads more by word of mouth at the events and social opportunities which it organizes.

A Time Bank or mutual credit system will never, and should never, take the place of all money. The goal is rather to provide an additional means of exchange that is sufficient to meet our needs for a variety of goods and services. It is fair to say that fossil fuels will never be traded in a mutual credit system; in fact, on that ride to the airport it is likely that you would pay some cash for the gas cost, since the airport is a 45 minute drive from Montpelier. However anything you can spend time on is fair game in a Time Bank. And there are always just enough Community Credits to go around—they only come into existence at the moment they're needed.

The Value of Time

Time ain't money when all you got is time.
GREG BROWN, FOLKSINGER

The value of time through history has been the subject of many economic theories, practices and terms. They include Marx's labor theory of value, opportunity costs, just in time manufacturing, discount rates and minimum wage. Time is clearly a critical piece of the economic system. The notion of scarcity casts a shadow on our idea of the value of time. We recognize that there are people with more skills and knowledge than we have, and so we pay more for their time as a result. Rocket scientists, brain surgeons and sports stars all have something that is relatively scarce—a talent or an ability that is highly valued. Jobs that require fewer skills, on the other hand, don't command as high a pay rate, largely because there are more people who can do them. The abundance of people with the skills makes the jobs more competitive, and the wages lower. There is only one Oprah, but house cleaners and street sweepers are numerous.

Yet just because there is an abundance of something does not necessarily make it less valuable to us as a species, even if its monetary value is relatively low. Every day we all need at least some of the following: child care, elder care, health services, food preparation. If we had to pay money for every moment of time that was spent on this part of our economy, we'd quickly go bankrupt even if the people we employed were not highly compensated.

Time is a great equalizer. We all only have 24 hours in a day, and how we choose to spend it is largely dictated by the economic system we're in. If we're part of a hunter/gatherer society, anthropologists have observed that we spend about 20–30 hours a week in activities that could be classified as *work* and the rest of the time playing games, making music and hanging around the camp. In the feudal system during the European Middle Ages, the breakdown of hours worked as compared to hours spent doing other things was about the same. Now, in so-called advanced civilization, we are spending many more hours per week working for pay and fewer hours in recreational, social and spiritual pursuits. Why have we chosen these priorities in our society?

Communities and cities run on time. Time is the glue that holds them together, the oxygen they breathe. The time volunteers spend serving on town committees, the time it takes city councilors to run for office, the time it takes citizens to participate in government — all of this is critical to community success, and almost none of it is work that comes with compensation. Service clubs who do volunteer work, church groups who staff the soup kitchens, food pantries and thrift stores, the girl scouts and boy scouts, the volunteer firefighters: all of these people and their time is what makes community more than a spot on a map.

In Bali, the people have recognized the value of community time for millennia and have a dual currency system that accounts for the time people need to spend on community activities. Community life is rich — each Balinese spends about 30% of their time on creative endeavors — dance, artwork, ceremony — that contribute to community life, particularly the elaborate ceremonies undertaken in their temples. The people are also part of a community group called a *subak*, which maintains the irrigation systems for rice production, and a *banjar*, which coordinates the civic life of the community, a bit like local government.

Each Balinese spends time in two ways — through conventional jobs in the businesses and other money-making enterprises on the island (being paid in *Rupiah*, the national currency), and also through *Nayahan Banjar*, which translated means "work for the common good of the Banjar." The *Nayahan Banjar* unit of account is a block of time, typically about three hours long. Each Banjar initiates between seven and ten projects per month, and each family is expected to contribute both *Rupiah* and their time, and both are accounted for. The governance system of a banjar can be described as hyper-democratic: for instance, the Klian Banjar leaders are not only elected at a majority but can also be un-elected whenever a majority chooses.

> In most cases, there is no problem finding enough people to contribute the time needed to complete an activity; thus contributions of time are not recorded. In some Banjars, however, where there is a scarcity in the contribution of time or when there are complaints from some members about the lack of contribution by others, the Klian Banjar records every contribution of time. Those who cannot contribute their share of time are asked to send a substitute person. If neither option is possible, they must then pay a charge of between 5,000 and 10,000 Rupiah (approx $1.20 US) for each time block missed.[5]

It may sound inexpensive enough so that you would assume people would buy their way out of community service, but in practice this is done only occasionally. So, the work goes on, and both time and money help pay for it.

The dual currency in Bali makes it possible for there to be a lot of flexibility with different projects, depending on the community. In wealthier communities where people have more money and less time, projects that cost more are easily approved. But in poorer villages more time and less money is available, but elaborate festivals and projects are still possible because the people choose to put in more time. There is less division between the wealthy and the poor for occasions like weddings and funerals as a result, because even people who are relatively poor in monetary terms can have big celebrations for major life events. The community work extends to other local tasks as well, such as improvements at the school or on roads, especially if the national government has not done its part.

Perhaps we have lost something in the West. Our affluence has made it possible to buy our way out of community service, even though we complain bitterly about all the taxes we pay to local and state governments. We don't spend our time on community projects in any official way, and that leaves the work to be done for pay, which is rapidly escalating out of control. On one level time isn't money, and the intrinsic value of time can be captured through different exchange systems like Time Banks.

Revaluing time can also move us towards a sense of sufficiency and abundance, since the things we need in abundance are impossible to fully value with a conventional money system. Child care is low paid work because it is abundant, and yet what is more important than raising our children? Elder care is low paid work for the same reason, and the abuses and neglect in that system make regular news as a result, a tragedy of epic proportions. Clearly something is not working when these critical life functions are systematically devalued by society. But every mother, father, son and daughter is caught in the dilemma of the cost of time. How can they give up the work paid at $30 per hour for tasks that people get barely above minimum wage to perform? It doesn't make economic sense — in most cases taking the time to do elder care or child care would mean economic hardship for the family. While it might be impossible to recreate the cultural norms that Bali has had in place for over one thousand years in the average US suburb, finding a way to revalue community time is important for a sustainable community.

The Two-Game Economy

A balance between competition and cooperation is critical for our civilization and our survival. Yet every morning when we get up, make breakfast and go to work, we are blindly participating in an economy propelled by a monetary system that values only one side — the competitive side of the equation. Even on a sports team, every coach knows that he needs to put in as much effort building the team as he does helping the members have the skills they need to beat the opposition. Players study the playbook and talk about how they need to work together on coordinated action.

Games of competition and collaboration are the polar ends of the way humans can interact. Another word for these two complementary qualities are Yin and Yang, the fundamental dyad that Chinese philosophy applies to all forms of manifestation. In *Creating Wealth*, we use the words cooperation and competition because they are more familiar terms for Western minds, but these characteristics are less all-encompassing. Yet for our purposes, they serve as a good reference point given their relevance to economic and community life.

What are the different values and characteristics of a system that fosters competition compared to one that fosters cooperation? Figure 1 presents the tendencies and patterns on each side of the game.

Values and Characteristics	Competition	Cooperation
Motivation	Having, Doing	Being
Operation	Peak Experience	Endurance–Sustainability
Thought Process	Formal Logic	Dialectical Logic
Causality	Linear	Non-linear, Cyclical
Problem-Solving	Technology	Interpersonal Relationships
Organizational Preferences	Bigger is Better	Small is Beautiful
	Hierarchy	Egalitarian
	Central Authority	Decentralized System
	Command and Control	Mutual Trust and Action
Spirituality	Transcendent God	Immanent Divinity

FIGURE 4.1. Competition and Cooperation

Obviously, in real life a balance needs to be struck between these two orientations. An exclusive focus on either one of those poles would be a problem. Yet the monetary system we have developed, which is now the primary one worldwide, focuses only on the competitive side, and therefore fosters competition at the expense of cooperation.

THE WAY OF YIN-YANG

The age-old philosophical framework of Yin-Yang makes it possible to provide a shorthand description of the entire thesis in this book. Conventional money is an extreme Yang construct: hierarchical, top down, with build-in interest which acts as a centralizing (by definition those with money get more of it, those without get less) and competition driving mechanism (see "The Eleventh Round" in Chapter 2).

A monopoly of a Yang currency will tend to induce a Yang bias in what is being honored with that currency. This explains why all the Yin functions tend to be underpaid in our societies. How many salaries of an average schoolteacher fit into an average investment banker's monthly check? Yet we entrust these underpaid teachers with what we hold as most precious: our children. In an environment where the monopoly of a Yang currency is enforced, all the caring functions—in fact all Yin functions—will systematically tend to be undervalued.

One irony is that it is government that enforces this monopoly by accepting only privately created bank-debt money as *legal tender* in payment for all fees and taxes. Taxes are what systemically enforce the demand for a particular currency.[6] The marginalization of any currency, including any Yin currency, would automatically stop whenever a government (at whatever level) requests annual contributions payable only in that specific currency. That same governmental entity could also issue this Yin currency interest free under whatever rules and principles that it chooses. Nonprofit NGOs would be among the logical organizers of the programs for which Yin currency would be issued. Such a dual legal tender currency strategy would empower civil society. Democratic control over the entity that has the power to require such a tax is important: it will be where the balance between the relative importance of the Yin and Yang economies will be decided. For instance, up to ⅓ of an adult Balinese's time is part of the Yin economy, and it has been proven that it is essential for a very democratic process to prevail for such a system to work.[7]

Much of the balance of *Creating Wealth* is about currencies which foster cooperative behavior that can counterbalance the existing system. One of the key questions is whether they can be introduced at a speed and scale adequate to face so many global crises. The evidence of their effectiveness (even when their existence was not introduced by design as in the cases of ancient Egypt, modern day Bali or the Central Medieval period in Europe) would suggest that a "two-game" economy could provide a more resilient prosperity over the long term. The chapters in Part II will describe in detail the problems in each sector of the economy caused by the constraint of a monopoly of bank-debt money and the alternatives that exist to address these problems.

Unmet Needs and Underutilized Resources

One of the critical faults of the national money system's tendency to value only those things that are scarce is its propensity to leave many economic resources undervalued and/or underutilized. Introducing complementary currencies links underutilized resources with unmet needs — this is the primary way these currencies create new wealth. Empty airline seats are transformed into customer loyalty and higher profits. Undervalued time is transformed into critical services needed to help elders be involved in their communities. Excess inventory can be liberated to serve people without the resources to buy it, in exchange for other things highly valued by the company.

There are a wide variety of *unmet needs*:

+ Social needs (e.g., elderly care or youth mentoring)
+ Economic needs (e.g., unemployment and underemployment)
+ Commercial needs (e.g., helping the locally owned groceries to better compete against the supermarket chains)
+ Ecological, cultural or educational needs (e.g., supporting local non-profit organizations, and community or regional identity building)

Similarly, *underutilized resources* can be found in the most unexpected places:

+ Any unemployed person who is willing and able to do something has some unused capacities
+ The next time you go to your neighborhood restaurant or movie house, count the tables and chairs that are empty: these are all unused resources that could be mobilized for your purposes
+ Schools or other buildings that are empty during part of the week or the year
+ College, university or vocational courses
+ Youth organizations and other nonprofits that have people ready to do things if supplies are provided

The idea is to design complementary currencies that are backed by or redeemable in some of those underutilized resources and can be mobilized to meet unmet needs. Empty stadium seats at sporting events might be offered to people who volunteer to coach student sports or who mentor youth in other ways. The marginal costs to the sports facility do not increase with more people filling the seats, and while they would always prefer to sell the seats, the fact remains that an empty seat is an unsold seat. The same principle applies to empty seats on public transportation systems, seats in the theater and tickets to public and private recreational facilities: amusement parks, swimming pools, golf courses and ski areas. Obviously there might be some interest in making the free passes available at times when the facilities are not at capacity, just as airlines black out times when their frequent flyers cannot use the seats.

The greatest underutilized resources of all are the people in every community. Our specialized economy has tended to make each of us focus on one fairly narrow task at work, and yet we have meter readers who are talented artists, store clerks who knit award winning sweaters and scarves, bankers who are expert cabinetmakers, insurance salespeople who love to teach. When you factor in the people who aren't working — the unemployed, the elders, the underemployed — the pool of skills, knowledge and time grows exponentially. But our current system doesn't have an effective way to mobilize people, largely because we are so dependent on money to do it.

THE CORE ECONOMY

A vast amount of services that meet our collective unmet needs are those which constitute what Edgar Cahn, the founder of Time Banks, calls the "core economy."[8] Here is an excerpt from his blog:

The Core Economy is not Wall Street or Main Street; it is the economy of family, neighborhood, kith and kin. Recently more and more economists acknowledge that something like 40–50% of productive economic activity takes place outside of the market and is not measured by traditional indicators. But even those percentages do not begin to convey either the scale or significance of an economic system that is pervasively ignored. Futurist Alvin Toffler captured the implications of what economists overlook with a question he puts to CEOs of Fortune 500 companies: "How productive do you think your workforce would be if it was not toilet trained?" That's a useful if disconcerting starting point for reassessing what we value and measure as *productive labor.*

A physician at a nationally renowned medical school puts this question to first year medical students: What group of people do you think delivers the most medical care and treatment in this country?" Doctors? No. Nurses? No. Allied health professionals? No. The correct answer is "mothers." Just compute the number of days school children are sick; then add infant care, preventive medicine, and chronic conditions, and a different profile of health-care practitioners emerges.

Who teaches children to walk? To talk? To obey the rules? To tell the truth? To avoid harming themselves? To avoid harming others? Who produces a workforce that gets up in the morning, gets to places on time, and knows it is wrong to steal and lie? Mothers, fathers, grandparents, families and those institutions that impart moral values.

Who keeps neighborhoods safe, keeps violence down? A $51 million study extending over ten years by renowned researchers from Harvard, Columbia and the University of Michigan finally pinned down the critical factor. They called it "collective efficacy"—which when translated into language we all understand turns out to mean: neighbors stopping kids from painting graffiti, having fights, hanging out on street corners. It is an invisible local culture that boils down to looking after each others' kids.

When an economist undertook to quantify the replacement value of just one function of this Core Economy, he found that the unpaid work done by family, friends, neighbors and kinfolk to keep seniors out of nursing homes totaled $196 billion in 1997. By 2000, when he updated his computation, it had risen to $257 billion. The value of just the informal caregiving portion of the labor produced by the Core Economy was *six times greater* [emphasis added] than the money spent in the market economy to purchase formal home healthcare services for the elderly; it is over twice what the federal government spends on nursing home care. Consider the monetary implications of even a small drop in the productivity of the Core Economy and if we were obliged to buy those services at market prices with increased private insurance or increased taxes for Medicare and Medicaid.

In recent decades, highly respected economists have undertaken to include the value of unpaid household labor that does not get included in the GDP or other standard economic measures of productivity. Rigorous estimates of the value of household labor have ranged from ¼ to ⅓ of the GDP.[9]

Feminine economists have tended to focus on Caring Labor as an essential component of productive labor missing from official economic indicators. But there are other kinds of labor that are equally essential and equally absent: Civic Labor, Social Justice Labor and Environmental Labor. And then there is another kind of labor that goes into Knowledge Acquisition that might be called Learning Labor.[10]

Caring, learning, civic engagement, the arts, social justice, a clean environment…what would our lives be like if people didn't spend their
time on these things? Yet the structure of the market economy based
on scarce national bank-debt money is systematically robbing us of our
ability to spend our time on these activities, even if we are employed.
People are spending more and more of their time earning a buck, and
less and less of their time making a living.

The Possibility of Sufficiency and Abundance

Complementary currencies that match unmet needs with underutilized
resources can be described as sufficient — in mutual credit systems they
come into existence as and when needed. The supply does not need to
be tightly controlled by a central authority, there is no inflation if they
are correctly designed, there is always enough of them to go around. The
idea of *enough* captures a sense of sufficiency. On the level of meeting
important needs, enough is exactly right. If we are hungry, we don't need
to overeat. If we are cold, we don't need to overheat. If we need to go
from our house to the doctor's office, we don't need to go back and forth
the same day — one trip is sufficient.

Yet finding sufficiency in matching unmet needs with underutilized
resources creates an abundance that is otherwise not as available. These
transactions are a source of real wealth, and can liberate all sorts of skills
and talents that are otherwise ignored. Thinking back to the definition
of wealth in Chapter 1, the word refers to well-being. We are in posses-
sion of well-being when our needs are met. We can have all the money
in the world, but if we are not healthy, in a loving relationship, with
access to a civic and cultural life to feed our soul, the money becomes
useless.

Further, the scarce money we depend on today creates a dynamic
all its own that pulls us away from the things that are really important
in life; how many people spend more time earning or managing their
money than they do with their families? How many days off come and
go where we are just too tired to go out and do anything fun because
the working week has robbed us of all the energy we may have had to
do something rewarding and fulfilling? Recapturing the value of the
cooperative currencies and integrating them into our everyday life can
restore the lost balance we need and make the circle whole again.

PART II

EXAMPLES OF COMPLEMENTARY CURRENCIES

CHAPTER 5

Building Equity

The reason saving comes before investing is that you need to have seed before you can sow it in anticipation of a harvest.

RAJEN DEVADASON

Neo-feudal Housing: The New Lords and Serfs

Home ownership has been one of the cornerstones of the American dream for almost a century. As early as in the 1920s, Better Homes in America, Inc. worked with the Department of Commerce to promote housing as an economic development strategy, knowing that the construction of homes would provide jobs and other multiplied economic benefits.

It wasn't until 1939 that the largest housing subsidy in US history was invented—the deduction on income taxes for the interest paid on mortgages. This, combined with federal mortgage insurance, the GI Bill for soldiers coming home from World War II and the mass production of automobiles, has shaped the ways in which our housing has developed ever since. Our homes are often our only source of equity—a cornerstone of the wealth we are able to accumulate in hope of securing a comfortable life.

In 2008, this clever combination of strategies—housing construction that creates jobs, mortgages that produce interest for the financial system and home ownership as a way to build wealth—collapsed on

73

themselves and brought the rest of the financial system with them, creating the largest economic crisis in the US since the Great Depression. The genesis of the sub-prime crisis of 2008 illuminates the problems at the root of the financial system, but also points to a way forward out of the mess.

Every person who buys a home in the United States triggers the creation of money. We go to the bank and apply for a mortgage. When we do this, some people imagine that the bank has the money to lend to us from the savings of other people. It's just a matter of making an application to get them to unlock the vault and hand out the money that's stored there. Not so. The banks are allowed to lend money based on the *fractional reserve system*, which means that they are only required to have 10% of the money they loan out in reserve. When you agree to take a mortgage for $100,000, the bank therefore needs to have only about $10,000 of that on hand. They give you a check for the mortgage, which is then deposited in another bank, freeing the next bank up to provide loans for up to 90% of that deposit, and on and on it goes.

When banks were deregulated and allowed to start giving mortgages to people who they knew would be unable to keep up with the mortgage payments over the long term, a LOT of money was created. But the money was only as valuable as the promises to repay the debt; once it became obvious that a lot of the mortgages were not going to be repaid, the whole system came crashing down like a house of cards.

The financial designers were clever — they packaged all of these mortgage notes into *derivatives* and sold big packages of derivatives in products with different risk levels. The built-in assumptions were that real estate would continue to go up in value and that all these mortgage notes would be paid back. When real estate started to decline and people started to default on their mortgages, suddenly no one wanted to touch all of the mortgage-backed financial instruments in circulation. The result was that the real market value of all these derivatives could not be determined. With $1.2 trillion in circulation, it was hard for the bankers to know who had the worthless ones. This uncertainty undermined the banks' trust in each other — they couldn't tell which banks or finance houses would be liable to fail, so overnight the credit market evaporated. Banks wouldn't even lend to each other overnight, a standard practice until that moment.

The money in the system that was created by all these suddenly worthless pieces of paper disappeared even faster than it appeared in the first place. The wreckage this has caused is staggering—in 2006, there were 268,532 people who lost their homes to foreclosure, in 2007 that number grew to 405,000.[1] During 2008, more than 1,000,000 people lost their homes to foreclosure! In 2009, the number grew to 2.82 million,[2] and in 2011 the current trend would appear to indicate that more than 3 million homes will go through the process.[3]

The problem is not with the people who are trying to buy homes—everyone needs a place to live. The problem is with the structure of money.

Sweating the Way to Equity

The foreclosure crisis left many US cities and towns with whole neighborhoods of empty houses. The economic crisis also left millions of people without jobs—in early 2010, the estimate nationwide in the US was 15 million unemployed, with over 1 million discouraged workers, people who had given up looking for work and so are not counted in that figure.[4]

The homeless population grows along with it—before the economic crisis of 2008, the National Law Center on Homelessness and Poverty estimated that each year over 3.5 million people, 1.35 million of them children, experienced homelessness. Since that time, accurate statistics are hard to find, but Reuters reported that local and state homeless assistance groups have seen a 61% rise in homelessness since the foreclosure crisis began.[5]

In response to the foreclosure crisis, the US Department of Housing and Urban Development created a new program—The Neighborhood Stabilization Program (NSP)—that is providing $4 billion to cities and towns.[6] The money cannot be used to prevent more foreclosures, but it can be used to buy up foreclosed properties, pay the bank, renovate/repair them and resell them. If public money is being used to purchase private homes from banks, this investment could be used to create new wealth by developing a means of exchange for housing that will create

jobs while at the same time moving homeless people back into homes —
all without spending more real taxpayer's dollars.

A model for doing this already exists — Habitat for Humanity routinely requires people to contribute sweat equity as part of their own
housing development. Sweat equity could be mobilized on a larger level
if the tax dollars are used to buy up groups of homes and sell them to
nonprofit community and economic development organizations that
provide job and skill training for unemployed workers.

Home renovation involves a wide variety of marketable skills: car-
pentry, plumbing, electric, renewable energy, HVAC, interior design,
gardening, sewing, painting, decorative arts, just to name some of the
more obvious ones. Professionals engaged for the renovation could
be required to provide skills training for people who need work, and
on-the-job experience could be provided with the publicly purchased
houses.

The people being trained wouldn't be eligible for very high wages
in conventional dollars — job training programs usually pay a small sti-
pend, if anything — but they could also be paid in supplemental vouchers based on a proportional division of the value of the renovated homes
they helped to create. The vouchers could then be used as a down payment on one of the homes or traded with other people for things that
the trainees need — forming the basis of a local complementary currency. This currency would not be based on debt (like our current dollars) but rather on the real value of a home. The equity produced by this
substantial infusion of tax dollars would therefore be captured by the
people who need it most — rather than going to gentrify neighborhoods
and displace low-income residents.

Community Land Trusts could play a vital role in this process — by
owning the land or other real interests in the housing that tax dollars
created, they can insure long-term affordability by having a role in the
future resale of the properties.

Saving Our Way Out of Poverty

An improved savings instrument would need to produce long-term
value from the original investment and be tangible enough to be readily
understood and easily convertible into real goods and services people
need. It also should ideally be based on actions that can be taken either

in the private sector for individual benefit or in the public sector for public benefit.

Our proposal is to introduce a savings currency that is fully backed by living trees. Their biological growth rate provides for the increased value over time. Trees offer us so many gifts we have come to take for granted. They are the lungs of the planet, inhaling CO_2 and exhaling the oxygen we need to breathe. Their fruit and nuts were our earliest and arguably our best food. Their wood has provided us with material for homes, fire for heat and cooking, ship making, electricity, furniture and paper. If you contemplate where humanity would be without trees over the long sweep of history, you can start to see that people and trees have truly been partners all along, although the trees have been silent partners and overexploited ones.

The tree savings system is simple. The key ingredients are land, water and seeds or tree saplings. A local government with underutilized land could make a parcel available to the community for tree planting. The people who do the work and the landowner — a local government or a private citizen — would receive shares in the final product, the trees that would grow over a period of time. The currency unit is simply a share in the value of a forest plantation.

These shares in turn could be either used as an inflation-proof savings account or be exchanged in the local economy for other goods and services — the people who earned them in the first place would not be limited to holding them until maturity. They could be denominated in whatever values would be useful for people, so if the total value of the trees you had planted was worth $1,000 over time from your initial investment of $50 plus the labor of planting and watering them, you could receive the shares in notes of $1, $5, $10 or $100, whatever would be useful for you.

Such tree notes would be based on an obvious value — the trees are very tangible, and ideally they are in the neighborhood where people live, strengthening the incentives to maintain them in good health and to harvest them at a sustainable rate over time.

Not all complementary currencies need to have something physically tangible, like real estate or trees as explained in this chapter. There are other currencies that deal with intangible activities like learning or the arts, as will be shown next.

CHAPTER 6

Growing Intelligence

[A] good education is another name for happiness.

ANN PLATO[1]

Educated Indentured Servants

The student loans provided largely by private banks for college and university education are reminiscent of an historic practice. As the United States was settled, people often bought their passage to the new land of opportunity through a relationship known as *indentured servitude*. They would get a ticket on a ship from a wealthier customer in return for a contract to be their servants for a fixed period—usually seven years. The practice was also used for professional training—to gain the skills you needed to be a shoemaker, for example, you would sign a contract with an existing cobbler that would obligate you to work for him for a period of time—typically three to seven years, after which point you could hang up your own shingle and work for yourself.

Indentured servants were only one small step removed from slavery, another common practice of the time. They could be bought and sold and did not have any of the rights under the law that *freemen* did. Regardless of how their employers treated them, or their health or the needs of their families, their obligation to work for their masters was enforced by the courts.

College loans have replicated this relationship, only now the service is in the form of debt. Indentured servitude was actually less constraining. The modern equivalent of indentured servitude lasts a lot longer than three to seven years. In the US, young people today leave college and professional school with indebtedness that will haunt them for most of their professional lives. The fact that their debt is guaranteed by the government makes it impossible for them to get out from under the burden regardless of their ability to find jobs that pay the salaries they need to make loan payments — student loans are the one form of debt that is exempt from the protections offered by US bankruptcy laws.

If we trace the history of education back in time, it began as a life process where young people worked alongside their parents and extended family to further the well-being of the group, learn critical survival skills and practice the customs of social exchange, all of which would have been seamlessly integrated with the spiritual traditions and values of the culture. While some members of the community or tribe might have more skill than others, the level of specialization tended to remain low compared to modern societies, and the general socialization and training people received to enable them to participate fully in the community needed to be equitable to insure the group's survival.

The earliest forms of a practice we might recognize as being similar to the educational system we have today were in sacred and spiritual matters — training for the priesthood, as healers, as ceremonial leaders and then later as scribes of sacred texts. Throughout the early history of Western civilization, the church and the learning institutions established by the church provided the majority of the formal education available in society. The trades also had systems of apprenticeship and training, but these did not resemble the college and university education we have today.

Today in North America, education makes a big financial impact on later earnings. As of the 2000 US census, those adults over 18 who had a high school diploma earned an average of $27,915 per year. Adults with bachelor's degrees earned an average of $51,206, while those with an advanced degree earned $74,602. Individuals who did not have a high school diploma only earned $18,734.[2] Only four states reported that over 90% of their young people earned a diploma. The Northeast region of the country had the highest number of college graduates — 30% of the population — whereas in the South the number of high school graduates dwindled to 25%.[3]

In the 21st century, the vast majority of people do not work on farms anymore. In 1800, over 90% of the US population was rural, with only 6% living in cities. At the turn of the 20th century, approximately 40% of the population lived and worked on a farm, but in 2009 this figure had decreased to only 2% of the US population.[4] Agricultural surplus has been supplemented with creative, technological and intellectual surplus as a basis for non-subsistence life, and the level of technological skill required to make a meaningful contribution to society has increased exponentially.

A form of education that systematically marginalizes the majority of the population can be seen in this light as a trend that will lead to our collective destruction if it is not reversed. Further, if those who do manage to navigate the barriers to learning are saddled with debts that prevent them from choosing the kind of creative endeavors that would utilize their knowledge to its fullest, this also works against our future.

The structure of college debt also plays a role in marginalizing the students who don't manage to climb to the top of the increasingly narrow hill of employment possibilities after college. If you finish college in debt, with average monthly payments on the debt (that ranged from $500 to $1,200 per month in 2009) and don't find a job right away, you don't have a lot of choices. Most student loans are guaranteed by the federal government, and so they are treated like obligations to the IRS — filing bankruptcy does not lift the ongoing obligation. Courts only grant forgiveness of college debt in cases where the person has a permanent disability that will prevent them from working. If you default on the loan, your wages through life can be garnished, your tax returns withheld, collection fees and possibly even legal fees imposed if the US Department of Education takes you to court. There are deferments, forbearance and consolidation programs available, but the bottom line is that the debt never goes away.

Contrast these practices to other countries where a higher tax rate insures that most students can attend college and university for little or no cost. Sweden, Venezuela, Qatar, Kuwait and many of the Eastern European countries subsidize college so that it's free to citizens. Canada, the UK and most of Western Europe offer subsidies so that college education costs little enough so that neither the students themselves nor their parents have to risk losing their homes, good credit or livelihoods to send their children to college.

Unfortunately, sometimes schools themselves can't resist usurious profit, extracting lifetime debt from young people who often don't know better than to sign loan agreements. In 2007, for example, the Attorney General of the State of Connecticut uncovered a scheme that involved over 50 colleges and universities. The schools were giving preferred status to lenders who provided the school faculty with benefits like cash, gifts and free trips to college staff, and yet these same banks were charging students higher rates of interest on their student loans than the going market.[5] There are even some for-profit colleges that cash in on the easy money represented by student loans through deceptive advertising. They claim that lucrative job opportunities wait for graduates, when no such opportunities exist.

---

60 Minutes, a popular US television news magazine, did an exposé of Brooks College in Long Beach, CA and Katherine Gibbs School, two of the holdings of the Career Education Corporation (CEC). Taking in more than $1 billion in annual revenue, with 100,000 students at 82 different campuses, CEC could be a poster child for what should be called an education racket.

Brooks College advertised a 98% job placement rate with salaries of $30,000 or more, when in fact for the much lower percentage (38%) of students who finish the program, the starting salary was less than $11 per hour. Katherine Gibbs advertised an 89% graduation rate, when in fact it was 29%. The admissions officers of these schools promised young people unattainable results, while at the same time extracting loan agreements that put them in debt for life. One admissions officer interviewed by *60 Minutes* said this:

> In that way, the job was a lot like a used-car lot, because if I couldn't close you, my boss would come in, try to close you... [The enrollment fee was $50.] You need three things... You need $50, a pulse and you've got to be able to sign your name. That's about it.[6]

The reason prospective students needed to sign their name is to commit themselves to indebtedness—many students amassed over $80,000 in debt at these schools. The government-backed debt cannot be forgiven when the highly paid job prospects turn out to be a myth. The result? Lifetime impoverishment on the part of the student, while the for-profit schools were clearly misleading their charges.

While this is an extreme example, it illustrates that there is a massive intergenerational transfer of wealth from the younger to the older members of society with the current education financing system we have in the United States. There must be a better way.

The Learning Currency

Human beings are born to learn. Learning is the common denominator of our species, the foundation of all other human needs. As infants and young children, we delight in figuring things out. A bit of the sparkle gets taken out of learning when we are pushed through an education system designed more for compliance than creativity. But for most of us, the need to learn enough to be productive and contributing members of society drives us on.

One of the few certainties we have about our future is that it will require a massive amount of learning by just about everybody, everywhere. In addition, it has been observed that learning—and even more importantly, learning retention—depends less on the person or the topics involved than on the delivery system of the knowledge. Indeed, average learning retention rates of children or adults are dramatically different depending on the process through which learning happens. In its simplest form, the result is Figure 1 below.[7]

What is striking is that our formal education system intently uses the two least effective learning methods available: lecturing and reading, processes through which respectively only 5% and 10% of what is being taught will be remembered. At the other end of the spectrum, a whopping 90% retention rate applies to whatever one teaches to others!

What would become possible if we reversed our entry into the learning pyramid by designing an incentive system that would encourage chains of *learning through teaching*? Such a system could operate in

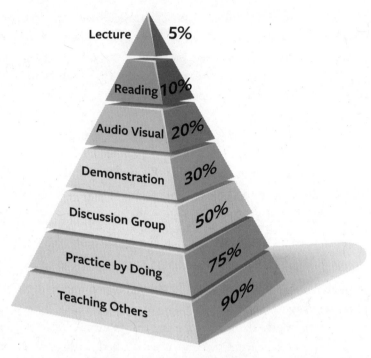

FIGURE 6.1. The Learning Pyramid.
Source: National Training Laboratories, Bethel, Maine

parallel with official schooling, as a special kind of extracurricular inter-generational game. Furthermore, it wouldn't have to deal with teachers' unions or ordinary school procedures and constraints. Although the model which follows was initially designed for Brazil, there is no reason to believe it couldn't be applied elsewhere.

The Brazilian Saber

When Brazil privatized its mobile telephone industry, it introduced a 1% special tax earmarked for higher educational purposes. By 2004, this education fund had grown to more than US$1 billion. A conventional way to use the fund would be to copy the GI Bill approach used in the United States after World War II, through which government funds were used directly for student scholarships. However, by introducing a complementary education currency, Bernard proposed that a substantial *learning multiplier* could be set in motion, so that a given amount of money could facilitate substantially more learning for a greater number of students. And a currency would fuel this learning multiplier without creating any new financial pressure on the economy.[8]

The proposal made to Brazil envisioned a project initiator called the Saber Administrator, which could be a nonprofit organization or the Ministry of Education itself. This Saber Administrator would issue a specialized paper currency, the *Saber* (pronounced saa-bear, meaning "knowledge" in Portuguese), which could only be redeemed to pay for tuition fees at participating universities for the academic year printed on the Saber itself—for example, year 2010. If the notes were not used to pay for tuition during that year, they could be exchanged for Sabers dated the following year—the year 2011—but with a penalty of 20%, giving a strong incentive to use the currency on or before the 2010 date.[9]

Let's assume that the additional enrollment capacity at participating universities is estimated at 10,000 students per year and that the average tuition amounts to 3,000 national money units per trimester. The Saber administrator would then make available 30 million Sabers per trimester, earmarked for each specific year concerned.

These Sabers would be allocated to primary schools in economically depressed areas where funding typically is not available for higher education. They would be given to the youngest students (seven-year-olds) on the condition that they choose a mentor from an older class (a ten-year-old) to work with the younger student on his or her weakest school subjects. The Sabers would be transferred to the older student in compensation for the hours spent mentoring. The 10-year-old could then do the same thing with a 12-year-old, and the latter with a 15-year-old, and so forth.

At the end of this learning chain, the Sabers would go to a 17-year-old who would then be able to use his or her accumulated Sabers to pay all or part of university tuition. The university in turn would be able to exchange the Sabers for conventional money through the Education Fund (see Figure 2), but at a discount of as much as 50%. This process is possible because most of the costs at a university are fixed, and the marginal cost of an additional student has little impact on those expenses.

In the above example, let us assume that the Saber circulates five times before it reaches the university. The total learning multiplier for the education budget allocated to this project would then be a factor of ten (five times for the exchanges among students of different ages, multiplied by two times for the arrangement between the Ministry of Education and the university). In this way, many more children would benefit from a better education, from a greater involvement with the learning process and from the chance to go to university than would have been possible if the education fund were used only for direct student scholarships.

Notice that this process would automatically encourage the spontaneous emergence of chains of *learning by teaching* from the bottom up among children of all ages. The Saber system would deliver total learning of an order of magnitude of $10 billion spending on the conventional scholarship model.

Furthermore, factoring in the change of the learning retention rate from 5–10% (normal education procedure) to 90% (teaching others), another tenfold effect becomes available, raising the total learning by teaching multiplier to one hundred. In other words, we estimate that spending $1 billion through the Saber system could produce a retained learning equivalent of $100 billion spent through conventional means… these are mind-boggling possibilities!

As this system develops, other ways of earning Sabers could be introduced. For example, why not eradicate illiteracy? Can you visualize an army of eight-year-olds proudly teaching their freshly learned reading and writing skills to grandparents? In the process, they would be developing a higher level of reading skill than any previous generation. Young people could also earn Sabers by helping the elderly and disabled with tasks they need accomplished.

Learning isn't only intellectual, but also about the social reality of the world of others. Learning beyond schools could become a vast and rich intergenerational game. All this would encourage intergenerational relationships and further learning, not to mention creating extra aid for the elderly without burdening governmental budgets. Given that all countries are expecting a higher percentage of elderly people that will require care, the learning currency could offer one integrated solution to two social challenges: education and elder care.

Rapidly changing environmental conditions, the pace of technical progress and the degree to which working opportunities have been transformed in recent years demand that we find new ways to learn and promote faster learning among all sectors of society. It is not suf-

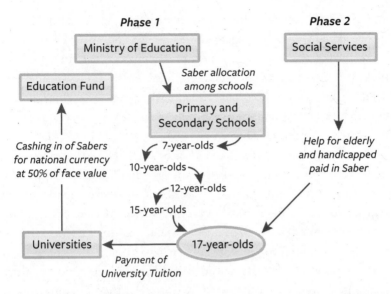

FIGURE 6.2. Saber Complementary Currency System = Learning Multiplier. Note: One Saber is equivalent to one national currency unit redeemable for higher education expenses.

ficient to merely repeat and imitate old patterns. Learners today must be creating new patterns and ideas. This can only happen if our learning capacity itself is transformed. The introduction of a learning currency could start this process in areas where accelerating learning faces the biggest challenges.

Buckaroos—University of Missouri, Kansas City

Beginning in 1999, The University of Missouri, Kansas City (UMKC) introduced an innovative complementary currency called Buckaroos (named after the University's kangaroo mascot). Students earn the Buckaroo notes when they participate in community service activities organized by area organizations. Students in several economics classes have to perform community service and earn Buckaroos as part of the course requirements. Each note is valued at one *roo hour*, representing one hour of a UMKC student's community service. UMKC's Center for Full Employment and Price Stability were charged with the administration of the program and issuing the notes.

Community service providers such as public schools, local government offices and nonprofit organizations apply to participate in the program — to be accepted they need to meet specific standards and be approved by UMKC. The organizations receive a number of Buckaroos to hire student workers and pay them one Buckaroo per hour of service. There is no maximum requirement for hours, and there is no need to list the names and service hours of students who work for each organization. Each organization is allowed to attract student workers to fill its specific needs for service hours.

The students can choose from a list of participating providers and are able to switch jobs and work as many or as few hours as they choose with approval of the provider. They are also able to barter, lend, borrow or purchase earned Buckaroos with other students — creating another level of economic activity within the system, because students who do not choose to do the community service have been known to pay cash to other students for the Buckaroo notes. The students need the notes to pay a tax each semester to UMKC's treasury; this tax can only be paid in Buckaroos. Students may also save Buckaroos for future semesters where course loads may be more restrictive.

FIGURE 6.3. One Buckaroo

In fact, according to Prof. L. Randall Wray who designed the program, the dollar value of the Buckaroo has appreciated over the life of the program, rising from a range of $5–$10 per note to the current value of $10–$20 per note. The value increases near the end of each semester, as procrastinating students scramble to get the notes they need to pay the tax so they can pass the class — their grades are the final value they get from the transaction.

In the future, UMKC may offer that a portion of tuition could be paid with Buckaroos. This would promote not only student involvement within the community, but a stronger network of community relations for the university. Students would have a strong incentive to earn Buckaroos, and the existence of the program would make university education more affordable.

Learning Our Way to the Future

If there will be a theme to life in the 21st century, it will be the need to learn. Rapid change actually requires a new kind of learning, and so creating new currencies that increase both the speed and capacity of learning is critically important. When social and material reality are stable, then learning by repetition and rote is an adequate way to learn — rely on the experts, do things the way they've been done over a long period of time because that works. When social and material reality are changing rapidly — climate change, economic dislocation, social upheaval — a new kind of adaptive and transformative learning is required.

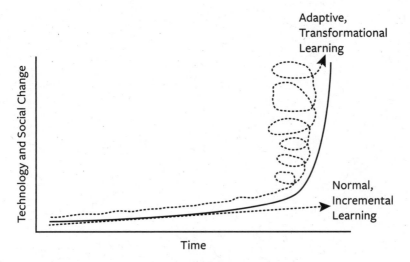

FIGURE 6.4. Rapid Change Demands New Ways of Learning

Adaptive and transformational learning is messy, and it requires a new mindset. Unlike normal, incremental learning, it does not rely on old patterns, but rather creates new ones. Mistakes form its pedagogy, and so developing a systematic patience toward mistakes can facilitate rapid learning. Thomas Edison captured this idea when he said: "If I find 10,000 ways something won't work, I haven't failed."[10]

When systems change is required by the times, learning may involve moving forward without necessarily knowing "the right" solution. Creating systems of exchange (which could function in parallel with official systems) that reward learning at all levels could help stay the course.

CHAPTER 7

The Creative Economy

It is better to create than to be learned,
creating is the true essence of life.

BARTHOLD GEORG NIEBUHR

The Arts: De-cultured Society

The arts shape our lives and provide the warp and weft for our cultures and societies. Without the arts, we would not be human. Yet the scarcity caused by our monetary system twists them beyond recognition. There are two deep human needs met by the arts—our need for self-expression and the need for aesthetic enjoyment or beauty. The arts form the footprints of human consciousness through time. The ancient cave paintings show our emergence as a creative species, our connection to divine energy and our aspirations. The graffiti on the walls of modern cities express the artistic voice of a lost generation. The arts open a window into our collective soul.

Sacred art in many religions takes on such symbolic importance that the forms, styles and even the paints are so closely prescribed that in centuries past breaking from traditional rules could result in the death penalty in some societies. Art historians spend a lifetime understanding the subtle gestures encoded in art from the era prior to mass literacy.

The arts have always played a central role in our ceremonial customs and forms of worship. The artifacts we have from ancient times were often created for ceremony—people coming together in shared expressions of joy, hope, sorrow, prayer, awe and power. Kings, queens, high priests and priestesses, chieftains, sultans and pharaohs all com-missioned music, visual spectacles, architecture, poetry, theater, jewels, clothing and other adornment to demonstrate their power, their piety and their generosity. Meanwhile, artisans, wives, laborers, children — if they had enough resources and time — created houses, furniture, fabric, clothing, lace, pillowcases, dishes, utensils and tools that spoke to their own creative sensibility. Whenever possible, people have surrounded themselves with beautiful things.

Some of our most enduring human creations demonstrate the link between the arts and everything we hold as sacred. We have used our creative energy to cultivate a relationship with gods and goddesses in the construction of our pyramids, megalithic stone circles, cathedrals, temples, tombs and statues. These endure while the vast majority of human endeavor has turned to dust.

Fast forward to the 21st century, and the majority of our creative workers no longer dedicate their life energy to the creation of enduring beauty and awe-inspiring celebrations of divine energy. Poets are put to work writing syrupy stanzas for greeting cards, visual artists are design-ing web pages, corporate logos and publications. Sculptors are employed making gravestones, musicians write jingles for television ads and the most lucrative form of theater is the 30-second commercial aired during the Super Bowl. The well-paid artists, in other words, are working for corporations. Recent statistics show, however, that 55.6% of the rest of the "fine artists, art directors and animators" in the workforce are self-employed, compared to 10% of the rest of the population.[1] Career advice for students thinking about majoring in the arts in college is clear: "the number of qualified workers exceeds the number of available openings because the arts attract many talented people with creative ability."[2] In short, there are a lot of people who want to be creative, but a real short-age of paid work for artists.

A study done by Michael Maranda, an assistant curator of the Art Gallery of York University in Toronto, Canada, on the plight of Cana-dian artists revealed the underlying truth of the near cliché image of the starving artist. In Canada in 2009, the average income for a visual artist was $20,000 per year, well below the national average for all incomes of $28,850.[3] In the United States, the situation is similar. The median in-come of all artists from 2003–2005 was $34,800, but this figure includes the income from all sources, not just the artwork they are producing. Full-time artists earned a median income of $42,200, fully $10,000 less than the $52,500 median income for other professionals. For the 45% of other artists who do not work full-time all year, their plight is the same as those in Canada, with a median income of $20,000. By contrast, office clerks in the United States earn an average income of $27,768, jobs which require a lot less training and creativity.[4]

Yet despite these figures, the *creative economy* has taken over a leading role in the US employment profile in the last 20 years. In the early 1990s, the people with jobs associated with the creative economy surpassed those employed in traditional manufacturing jobs for the first time in history. This trend is as much due to the decline in manufacturing jobs as it is to a new wave of creative jobs, but the numbers still tell an important story.

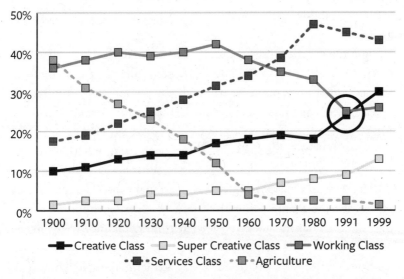

FIGURE 7.1. US Class Structure, 1900–1999 (% of Workforce). Source: Academy for Entrepreneurial Leadership, University of Illinois at Urbana-Champaign

There is no shortage of people who want to do creative work and no shortage of creativity. What is scarce is the money to pay them. If the creative class were a marginal, fringe sector of our economy, this apparent lack of collective value might make some sense on a superficial level, but in fact research shows that the creative class is central to economic success.

The shortage of decent livelihoods in the arts can't help but have an impact on both the amount and diversity of art, music, dance, theater and other work available to us. When the for-profit arts take over the television airwaves and the music companies are able to control the content of music played on radio stations, the ability of smaller artists to have success declines. The increased availability of professional art also reduces the practice of art in general — after all, if you can't sing like Madonna why would you even try? A society awash in popular culture could actually be starved for authentic culture. The scarcity produced by an economic system based on private money simultaneously homogenizes and eradicates our unique cultural identities.

Art Tokens

What if it were possible to pursue creative endeavors without worrying about the money required? What if every creative person had the opportunity to follow their dream and bring a creative work of some sort into being?

Right now in the United States, if you are a child who is dying from cancer, the Make a Wish Foundation raises money to allow you to experience something you never had a chance to do. Some children, for example, meet their favorite sports hero, some go to Disney World; one young boy was able to go on a shopping spree at Toys R Us.

It would be possible to extend this model, using a complementary currency, to the wishes of other young people and let them do something creative as a key part of their educational experience. In the next chapter, the model for doing just that is discussed: the prefecture of Shiga in Japan has introduced it for environmental improvements, but their model has many applications.

For example, your city decides that attracting people who are involved in the Creative Economy is an important economic development idea. Many cities have already made this decision, since research shows the importance of this kind of initiative in the 21st century economy. So, the city institutes an Art Token system. Imagine a scenario where every taxpayer in the city would need to turn in at least ten Art Tokens when they pay their taxes.

To earn the Art Tokens, citizens would need to participate in some type of creative endeavor. This might be taking a class in music, art, dance or theater, attending a performance or supporting a creative activity a young student was initiating. People with money and no time could buy tokens (using bank-debt money) from people with a surplus. Such exchanges could take place, for instance, through a local e-Bay type electronic market. Artists, students, theaters, studios and galleries would all certainly have a surplus. By valuing the currency on the city level as a partial payment of something like a tax, the city could create an *economy* in the type of activity it is trying to encourage.

Notice that this approach would ensure that more of the creative activity would take place in town, that its creative people would obtain income in dollars, but that this wouldn't cost the city any additional dollars. By setting up a foundation, for example, an organization could make the Art Tokens even more valuable to its users than bank-debt dollars.

Living the Dream

The city could offset some of its bank-debt dollar costs by paying people in Art Tokens for work that would normally cost dollars. These dollars saved could go into a fund to support a foundation in the city that supports the arts. Or those in the city who provide opportunities for youth could pay individuals in Art Tokens for participating in their activities. Instead of making grants to organizations as the sole way they achieve their goals, the city could sponsor activities where people earn Art Tokens. In these ways, both the time and money needed to allow students and artists to engage in a new creative endeavor could be found, where none exists now.

For example, imagine that you are a high school student and your dream has been to go to Rome to study Michelangelo's work in the Sistine Chapel. Your high school requires that you undertake a creative or community project as part of the requirements for graduation, and they assign an adult mentor to work with you on the project. At the end of the project, you are required to produce a written report, a work of art, a performance or some product that demonstrates you have met your learning objectives.

Obviously, travel to Rome requires two things — money for the journey and time of your mentor to help you understand all that is involved. The mentor could earn Art Tokens for their time, which frees up some of the adult creative energy you'll need. The money for the journey could come out of the fund created by the foundation or from the city by using real dollar offsets that other people earning Art Tokens have allowed. Another approach could be to have this foundation or city collect unused airline miles for this purpose.

As the recipient of the money and time in the Art Token account, you would engage in a contract for the work. Each contract could reflect the level of mentoring and cost required, and you, the student, would need to contribute as well — either through the more traditional ways of raising funds (finding sponsors, doing a fundraising event, selling things) or by earning Tokens by undertaking activities supporting the arts that normally cause the city, the foundation or the arts organizations in the community to incur conventional money costs. Everything from ushering at the theater to mentoring younger children might qualify as a certified activity that earns you the Tokens you need for your dream to be realized.

The critical leverage point for Art Tokens is the same for just about any complementary currency. If a city makes it mandatory for everyone to pay some contribution every year in a form of complementary currency or accepts partial payment in complementary currencies for some regular taxes and fees, the demand for that currency will significantly increase and therefore obtain a value that it has not had previously. Remember, the main systemic reason we universally accept privately created bank-debt dollars right now is that they are the *only* legal form by which we can pay our taxes. If we expand this mandate to a more democratic form of community currency and no longer grant banks a monopoly in this area, whatever functions that this currency is compensating will predictably flourish.

City Money in History

If the idea of a city issuing a currency and accepting it for payments in taxes sounds strange, there are clear historical precedents for it including in the US only a generation ago. For instance, during the depression of the 1930s, cities issued their own currencies as a way of counteracting the economic hardships everyone was experiencing. *Scrip* was another local currency that appeared spontaneously all over the country, as local businesses and business associations issued currency so that people could continue to exchange products and services and keep the local economy going, even in the face of a national economic crisis and "bank holiday."

Figure 2 shows a note issued by the City of Detroit in 1934. Hundreds of cities did the same thing during the bank holidays of that time.

Private companies also got into the currency business as a way to provide their customers with a means of exchange. Figure 3 is an example of local scrip from a gold mining company.

These depression scrips were introduced in full replacement of conventional, centrally controlled dollars. They could be used to pay for any type of activity, competing directly with the dollar. When cities all over the US started to do the same, an Executive Order was issued prohibiting cities from

FIGURE 7.2. City of Detroit note

FIGURE 7.3. Scrip from local mining company

issuing currency even though it was helping to address the economic crisis. What we are talking about in this book is not such a full replacement, but a more narrowly targeted application. Any city can issue tickets for any event it chooses, and impose conditions for people to obtain such tickets. From a legal viewpoint, the city scrips we are recommending would fall into the category of such "tickets." This is what is being done in Japan with the ecological scrip described in Chapter 8.

Given their proximity to the people and the role they play in delivering critical public services, cities can help make economic institutions more accountable democratically. It is important to realize that any choice of activities to be rewarded could also be a democratic choice.

Culture Cards in Flanders

In Belgium over the last several years, an idea like Art Tokens has taken root, although to date it has not been fully implemented and involves payments in Euros. A proposal was made to take a percentage of regular art subsidies — which are given by the government for a play, an orchestra or another event—and to put their value on a Culture Card—the equivalent of a debit card that would be issued to everyone. Each taxpayer in Flanders could in turn use their Culture Card to buy tickets to cultural events of their choice. The money on the card can only be spent on certified cultural events. The citizen chooses what she or he wants to go to, but within some boundaries. There would be some criteria that applied to how events were certified—for example, you couldn't use the Culture Card outside the country, and going to a foreign film also might not be eligible.

Since most artistic work incurs its costs in advance of the actual event, it was important to find ways to help with the production costs. One idea offered was to allow people to subscribe to artistic events and productions in advance using the Culture Card, in much the same way that you would buy a season ticket to the local theater. Obviously, this makes it easier to use the credits on arts that are events, a bit harder to use for things like paintings. Yet going to gallery shows where visual artists present their work would be an eligible activity.

One beneficial effect of the Culture Card would be that a local production, like a neighborhood group, could have access to funds that normally would go to arts organizations with the wherewithal to do high-level fundraising. It would make arts funding much more accessible to smaller, local productions rather than being reserved exclusively to a small elite. The voice that people would have in the types of creative activities they prefer would also be beneficial insofar as cultural minorities are concerned.

The Belgian government has been planning to implement the program with stickers embedded with radio signals that would credit the account when a purchase is made. Evolving technology has made it more likely that a mobile telephone payment system will be used when Culture Cards are finally issued. In Flanders, it is already possible to find which artistic events are available locally using a mobile telephone application, so it is not going to be a big leap to have the same list indicate what events and productions are eligible for payment with a Culture Card.

There are several reasons why the system hasn't been implemented yet. One issue has been that there are many cards for different purposes in circulation already. Another problem arose during the financial crisis:

most governments are cutting costs at this point, so adding the expense of a new system when other things are being cut is harder to do, even if the new system might save a lot of costs over time. In the longer run, the time required to oversee large grant programs could be reduced if payments to artists become more automated.

Core Support for Artists

It is clear artists and the arts need a more stable source of support, especially in North America. The creativity required to innovate and to make our world beautiful is not something that should be relegated to the impoverished sidelines. Partly because they are creative, there are some artists who have thought of some new ideas for general support. Here are a few of them.

United Artists of America Reserve Note

Joseph Gray and Peter Nelson in Seattle, Washington have designed a large bill with one printed side — the United Artists Reserve Note — and one blank side. The idea is that the bill can be issued to artists, who in turn can decorate the blank side of the note with some of their artwork. The value of the artwork will help determine the value of each note.[5] The idea was inspired by an urban legend — that Picasso had lunch with Nelson Rockefeller at the Four Seasons restaurant in New York City. When it came time to pay the rather expensive bill, Picasso suggested that he could pay for lunch by drawing something on the bill and signing it, which would turn the bill itself into something much more valuable than the lunch.

Credit: artistreservenote.com

Fluxus Bucks

Started by Julienne Paquette in the 1990s, the Fluxus Bucks movement uses dollars as a background stamp for art. They are traded through the mail as a form of mail art and can also be used for purchases in stores that will accept them.[6]

The system we use for exchanging goods and services with each other is only limited by our imagination. As artists demonstrate, there are many possibilities for new kinds of notes and exchanges. Value is not based in a governmental promise; it's based in our own social contract and the agreements we are able to make with each other about value. We created the system, and we can change it.

CHAPTER 8

Exchanging Ecologies

There are no passengers on Spaceship Earth. We are all crew.

Marshall McLuhan

For centuries we humans have been replacing healthy natural ecosystems and environments for less healthy ones. We've cut forests, polluted rivers, excavated mountains and generally taken the environmental services offered to us by nature for granted, without concern about maintaining their productive capacity. For most of human history, nature was abundant and humans did not pose a significant ecological threat — it was enough that we managed to survive. The tipping point came with the human population explosion and the systematic commoditization of products extracted from nature.

The rate at which we used natural resources has increased markedly over the past half-century, and that in turn has resulted in the increased degradation of our natural environment. Now, another tipping point is rapidly approaching — one in which the atmospheric concentration of greenhouse gases pushes climate change beyond the brink of our control. Instead of exchanging our environment for money to make more money, can we use a new form of money to help renew nature? Could complementary currencies help us on our way to a healthier environment? Absolutely.

One of the great strengths of complementary currencies is that you can choose to make them local, and local tends to be good for the environment. No matter the specific function of the currency, in this respect local currencies are always greener than bank-debt money. Because they circulate locally among community members and businesses, they encourage the purchase or exchange of local goods and services — exchanges that come from the community or from its immediate surroundings, thus reducing realities such as the carbon footprint of long-haul transportation. The lettuce and tomatoes you buy at the farmers market using a complementary currency, for example, most likely come from a local farm, not from the other side of the planet. Thus you reduce your carbon footprint. Other things being equal, the more we exchange international and national commerce for regional and local commerce, the more we act as responsible stewards for our world.

> We abuse land because we regard it as a commodity belonging to us. When we see land as a community to which we belong, we may begin to use it with love and respect.
>
> Aldo Leopold, *A Sand County Almanac*

Beyond the simple fact that local is more ecologically sustainable, and complementary currencies are usually local, we can also help restore the environment with eco-currencies, including carbon credits associated with a cap and trade system, which can be local, regional, national or international.

Mitigating Carbon

We see the impacts of the roller coaster economy every time we pull in to a gas station. The ubiquitous roadside signs announce the cost of a gallon or liter of gas and tell us something about our relationship with the economy. And when it comes to the environment, when we fill our tanks we are also playing our part in pumping into the air more toxins, carcinogens and greenhouse gasses. The burning of fossil fuels is recognized by the vast majority of climate experts as one of the leading causes of climate change. When we fill our tank and then turn the key, we step into the middle of the carbon cycle, initiating an action which results in the release of carbon dioxide (CO_2) into the atmosphere. That CO_2, in turn, traps the heat from the sun and acts to create a greenhouse effect.

In a healthy biosphere, the amount of CO_2 in the atmosphere would be relatively constant as it cycles from Earth, through living organisms, to the atmosphere and into the ocean — a balanced series of feedback loops. Human ingenuity and advanced technology have allowed us to circumvent the system, however. We remove ancient fossil fuel — coal, oil, natural gas — essentially long-sequestered carbon, from Earth and release it into the atmosphere. And as the human population grows, our appetite for convenience continues in parallel and the supply of fossil fuel diminishes. We find ourselves at the mercy of the market, which is, of course, tied to everything from weather to war, and many things in between.

In short, the natural world is now at our mercy. So, can we change the equation once more? Can we reestablish ecological balance, and perhaps, in so doing, step off the roller coaster as well?

At this point, you might well say, "I'd buy a hybrid, if only they were more affordable," or "I'd walk to work if I could find a job near my home." In other words, although you possess the power of choice, you do not have sufficient good choices at your disposal. So how do we create a world where environmentally-friendly choices are widely available and a sustainable lifestyle the norm? We can begin by reducing the amount of CO_2 in the atmosphere. Could a complementary carbon currency be part of the solution?

Global Cap and Trade: The Kyoto Treaty

As of November 2004 the Kyoto Treaty on climate change has been legally binding for 141 countries. Among the developed nations, only Australia and the US have abstained from the treaty. Its Clean Development Mechanism (CDM) allocates a specific amount of carbon credits to various countries and industries, but allows credits to be bought and sold internationally. A company that produces more greenhouse gases than its allocation needs to purchase carbon credits sold by another producer who has reduced emissions beyond what is required. International trading in carbon contracts on the basis of the CDM protocol of the Kyoto treaty has successfully started.

Reducing Greenhouse Gases Using the Market

Although the burning of fossil fuel results in the creation of CO_2, there are other greenhouse gases (GHGs) including, most notably, methane which have an even stronger atmospheric climate effect. CO_2 is just the most prevalent of these gases and has the most recognizable name. Some recent technical approaches to reducing GHGs range from sequestering carbon deep in Earth to capturing the methane produced by livestock in order to generate electricity. Raising animals for food has now surpassed burning fossil fuel as the leading source of GHGs. The two most comprehensive market strategies for reducing GHGs, however, are a trading system known as cap and trade, and the carbon tax. *Cap and trade* regulates the total supply of carbon credits, letting the market regulate price. A *carbon tax* raises the price of things that produce CO_2 and leaves supply and demand to the market. Both have strengths and weaknesses. Both can be part of the solution.

The Theory of Cap and Trade

In Environmental Trading Markets (ETMs), the *cap* in cap and trade is the limit put on the amount of GHGs that can be released into the atmosphere. This is the strong aspect of cap and trade. It puts limits on emissions up front. Permits to release CO_2 or another GHG are made available, usually by the government. These permits can be auctioned or distributed for free to those entities being regulated, usually fossil fuel users or power producers. These are known as *upstream* producers. Consumers are *downstream*. There are only a limited number of permits and that number is decreased every year, in theory moving us toward an overall level of CO_2 in the atmosphere that stays below 300 parts per million (ppm), the level that historic geological and ice core records show we can't exceed if we hope to maintain ice caps and glaciers. The *trade* in cap and trade comes from the fact that the permits can be traded, subject to regulations, among permit holders. So if one producer of GHGs, say a power plant in California, emits less CO_2 than expected, i.e., pollutes less, it can sell its extra credits to another power plant in Ohio that hasn't met expectations and needs more credits. The idea is to create an incentive for greenhouse gas producers to produce less greenhouse gas. The less they produce, the fewer credits or permits they need.

In theory, it's a great system. In practice, things get more complicated.

The value of carbon credits has rapidly increased since the Kyoto Protocols. The World Bank has estimated that the size of the carbon market was $11 billion (£6.6 billion) in 2005, $30 billion in 2006 and $64 billion in 2007.[1]

Cap and Trade in Practice

Like other government policies, cap and trade is subject to the same pressures and interests as other policies. In the United States, California has passed a law that places a cap on carbon production, but no such law exists on a national level at this point. Although there are several functioning carbon exchanges in the US, all of them are either voluntary or in response to the California law, as people and companies who are genuinely concerned about carbon emissions buy credits to offset their use of CO_2 for other things.

Another weakness of cap and trade is the measurement and regulation of GHGs. If one were to try to measure how much GHG-producing fossil fuel was dispensed by all gas stations, propane sellers, households and heating oil supply trucks, the task would be enormous, complex and likely inaccurate. These distributors of fuel are too far down the supply chain. The most effective regulation takes place as far upstream as possible — at the well head or the coal mine. It is relatively easy, using currently available information, to calculate the amount of GHGs an upstream producer sells (which is the amount that will eventually get released into the atmosphere). But the producers have been successfully lobbying so that this more simple and effective approach isn't chosen.

Another crucial aspect of cap and trade is the cost to the consumer. If we cap production of fossil fuel, we cap supply and drive prices up, or so the theory goes. If, however, those permits are sold (rather than giving them away for free as was done in Europe), the system provides a new windfall. Those monies can be used for a variety of things, including rebates to consumers, particularly to those in low-income brackets. Funds can also be used for other green programs like weatherproofing, green job creation, green technology research and development.[2]

The Carbon Tax

A carbon tax places a tax on all activities that produce carbon dioxide. This makes the price of fossil fuels higher (because of the tax), and supply and demand theory would suggest that higher prices will reduce consumption, while the taxes collected can fund programs that mitigate the impacts of climate change. Mitigating programs can include better public transit to replace automobiles and renewable energy installations to reduce GHG emissions. Advocates of a carbon tax often tout it as an alternative to cap and trade. A carbon tax can act as an incentive to use less fossil fuel.

With higher prices, we might think twice about driving to work alone when we could carpool or take the bus instead. Germany, British Columbia and Quebec have recently implemented different forms of a carbon tax. The primary weakness of a carbon tax is that it doesn't put limits on the production of GHGs, so it can't guarantee a given reduction in their levels. A secondary issue with a carbon tax is that it is a regressive tax, which impacts the poor more than the wealthy. This can be addressed, as in British Columbia, with a compensating rebate for the poorer families.[3]

A New Approach: The Vision of a Carbon Currency

Both cap and trade and the carbon tax are tools we should have in our green toolbox. But that doesn't mean we should simply sit back and wait for the results. What other tools might we design? What if your carbon-producing and carbon-reducing activities were automatically counted and banked? What if you could see your net carbon effects simply by swiping a card or clicking your mouse? Would that active awareness of your place in the biosphere, of your role in restoring balance to our world, not change your actions? And what, if as an added bonus, a new carbon currency also created new economic opportunities?

A Carbon Currency System

Carbon currency[4] would be a voluntary carbon reduction program whereby consumers receive electronic credits for purchases or investments that contribute to measurable carbon emissions reductions. It could mobilize people who are already engaged in reducing their carbon footprint (for example, they may currently own a fuel efficient car or solar power generator) and also the much larger group of consumers who have adopted a wait and see attitude. Furthermore, a carbon currency could provide individuals and communities with a reliable way to track and compare their carbon emission reductions, as all transactions can be recorded and verified.

Businesses providing goods and services that reduce carbon emissions or those that have formally engaged in sustainability activities (green businesses) could accept carbon currency units (CCUs) as a loyalty currency in partial payment for additional carbon-reducing goods and services. Each business would decide what percentage of an invoice or bill they are willing to accept in CCUs (which in turn could be tied to its value on the carbon market). An electric or hybrid car dealer, for example, could decide to accept 10% of the purchase of a new car in CCUs, whereas a shop selling energy efficient light bulbs or solar panels might accept 20% of their payment in this currency.

The participating businesses that sell the carbon-reducing goods or services to the customer provide the data relevant to the transaction — the amount of carbon reduction achieved with the purchase. For example, a consumer could earn a CCU when they take a bus to work in the morning instead of driving their car. They would pay for the trip in dollars, and would swipe their CCU debit card for the carbon currency credit. The transit company would have a standard carbon value for bus riders.

Later, the same consumer might go shopping for solar panels to replace electric generation using fossil fuels. If the consumer had a number of the carbon currency units on their card and the solar panel store accepted up to 10% of the purchase price in the units, they could partially pay for their panel with CCUs.

In turn, participating businesses like a car dealership, hardware store or solar panel distributor would have two options for the use of the CCUs they receive. They could make purchases with other businesses participating in the program (B2B transactions) or sell the CCUs through the program's administrator to the carbon market.

Final redemption of CCUs would be at a fixed price previously agreed upon between the carbon market administrator and the businesses. The administrator could be any organization willing to pay for carbon emissions. Given additional sales tax generated by this program, it would be ideal if the tax authority of the particular municipality, county, state or local government that has a mandatory reduction in carbon emissions would play this role.

For homes, professional raters could make an evaluation of the carbon credit consumption of different types of dwellings. (In the US, many have already been trained and certified by the trade association called Build it Green.[5]) Residential homes could then be rated on performance beyond their city/county's energy code minimum standards. If a house scored 25% better than code, then that fact could be logged and certified and corresponding carbon savings are computed. Adding better insulation or double-paned windows, for example, are ways to reduce heating bills and carbon consumption.

For transportation, the type of car used and any reduction in mileage driven compared to some benchmark like the state or city's average vehicle miles traveled, could similarly provide CCUs to the consumer. These would be credited to his or her CCU account following a smog test or a comparison of the driver's previous annual mileage.

Keeping the System Honest

The burgeoning regulated international market for carbon credits is expected to more than double in size to about $68.2 billion by 2010, with the unregulated voluntary sector rising to $4 billion over the same period.[6] Yet, companies and individuals rushing to go green have been spending millions on carbon credit projects that, on deeper inspection, yield few if any environmental benefits.

A *Financial Times* investigation has uncovered widespread failings in the new markets for greenhouse gases, suggesting some organizations are paying for emissions reductions that do not take place.[7] Others are meanwhile making big profits from carbon trading for very small expenditure and, in some cases, for cleanups that would have been made anyway.

In contrast, the CCU approach provides carbon savings that are locally certified, can be tracked within the vicinity in real time and whose use can be electronically audited back to their origin. Each CCU has its own electronic certificate, through which one can follow where and by whom it was created, for what specific purchase and at what time. This gives a much higher degree of verifiability than is typically available with the carbon credits traded under the Kyoto agreement. Finally, as the CCU system is electronically integrated in real time, it enables each community to announce the carbon savings it has generated, providing on the spot feedback on how well it is doing compared to other communities. That way, everybody participates through their own daily decisions.

Advantages Compared to Other Approaches

Besides the advantage of providing an instantaneous tracking system for carbon-reducing activities and leaving an auditable trail of these carbon reductions, the CCU leverages the efficiency of tax dollars to multiply carbon reductions. In most existing schemes, a consumer or business receives a tax credit or subsidy for a carbon-reducing investment, but these tax dollars only have a one-time effect.

In contrast, CCU are used at least twice, and possibly more, before they are cashed in. The sales taxes on these multiple transactions compensate for the cost of their redemption. As already noted above, the cumulative sales taxes can even be larger than the redemption costs, changing the carbon reduction program from a cost item to an income-producing one for the tax authority.

Other Ecologically-Positive Currencies: the Biwa Kippu System in Japan

Japan has hundreds of complementary currencies designed to benefit local communities and their needs. In the case of the Shiga Prefecture (a Japanese Prefecture is roughly equivalent to a County in the US) near Kyoto, protecting Lake Biwa is of critical importance to the community. The lake, which is one of the oldest and most diverse lakes in the world, is inextricably linked with the culture and industry of the area. Poor upstream watershed management, pollution from industry, agriculture and households and the arrival of invasive species now threaten the lake and its once healthy ecosystem. Enter the Biwa Kippu — a complementary currency designed specifically to rehabilitate the lake. Although it is currently in evaluation stage and not yet implemented, this is how the Biwa would work once in place.

The Biwa system will promote environmental activities by residents and nonprofit organizations in Shiga Prefecture without creating any additional budgetary deficits. Job creation and community building, while not direct objectives, are expected as positive side effects. Focusing on residents and nonprofit organizations, and only indirectly on businesses, the system is designed to be able to expand in both scope and range over time.

To begin, the prefectural government would enact an ordinance requiring residents to contribute a certain amount of environmental Biwa Kippu each year, for example 10 Biwas per family, with appropriate exceptions for special circumstances (e.g., people with disabilities or other valid grounds for exception). One Biwa might correspond roughly to one hour of environmental service. The Biwa would be issued by the Prefecture itself (or by an appropriate entity such as the Lake Biwa Environmental Research Institute) only for specific measurable environmental activities as determined each year by the Prefecture. Residents or nonprofit organizations that engage in such work would be rewarded with Biwa Kippu. Biwa obligations could not be paid in Yen, nor would the government set a fixed exchange rate between Biwa Kippu and Yen. Participants, however, would be free to exchange Biwa Kippu should they choose, including for Yen, on free market principles through an electronic e-Bay type market.

Biwa would be issued via mobile telephone and collected using the online prefectural taxation system. In addition, real-time progress could be tracked and feedback given using the electronic Biwa system.

Aside from the obvious advantages of creating a supplementary eco-currency like the Biwa Kippu, the system has several additional benefits. The sale of Biwas to those who haven't earned enough Biwas through their own environmental activities would provide an income source for environmental non-governmental organizations and activists. Research has shown that more people volunteer and that the turnover of volunteers in nonprofit organizations is significantly reduced when a complementary currency is used to reward volunteers.[8] Because of these two effects, more nonprofit organizations that focus on environmental needs will tend to emerge spontaneously in Shiga Prefecture.

By balancing the quantity of contributions and the opportunities for earning Biwas, an *ecological economy* can be activated at whatever scale is deemed appropriate for the Prefecture.

Conclusion

In addition to the specific examples of how currencies can be used to address the environmental issues described here, it's important to note that local currencies issued without interest help reduce the environmental impact of the monetary system. They do this by striking at the heart of the growth imperative described in Chapter 2. This growth imperative drives the practices that require the environment to be used up without adequately pricing the services it provides.

CHAPTER 9

Minding
the Community's Business

Do businesses ever look out for anything besides the bottom line? The answer is yes. In fact, both corporate social responsibility and corporate sustainability are growing movements in the business world, with a history that goes back centuries.

In the 21st century, businesses — corporations, partnerships, sole proprietors — are omnipresent. We don't think twice about being able to find familiar national chain stores thousands of miles from where we live, even in other countries. Small businesses get a lot of our attention, too, and a lot of our cash. Let's face it, without businesses, most of us wouldn't be able to feed or clothe ourselves, or even live under a roof. We rely on businesses, big and small, to make the necessities of life available to us. But this wasn't always the case. Business of today's scope and scale is a relatively new phenomenon, and it has changed our most basic relationships — with food, land, housing, clothing, transportation, work and even ourselves.

Before the Industrial Revolution, industry was usually small scale, and much was done at home. The big trading corporations, like the East India Company and the Hudson's Bay Company, were notable exceptions.

One of the earliest corporations in the United States, the Massachusetts Bay Corporation, began as a group of religious refugees, pooling their money and resources to begin a new venture in a new land. Led by John Winthrop, who famously preached social responsibility and called upon the wealthy to help the poor, these Puritans founded a new colony which eventually became the Commonwealth of Massachusetts. (Of course, social responsibility in the early colony included mandates and practices that we would consider inappropriately invasive today.)

Since the days of the Puritans, our sense of community and many of the institutions that form it, like our spiritual traditions and the need to help our neighbors bring in the harvest, have changed in our modern industrial world. But our core sense of social responsibility has not changed. Many of us are now beginning to expand the notion of responsibility to *community* so that it goes beyond the responsibility to our fellow human beings to the whole ecological community of life. We expect the businesses we buy from to share these values and reflect them in their supply chains, the products they offer and the energy they use.

From Social Responsibility to Sustainability

Green sells. Turn on the television, and chances are good that you will see a commercial proclaiming the ways in which some company or other is helping the environment. And many are. In some cases that ad reflects a deeply held corporate value. In other cases, that 30-second spot serves both the bottom line and consumers' calls for corporate environmental responsibility.

The notion that businesses have a responsibility to society isn't new, but the extent and shape of that responsibility, as well as the rationale behind it have changed. Some robber barons of the late 19th century were also great philanthropists, founding universities, museums and public libraries. Meanwhile, working conditions in steel mills and mines, shoe factories and sardine canneries were abominable. The labor movement was born from inhuman working conditions: organized workers demanded fair wages and better workplaces, asking management to be socially responsible to at least their employees. The road from child labor to the corporate sustainability report took just over a hundred years to travel (the first child labor laws were introduced in the 1830s).

Our modern idea of corporate social responsibility (CSR) is only about 60 years old and owes much to the time and place of its birth. In the early post-war years, as the Cold War (a battle between two economic systems, capitalism and state socialism), began to take shape, the call for corporate social responsibility was championed by the most prestigious business schools in the US. The idea that business and business managers had the aptitude and means to positively influence society, and a responsibility to the public, became ingrained in several generations of influential businesspeople.

With the advent of the modern environmental movement in the 1960s and subsequent regulations, particularly of toxic substances, the expectation that businesses had some responsibility not to pollute grew. Corporate responsibility was gaining a new face.

In the 1980s the public, and particularly investors, began to pay more attention to where their money was going. The idea of socially responsible investing (although again, not new) took off, spurred largely by the call to end apartheid in South Africa. Wall Street heeded the call, and soon investors could choose *socially responsible* stocks and funds. By 1999, the Dow Jones Sustainability Indices had been created, and the idea of selling "green" was catching on.

Just as business was beginning to embrace the idea of corporate environmental responsibility at the end of the 20th century, a shift took place within corporate culture. Managers began to manage funds to increase their own profits, and those who were most successful rose to the top where their salaries and bonuses quickly set them apart. Shareholders, employees and certainly the public good took a back seat. The excesses of Enron, whose traders mocked the idea that old ladies were going to lose their pensions, became the icons of corporate irresponsibility.

Strangely, while many businesses were losing ground when it came to actual indicators of social responsibility, more and more were taking on the challenge of sustainability, whether by ordering recycled paper or supporting green causes in their local communities. And of course, some were doing both at the same time. But could you do good AND make a buck? While many of us wondered, others got to doing just that — building successful, sustainable businesses.

Progressive Profitability

In 1983, a small, organic farming and homesteading school in New Hampshire needed a way to stay afloat. They decided to make and sell organic yogurt. The venture was so successful that they closed the school and devoted themselves full-time to yogurt-making. Today, Stonyfield Farms is a fixture in grocery stores across the US, with enviable profits, a firm track record of environmentally and socially responsible actions and a plethora of awards to show for it. Although their rise to success wasn't always smooth, the company persisted through everything from runny yogurt and market flops (prunewhip yogurt) to a serious economic crisis brought on by an insolvent supplier.

As Stonyfield grew, becoming economically more and more secure, they increased their commitment to the environment, tackling everything from global warming to cow emissions. (Yes, their cows now burp less, emit less and produce milk higher in Omega-3s!) In 1997, long before most people had heard of carbon offsets, Stonyfield began offsetting their carbon footprint and teaching others how to do the same. It turns out that producing a good product, making good money and doing good with that money isn't as hard as we might have thought. It just takes a little imagination, a lot of hard work and a healthy dose of persistence.

Businesses that Change the World

Like Stonyfield, Seventh Generation also models what a company can and should be. From a first glance at their website, it's clear this is no ordinary company, no business as usual. "Protecting Planet Home," is front and center, along with their mission, "help[ing] you protect your world with our naturally safe and effective household products." You can participate in "Ask Scienceman," a Q&A, or purchase a copy of "The Responsibility Revolution." Seventh Generation isn't just selling eco-friendly products, they are teaching people how to steward Earth. Recently, the company began a crowd-source project to produce an online book featuring best practices in corporate social responsibility and sustainability. Contrast this with a large, conventional competitor whose website proclaims "Everyone is an innovator" and lists "Investor Relations" as the first tab.

The difference between a conventional business and a sustainable business isn't merely adherence to the triple (economic, social and environmental) bottom line. It's something deeper: a real commitment to community and the values that underlie it. This, and the business culture within the company itself, can make all the difference.

Within the business itself, there are elements of how it operates that add value to the enterprise which are hard to quantify in dollar terms. Often described as *intangible assets*, these things include brand recognition, employee loyalty, intellectual property and the reputation the company has in the community and among its clients. These intangible assets are fertile ground for the creation of complementary currencies. Perhaps employees can earn points for mentoring other employees into higher levels of leadership and responsibility. Or they could get credit for different types of community service that can be exchanged for lunch at the company cafeteria. Anytime there are underutilized (or undervalued) resources and unmet needs, there are opportunities for new ways to mobilize people to increase productivity and value.

Rewarding Loyalty

Maybe you've never heard the term *loyalty currency*, but you know what it is. It is ubiquitous these days. Every store seems to have one. The store tracks your spending, encourages more and rewards you for coming back. Rewards cards, frequent-flyer miles, co-op memberships, even those little punch cards that coffee shops give out — they are all loyalty currencies, and they are the most widespread type of complementary currency today.

Although customer loyalty programs have proliferated lately, the granddaddy of loyalty currencies, the trading stamp, dates to the 1890s, when merchants, hungry for cash during that era's depression, began to issue stamps as a reward for cash payment. Eventually most chain supermarkets, as well as a host of other retailers, issued stamps to all customers, regardless of payment method. The stamps, which retailers bought from a stamp company (like Blue Chip or S&H) were issued along with one's receipt. They could then be pasted into stamp books and redeemed for goods at the stamp store. Except for the extensive licking required by the enterprise, it was like getting things for free.

Another older, and still very common, paper-based, loyalty currency is the *discount voucher*, redeemable for goods or services in retail shops and supermarkets. In the UK, Tesco has grown to become the largest supermarket chain on the strength of its loyalty currency system, which it developed into a fully fledged complementary currency system. Introduced in the mid-1990s, the Tesco loyalty program was so successful that it forced rival retailers to follow suit. One in three UK households now are Tesco card members, and the *Clubcard* magazine is Europe's largest circulating customer magazine.[1]

Loyalty currencies are becoming so pervasive that new ventures are being established that enable people to trade in the currencies themselves, without respect to the original company with whom the points or miles was designed to benefit. Whether it's LoyaltyMatch in Canada[2] or a patent filed recently in the US that will enable transactions to occur between multiple "non-financial loyalty currencies held by different loyalty issuers,"[3] these currencies have intangible value for companies but real value to their customers.

Loyalty currencies are also often used as just another marketing strategy. But by themselves, they don't provide a complete, sustainable business strategy.

Recession-Proof Commerce

Back in the 1930s, the world was reeling from the banking crash that caused the Great Depression. Then as now, banks were cutting back on their lending, and money was scarce; there were also several instances around the world where hyperinflation took over. For example, there are many stories of people using suitcases full of money to pay for simple things like a loaf of bread.

When money is not available at all, the first option is a return to barter. Barter is one of the oldest exchange mechanisms in history. With the advent of currencies though, barter slowly fell out of favor. It's easier, after all, to give the shopkeeper a few coins or bills than to haul a bushel of corn or a squealing pig into the shop. Now, as we try to recapture community, create sustainability and find stability, barter is making a modern-day comeback. Some of barter's popularity is about lifestyle choices — local choices in particular — but it is also about economic security in an unpredictable economy.

Like individuals, businesses, too, can have a cash flow shortage but a surplus of goods. Again in this case, it's not terribly convenient to pay in corn, pigs or saddle shoes. And doing so might limit what you can purchase. The shoelace supplier probably doesn't want a warehouse full of shoes.

In 1934, a small group of business owners in Switzerland convened to talk about their troubles. It didn't take long before they realized that one of them needed his credit line from the bank to pay a supplier. That supplier's business in turn needed the same kind of credit line for similar purposes. They all decided to work together to create a mutual credit system, where instead of borrowing money from banks, they issued credits and debits to each other at the moment of an exchange to keep production going so it all would balance out in the end.

Needless to say, the banks did not like the idea, and they tried to stop the new currency, called the WIR, in its tracks. (WIR is derived from the word *Wirtschaftsring* or economic circle — but *wir* also means "we" in German.) Nevertheless, the system survived. The WIR system evolved into a full-scale dual currency bank which manages and lends in both WIR and Swiss Francs.

Today, over 75 years later, the WIR Bank has grown into a major financial institution in Switzerland. Some 75,000 small and medium sized businesses (SMEs) in Switzerland are members, ¼ of the total number of businesses in the country. SMEs make up 99.7% of Swiss companies and provide jobs for 66.8% of the workforce. The total value of WIR traded in 2008 was over $1.58 billion. The WIR bank in addition issued 2.74 billion Swiss Francs in loans in 2008.[4]

Notice that, in the case of the WIR, the complementary currency is not convertible into Swiss Francs: a debt incurred in WIR needs to be compensated by a sale in WIR of a good or service to another member of the network. The next system considered, Commercial Credit Circuits, improves on that approach by making the complementary currency automatically convertible into conventional national currency.

Commercial Credit Circuits (C3)

Commercial Credit Circuits, or C3s, developed only over the past decade. They are based on businesses paying for goods and services completely electronically.

Here's how a C3 works. The process starts by having one participating small or medium sized business get insurance on an invoice or other payment claims. This insured invoice is then used as backing for a complementary currency for the same amount as the invoice. The proceeds in complementary currency are then used as a liquid payment instrument within a business-to-business network. Each recipient of such an invoice can either cash it in for conventional currency (at the cost of paying the interest to the maturity of the invoice) or pass the proceeds on to pay its own suppliers. At the maturity of the invoice, the amount gets paid in conventional money (normally by the company to whom the invoice was issued, or in case of default, by the insurance company). At that point, all the C3 units that were created become convertible to conventional money at no cost.

This process injects working capital into the C3 members' network at a cost substantially lower than what would otherwise be possible. Given that small and medium sized firms provide the vast majority of all private jobs, the C3 mechanism systemically contributes to the stability of both employment and the entire economy. The software for implementing the C3 approach is open source, called Cyclos.[5]

If governments, particularly regional governments, would accept C3 currency in payment of taxes (as the country of Uruguay has now begun to do), this would not only encourage all other businesses to accept C3, but would also provide additional income to the government from transactions that wouldn't otherwise take place. Furthermore, that additional income would become automatically available in conventional national currency at the maturity of the original invoice. Thus accepting C3 units does not upset any existing procurement policies. The first country that has agreed to accept C3 units in payment of all fees and taxes is Uruguay.[6]

The C3 approach is probably the most dependable way to systemically reduce unemployment, and accepting C3 units in payment of taxes is the most effective way for governments to support the spread of the C3 system. Businesses with an account in the same regional network have an incentive to spend their balances with each other, and thus further stimulate the regional economy. C3 provides a win-win environment for all participants and therefore promotes other collaborative activities among regional businesses.

The win-win approach of C3 also benefits the financial system itself. As the entire C3 process is computerized, it significantly streamlines the lending and management for its insurance and loan providers. SMEs can thereby become a more profitable sector for banks, because credit lines are negotiated with the entire clearing network, providing the financial sector with automatic risk diversification among participants in the network.

A Role for Businesses

Businesses are poised to play a greater role in the trade and exchange world — they often are the leaders that step in whenever monetary systems fail. During the Great Depression, it was often individual businesses or business associations that introduced alternative forms of currency (such as scrip) that circulated on a local level to keep doors open and people employed. Businesses have developed the most widely circulated complementary currencies in the world — the loyalty currencies — and the most stable alternative exchange systems. The WIR and the C3 systems are clear examples of this.

We can do a lot to foster a healthy business climate by expanding the ability of local businesses to use either loyalty or commercial barter systems in new ways. When our cities and other local governments accept C3 units in payment of taxes and fees, this will be one of the most effective ways for local governments and businesses to collaborate in solving local economic problems.

CHAPTER 10

Putting the Care Back in Healthcare

The greatest wealth is health.

VIRGIL

In Sickness and in Health

Healthcare in the US is one of the glaring examples of the failure of money, insurance and the privately held healthcare companies' ability to meet human needs. The US Constitution affirms that we all are created equal — no one born on Earth is more deserving of basic human rights than anyone else. However, the same centripetal forces that consolidate wealth and power in the marketplace and in society are also at work in the healthcare system.

The starting point should be to recognize that we don't have a *healthcare* system — instead we have a *medical care* system. Furthermore, income for that medical care system is produced essentially by people who are alive and sick. Therefore only more sick people — not healthy ones — lead to more growth and income in that sector. With such an incentive scheme, that system has become remarkably adept at keeping sick people alive. Over 60% of total lifelong medical expenses are typically incurred in the last three months of a patient's life; and emergency care is clearly a domain in which Western medicine excels.

Sickness Treatment vs. Wellness Promotion

When industries are built around a medical model that rewards the proliferation of illnesses rather than the provision of genuine health, there are fewer incentives for participants in the system to discover and promote treatments that will keep people healthy. A good example of this is the relationship of food to our health. "You are what you eat," is a statement to be taken seriously: nutrition plays a pivotal role in our lifelong health. Obesity, cancer, heart disease, diabetes, high blood pressure, stroke and infections — all of these are on the list of the top killers in our society, and every one of them has a direct causal relationship to the food we eat.

Are doctors and medical students flocking to nutrition programs as a result? Far from it — nutrition is not even a required course in medical school. Few doctors know any more about nutrition than the general population. The response of the sickness treatment industry to these epidemics is to create more patented and expensive drugs for people to take rather than to provide nutritional advice, to advocate for safer and healthier foods or to intervene when children are being raised eating junk food.

The number of children in the US who regularly take drugs like Ritalin, an amphetamine used to treat hyperactivity and attention deficit disorder when there is a clear link between these behaviors and food that is loaded with sugars, chemicals and artificial colors, is an example of how drugs are used as a substitute for common sense. "The science shows that kids' behavior improves when these artificial colorings are removed from their diets and worsens when they're added to their diets," said Dr. David Schab, author of meta-analysis published in the *Journal of Developmental and Behavioral Pediatrics*.[1] Links between artificial colors and flavors and hyperactivity have been known for years, yet the amount of these chemicals certified by the US Food and Drug Administration (FDA) for use in food increased from 12 mg per person per day in 1955 to 59 mg per person per day in 2004.[2]

The Scarcity of Health

Health is perhaps the best example of something that human beings need in abundance. There is never "too much" health. Our spiritual traditions are full of stories of healing — it is considered a form of divine intervention. Being a healer is one of the highest callings and has always been one of the revered positions in society.

We might legitimately hope that when we go to a doctor, the doctor's goal would be to provide us with the care we need to get well. The system isn't called health *care* for nothing. We expect the doctor to serve us in a compassionate way, to genuinely care about us as a human being and to take all the steps necessary to help us be whole again. The root of the word health is wholeness. Yet slowly and insidiously the monetary incentive scheme we have developed has twisted and deformed the institutions we hope act as healers into institutions that work more like hard nosed businesspeople than compassionate caregivers. How did this happen?

Much has been written about the problems with the health insurance industry in the United States. Michael Moore's film *Sicko*, released in 2004, provided a sometimes humorous but relentless exposé of the number of people with health insurance who are turned away — denied coverage — as soon as they get sick. The Health Maintenance Organization (HMO) industry has brought the concerns of an insurance industry right into the doctor's office. People who enroll in HMOs no longer have the ability to go to specialists who might know more about their condition without the pre-approval of primary care doctors who don't. The primary care doctors are often in the position of needing to keep costs down, so testing and specialized care is denied to people when their illness is still in the early stages, causing more people's diseases to advance to much more serious forms — leading often to more treatments, hospitalization, disability and death.

For a sickness treatment industry, however, the more treatments they provide, the more drugs that are sold, the more billable hours doctors, nurses, technicians and other healthcare workers spend with patients, the more tests that are run, the more of their product is sold. If a pharmaceutical company invents a drug and then owns the patent on it, it means they have a monopoly on the ability to sell that drug anywhere it's needed. If you have ever taken Economics 101, you know that monopoly pricing is not necessarily fair or competitive — patented drugs can cost astronomical amounts of money. The companies argue that the costs of the drugs have to pay for the research and testing that went into developing the drugs, but in reality these companies spend three or four times more on marketing their products than on researching and developing them.

When you understand how the variables in the system relate to one another — the positive and negative feedback — it is also possible to discover ways that interventions could change the system for the better. In the admittedly simplified system diagram below, one intervention that would have a beneficial impact on human health — and that would change a vicious cycle into a virtuous cycle — would be to increase access to treatment. Higher access to (presumably preventive and early diagnosis) treatment would (because of *positive* feedback) lead to higher individual health, which in turn would lower demand for (more expensive sickness) treatment (*negative* feedback), lower costs (*positive* feedback) and allow for increased access over time as a result of the lower costs (*negative* feedback).

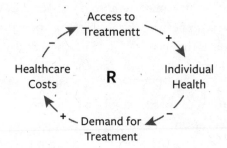

FIGURE 10.1 Caption: A Healthcare Feedback Loop

To sum up this section, our health itself is being systematically undermined by the flawed systems we are using to provide health services and pay for them. The insurance and sickness treatment industries are required to put profits first in the services they offer, which creates a vicious cycle where people are getting sicker and needing more expensive forms of treatment because of a lack of preventive health services.

The Cost of Failing Health

Lack of preventive care also means higher costs to society. Since 2000, the cost of medical care increased by 4% per year in real terms on average across OECD countries, whereas real GDP growth averaged just 2.3% per year. This gap led to a further rise in healthcare spending as a share of GDP, reaching 8.4% on average in 2001, up from 7.3% in 1990 and just over 5% in 1970.³ For the US, according to the General Accounting Office, the cost of healthcare has risen from us$666.2 Billion in 1990 (12.2% of GNP) to us$1,615.9 Billion in 2000 (16.4% of GNP) and is expected to reach $3.1 trillion (17.7% of GNP) by 2012. For Germany, the actual costs in the health sector amount to 234.2 Billion Euro and are estimated to double by 2020.⁴

Figure 2 shows the expenses paid for healthcare as a share of GDP in OECD countries — our peers. The US stands out as spending almost double the average of all industrialized countries.

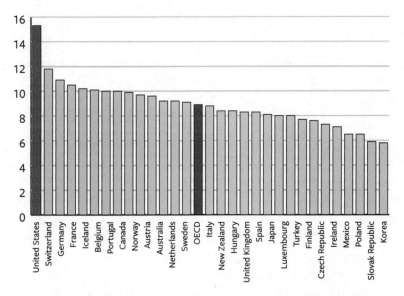

FIGURE 10.2 Per Capita Expenditure on Healthcare as a share of GDP, 2006. Source: OECD Health Data 2006.⁵

In 2004, more than one million Americans were financially ruined by illness or medical bills. Most were middle class. Each year, two million Americans face the double disaster of illness and bankruptcy. But the bigger surprise is that ¾ of the medically bankrupt had health insurance. Too sick to work, they suddenly lost their jobs. With the jobs went most of their income and their health insurance — ¼ of all employers cancel coverage the day employees leave work because of a disabling illness; another ¼ do so in less than a year.

Bankrupt families lost more than just assets. One out of five went without food. One third had their utilities shut off, and nearly ⅔ skipped needed doctor or dentist visits. These families arrived at the bankruptcy courthouse exhausted and emotionally spent, brought low by a medical system that could offer physical cures but that left them financially devastated.

Without better coverage, millions of more Americans will be hit by medical bankruptcy over the next decade. It will not be limited to the poorly educated, the barely employed or the uninsured. The people financially devastated by a serious illness are at the heart of the middle class. Every 30 seconds in the United States, someone files for bankruptcy in the aftermath of a serious health problem.[6]

It is hoped that the healthcare reform passed by the US Congress in 2010 will be able to correct some of these problems. However, we should consider that the jury is still out on this topic, because there are systemic forces at work that this reform has not addressed.

From Sickness Treatment to Healthcare

A US Committee on Capitalizing on Social Science and Behavioral Research to Improve the Public's Health concluded that "Behavioral and social interventions therefore offer great promise to reduce disease morbidity and mortality, but as yet their potential to improve the public's health has been relatively poorly tapped."[7] Approximately ½ of all causes of mortality in the United States are linked to social and behavioral factors such as smoking, diet, alcohol use, sedentary lifestyle and accidents. However, less than 5% of what is spent annually on healthcare in the United States is devoted to reducing risks posed by these preventable conditions.

The proof that there is a systemic cause underlying this entire issue can be found in evidence from traditional Chinese medicine. Until the late 19th century, very different monetary incentives were applicable to healthcare in China. A doctor would get paid by a patient as long as he or she was healthy. But the doctor would have to pay the patient whenever the latter was sick. Furthermore, if a patient died while under the care of a doctor, a metallic ball was hung at the entrance of that doctor's office: a long string of such balls would therefore constitute a clear warning for any new client. With this incentive scheme, is it surprising that traditional Chinese medicine was focusing on preventive measures and healing chronic diseases? Or, that typical Chinese medical interventions such as acupuncture, moxibustion and even herbal treatment are extremely cautious in not generating any negative side effects? This financial enticement explains why preventive medicine is emphasized so much more systematically in traditional Chinese medicine than in the Western approach.

Studies on employee activity programs reveal that the productivity of the people involved increased by 12%,[8] and absenteeism dropped by up to 45%.[9] Estimates of the impact of healthcare costs on corporations show a rise from 7% thirty years ago to up to 50% of the corporate profits now. This is why some individual companies are investing in wellness directly. For instance, Johnson & Johnson spends $4.5 million per year on staff wellness programs, avoiding thereby medical costs estimated at $13 million per year. But individual corporate solutions may not be the most effective way to solve the problem.

Wellness Tokens: Promoting Preventive Care

What systemic solutions can become available to help shift society as a whole towards more sustainable wellness? Trying to shift the modern Western medical model to simply adopt the ancient Chinese incentive system is unrealistic. But another way is available with a complementary currency that is specifically designed to promote wellness, rather than sickness.

Today, the conventional Western medical system focuses on four areas:

+ Sickness treatment — treatment of diseases and injuries
+ Emergency care — treatment for acute health problems that carry significant risk of death or imply severe changes in lifestyle
+ Long-term care — treatment for chronic health problems
+ Elder care — treatment for people who have entered a phase of their life when caring for their own health becomes a difficult challenge for them to do alone

In addition to addressing some of the issues generated in these areas, the framework proposed below would add consideration of three additional domains:

+ Prevention — taking actions to keep health issues from escalating into medical breakdowns or emergencies. This could include medical procedures that might prevent more serious complications in the future, or alternative treatments that use mainly the body's own energy for healing, like acupuncture and dietary changes.

+ Wellness — taking actions to maintain a healthy body and lifestyle that is less susceptible to many common health problems. This could include personal practices like better diets, daily walks or yoga classes, as well as other healthy habits.

+ Holistic/Optimal Health — taking actions to create a level of health that seems impossible to many today. Imagine practices that would allow 80-year-olds to retain physical activity comparable to today's active 40-year-olds, or people living well into their 100s. Such results have already been demonstrated by exceptional individuals, and we know enough about the human potential today[10] to conclude that there is no reason that such results, if considered desirable, could not become more generalized with the appropriate incentive schemes.

We know how frequent flyer miles can successfully encourage particular customer behavior patterns, i.e., loyalty to a particular airline alliance. Now imagine a complementary currency — let's call them Wellness Tokens — that would encourage people to take on healthy habits and practices. For example, one hour of exercise at a gym would earn one Wellness Token; or specific preventive treatments could similarly be encouraged with Wellness Tokens.

The role played by the airline alliances in issuing and administering frequent flyer miles would be performed by a Wellness Alliance — an association of organizations which have a financial or other interest in promoting healthy behaviors. Such an alliance could include health insurance companies, HMOs, corporations that want to reduce the healthcare cost of their employees and their families and local, state and federal governmental agencies.

The process starts with a Wellness Alliance issuing Wellness Tokens for two types of activities:

+ Help of a non-medical nature to elderly or handicapped persons who need chronic support, similar to the *Fureai Kippu* system (and other time currencies) in Japan and the Care Bank in Vermont (e.g., help in shopping, reading to visually disabled people, help with house living conditions). Home care programs typically cost five times less than hospital care systems. See Chapter 11 for more details.

+ Taking an active part in specifically qualified preventive health programs (like voluntary vaccinations; obesity reduction programs; primary, secondary and tertiary prevention; health educational programs). The Return on Investment (ROI) for these activities has been estimated at a striking 300% to 1000%, depending on the program.[11]

These tokens could be redeemed in part for other services or goods that further promote health, ranging, for instance, from partial payment for preventive therapies to buying or repairing a bicycle or buying appropriate foods. Another use of the tokens could be in partial payment for the insurance premiums, given that participants in this system should have a lower probability of getting or remaining sick. This logic is what justifies the Elderplan Insurance Company in Brooklyn accepting 25% of its health insurance premium for elderly participants in a local Time Bank.[12]

There is ample evidence that support groups for encouraging long-term wellness activities (e.g., weight reduction groups, Alcoholics Anonymous, running or gym exercise buddies or simply direct family) are important. Therefore, a Wellness Token system could meet not only the needs of individuals, but also those of groups: a family unit, a group of friends, professional colleagues or other support groups.

Participants in such a group would agree to a mutual *wellness contract*, so that the whole group would be affected by the results of each member. For instance, assuming that a group of five people are involved in an obesity reduction program, both the individual and the group weight reduction objectives could be used as a criteria for obtaining Wellness Tokens. In this example, independently verifiable, quantitative results could even be used in a contract with the Wellness Alliance.

Figure 10.3 shows schematically the flow of Wellness Tokens through economic circuits for prevention programs and home care support systems.

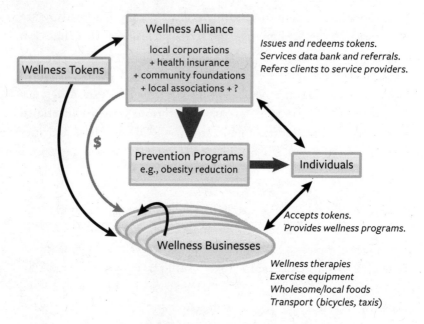

FIGURE 10.3. A Wellness Token System

Businesses or care providers could accept Wellness Tokens in partial payment for their services, and the balance in national currency. Each wellness provider would decide the percentage they accept in Wellness Tokens in payment for their services. The amount that they accept in Wellness Tokens could also be modulated to fit their own specific business needs (e.g., some may want to accept a higher percentage in Wellness Tokens during weekdays when they are less busy). Others may want to accept larger percentages if it would attract additional customers or because they have a good use for tokens themselves.

What can businesses or care providers do themselves with the Wellness Tokens they accept? First of all, the owners or employees of those businesses could use them exactly as anybody else, for their own health improvement. However, a bicycle shop, for instance, may receive more Tokens than it can use personally. That is why businesses accredited by the Wellness Alliance as providing valuable services would have the option to cash in Wellness Tokens in national money, but at a discount calculated to be a win-win between all the parties.[13]

Wellness Tokens would help people to become or remain healthier than they otherwise would be, reducing current and future medical costs. The system would create a wider market for goods and services that promote wellness. Even the pharmaceutical industry could benefit by producing more preventive medicine products and services, as it amplifies their market to the 93% of people in the society that are currently healthy. In the cases where governments provide universal healthcare, a Wellness Token system also helps to reduce the pressures on government to go into deficit for healthcare spending.

For there to be any hope of the adoption of new systems, like Wellness Tokens, where the incentives work to reward wellness instead of sickness, we need to strengthen the industries that are more profitable when people are well. Fortunately, this includes the vast majority of businesses in the country who suffer when people are out of work, or when their insurance premiums increase because of higher risk employees.

Already, some corporate wellness programs offer incentives to employees who go through a year without taking a sick day — some workplaces offer cash bonuses to workers with a good record. Others introduce weight reduction competitions with prizes for pounds lost, or miles walked or health programs attended. In 2008 over 60% of the companies in the US who have more than 10,000 workers offered wellness programs, up from 47% in 2005.[14]

For instance, IBM self-insures its workforce, and spent $1.3 billion on healthcare for its employees, dependents and retirees in 2008. They have been offering financial incentives to employees who participate in wellness activities since 2004, and through the end of 2008 had invested $133 million to date in these incentives. To determine whether or not all this money paid into wellness was a good investment, the company hired the University of Michigan's Health Management Research Center to analyze their program; the Center found that the wellness programs had saved the company over $80 million in reduced health claims since its inception.[15] If that is combined with the reduction in lost productivity that comes with sickness, and sick and disability leave for employees who are out sick, the program clearly offers benefits to the company as a whole.

In addition to wellness programs, some companies are getting a lot more serious about making employees with unhealthy behaviors pay higher costs for health insurance. PepsiCo, Northwest Airlines, American Financial Group and others charge employees who smoke between

$20 and $50 per month surcharge on their health insurance. Gannett, which owns 99 newspapers and 21 TV stations in 41 states, charges their employees who smoke more than $50 per month more for health insurance.[16] When PepsiCo increased the health insurance surcharge for smokers in 2008, it also added some additional smoking cessation programs, including nicotine replacement therapy such as patches and gum. "The combination of those two elements led to a tenfold increase in participation and increased the quit rate from 20% to 34% in 2008 over 2007," said Greg Heaslip, Benefits Vice-president.[17]

A wide variety of wellness programs have been around long enough now for their efficacy to be well-researched and documented. Several kinds of incentives have been tested and evaluated, and these too have had sufficient results to understand what works and what doesn't. The introduction of Wellness Tokens is not an experimental, unknown approach; it is rather a new way to systematize and support what is known to be a very successful approach to increased health, rather than merely the treatment of disease.

CHAPTER 11

Honoring Our Elders, Caring for Children

*I can think of no better way of redeeming this tragic world
today than love and laughter. Too many of the young have
forgotten how to laugh, and too many of the elders have
forgotten how to love. Would not our lives be lightened if only
we could all learn to laugh more easily at ourselves
and to love one another?*

THEODORE HESBURGH

In traditional cultures, many of which still exist today, children and elders are treasured members of both family and community. The beginning of life and the end of life have a special place, as do those closest to these sacred rites of passage.

Throughout most of human history, childlessness has been a serious hardship. The biblical story of the long-childless Abraham and Sarah, who finally conceived a child well into their ninth decade, is celebrated across three of the world's major religions: Judaism, Christianity and Islam. These two citizens of Ur, an ancient city,[1] received God's miracle in the form of a child, Isaac, who later became the father of a royal lineage, that of King David, King Solomon and eventually of Jesus of

Nazareth himself, whose birth is also considered miraculous by the majority of Christians. Abraham's other son, Ishmael (whose mother was Hagar), is believed to be the shared ancestor of the Arab people, and even possibly of Muhammad himself.

Elders play a critically important role in most traditional communities. They are wise ones, the mediators of conflict, the healers, the teachers, the spiritual leaders. Yet now, in the 21st century, they are relegated to the sidelines, discredited "senior citizens," a term which devalues the idea of an elder. The facilities and programs created for them focus on keeping them entertained rather than keeping them engaged. Modern society has created leisure time for elders, with social security, pensions and retirement programs which give them the potential to make enormous contributions to our communities. Unfortunately, deteriorating health, isolation and the culture of youth, with its inherent disparagement of older people, robs society of the values that elders offer.

We need child care and care for our elders in abundance. Yet, child-care workers and elder-care workers are among the lowest paid workers in our society. As a result, the quality of the care is also quite low, since these professions do not attract people who are educated and who have the ability to do other things at higher wages.

In the United States, there were more than 90 million people over the age of 60 in 2008, close to ⅓ of the country's population. More than ½ of these people require some level of care, and one in ten jobs are generated in this area. According to US Census data, in 2005 there were 11 million children under the age of five. Anyone who has had to care for a young child knows that at this age, the optimal ratio for attention is 1:1. So, ideally there would be 11 million people engaged in this level of child care. Yet in 2005, 21% of the children under five in the US were cared for by their parents, 25% by their grandparents, 23% in a daycare facility, 15% in what is described as "non-relative care," and fully 13% with "no regular arrangement." The number of child-care workers in the US is hard to determine with any accuracy, because the census number (456,232 in 2002) doesn't include self-employed daycare providers, pre-school teachers, teacher assistants and all the parents and grandparents i.e., the majority of the people who are actually doing this work today. The mean hourly wage for those who were counted in 2002 was $8.32, just over minimum wage in most states. The mean hourly wage for elder-care workers in the same year was a bit higher, ranging somewhere between $9.45 per hour and $10.25, depending on the level of skills required.[2]

The low wages and lack of quality care for the people who traditionally were the most important members of our community is one important way we neglect them — it is nothing less than economic abandonment. The ramifications of this neglect are staggering — the statistics describing child and elder abuse in the US are truly a national tragedy, as the weakest members of our society take the brunt of our dysfunctional economy. Studies done on a national level indicate that between one and two million people over the age of 65 have been injured, exploited or otherwise mistreated by someone on whom they depended for care or protection.[3] Every year, there are over three million reports of child abuse — one report every ten seconds. In 2003, there were 906,000 convictions of people who abused children in the US. Four children die every day as a result of neglect and abuse, with three out of four of these victims under the age of four.[4]

These raw statistics can't help but break your heart. It is hard to read them without feeling a sense of despair and helplessness. Recognition of the systemic underlying causes of this national shame would be the starting point to correct it.

A Scarcity of Care

Several converging systemic patterns form the roots of the economic vice that squeezes our children and elders. The time crunch everyone experiences (caused by a competitive currency dominating our exchange system) is a key factor, combined with the low wages paid for jobs with skills we have in abundance, and the lack of value our system places on people who are not in the workforce.

Child care and elder care takes time. It does not typically require years of study or apprenticeship, although higher skill levels in issues like nutrition, first aid and healthcare can make the difference between quality care and neglect. The main factor is time — young children and disabled elders can require someone's focused attention 24 hours a day, seven days a week. In an economy where all able-bodied adults typically need to work full-time to earn enough dollars to pay for basic necessities, time is scarce.

The skills and capacities we need to take care of each other are not scarce, however. Human beings are richly endowed with the capacity to love and nurture each other. It is arguably one of our innate survival skills — everyone knows how to do it, with the rare exception of people who are born with mental disabilities or illnesses that make them sociopaths on some level. In an ideal world, the knowledge and skills we would need to provide adequate nutrition and healthcare would be something we learned as we matured, since these would have been provided to us by our parents and extended family.

Yet in this current economic system all the caring functions, even those needed in abundance, are not valued adequately. In the case of child care and elder care, this translates into low wages for the people who are arguably carrying out some of the most important and sacred tasks in our lives. The low wages paid for these jobs mean that people who do the jobs are often living in poverty themselves.

Time Banks and Care Banks

When the effective delivery of an important service requires a substantial amount of time, the competitive, scarce exchange system will inevitably prove to be inadequate. The clichéd expression "time is money" states the problem pretty clearly — the more time something takes, the more it costs. If lots of time is required, then the costs will be substantial, and this grows in direct proportion to the level of skill involved.

Raising children challenges even the most intelligent minds, and elder care can be equally confounding. When all we expect of our child-care and elder-care providers is the bare minimum — physical safety — we take the care from the equation. Providing "care" becomes merely a job, performed by low-skill, low-pay workers. When the world of a child or elder is allowed to fall into hands that don't care and don't know, that world shrinks, in danger of becoming an unbearable monotony, where humanity is forgotten and individual potential ignored.

Parents face the hard reality of child care on a daily basis. It is a problem that has become more pressing in the last 50 years as opportunities for women in the professional workforce have expanded and the economy has made it harder and harder to raise children on a single income. Child care co-ops have emerged in larger cities, where groups of parents arrange their schedules around shared child care, and where parents themselves provide a lot of the service rather than relegating it to lower paid child-care workers. These baby-sitting co-ops can actually be considered as very small scale complementary currency systems, with typically one hour of baby-sitting as the unit of account. While a co-op is a nice alternative to much of what passes for child care, it doesn't work for everyone. What other creative solutions can we find? After all, the need for child care is not going to go away. We need to turn again to our children as an important center of our purpose here, and stop relegating them to the sidelines.

One way to meet our child-care needs, and a lot of other needs as well, is to turn to a Time Bank — a system which allows people to exchange time without using dollars or other forms of national currency.[5] Time Banks work like this: people sign up as members, listing the services they are willing to perform and the services they want to receive. *Time dollars* are exchanged, based on the amount of time spent on the service, not on the level of skill or perceived economic value. All time is valued the same — an hour for an hour. In a Time Bank system, time is the great equalizer because each of us only has 24 hours in a day. In this system, it is considered that all time has the same value.

Time Banks can be used in many situations and on various scales. A shared living facility might record time dollars on a chalk board, while a city might track time and requests electronically, matching people up using a database. A new county level Time Bank was recently formed in Wisconsin that will coordinate services throughout a region. Time Banks can serve a relatively narrow purpose, as they do in Washington, DC, where Time Banks are used in the juvenile justice system to motivate young people to get out of trouble and learn job skills, or they can serve many different goals, as in Portland, Maine, and Montpelier, Vermont, where Time Banks encourage community building, economic development, poverty alleviation and even health service provision.

The core values of Time Banking grew out of the anti-poverty work done in the 1960s by the founder of the movement, Edgar Cahn. Frustrated by a War on Poverty that reinforced poverty by creating classes of beneficiaries and benefactors, Edgar felt it was important to affirm the value and dignity of every human being, regardless of their economic value to the system. This conviction led to the five core principles that are part of every Time Bank.

Assets

We are all assets.
Every human being has something to contribute.

Redefining Work

Some work is beyond price.
Work has to be redefined to value whatever it takes to raise healthy children, build strong families, revitalize neighborhoods, make democracy work, advance social justice, make the planet sustainable. That kind of work needs to be honored, recorded and rewarded.

Reciprocity

Helping works better as a two-way street.
The question: "How can I help you?" needs to change so we ask: "How can we help each other build the world we both will live in?"

Social Networks

We need each other.
Networks are stronger than individuals. People helping each other reweave communities of support, strength & trust. Community is built upon sinking roots, building trust, creating networks. Special relationships are built on commitment.

Respect

Every human being matters.
Respect underlies freedom of speech, freedom of religion, and everything we value. Respect supplies the heart and soul of democracy. When respect is denied to anyone, we all are injured. We must respect where people are in the moment, not where we hope they will be at some future point.[6]

While they are not focused on child care or elder care, Time Banks provide a system where care for children and elders can take place more easily. In fact, a high percentage of Time Banks find that child care is one of the things people are seeking when they join. The fact that the activities in Time Banks are officially tax-exempt (which means they do not count toward members' income) also means that when people use services through a Time Bank, they do not put income-based government benefits at risk.

In 2009, the concept of Time Banking was taken a step further, so that it could be used reliably for elder care. Through a grant from the Ashoka Foundation and the US Administration on Aging's Community Innovations for Aging in Place (CIAIP) program, the idea of a Care Bank was born.[7] A Care Bank adds an additional level of coordination and reliability to the Time Bank model. If a Time Bank is like a marketplace, where people enter their offers and requests and trade them as often as they like, a Care Bank is more like an insurance program. Members of a Care Bank make a commitment of time and money to the system each month, and in return they are able to receive care when they or their family needs it.

Montpelier, the capital city of Vermont, has created both a Time Bank and a Care Bank. The Onion River Exchange is a standard Time Bank, where members post their offers and requests and trade with each other as often as they like. The city also received a federal grant from the US Administration on Aging to create the Rural Elder Assistance for Care and Health (REACH) program. REACH expands traditional Time Bank membership types to include three levels: basic, assisted and specialized.

At the *basic* level, REACH works like a Time Bank. You make a donation to the organization of either $25/year or offer two hours of assistance with a fundraiser for the organization. Then you post the things you are willing to do for the Time Bank — your offers — and the things you would like someone to do for you — your requests. The posting is made using the Community Weaver software developed by Time Banks USA. A central website keeps track of all the members, their requests, their offers and the time dollars or, in Montpelier's case the Community Credits, that are exchanged by members.

At the *assisted* level, you make a commitment of time and money each month — four hours of time and $5 per month for each service cluster you need. So if you want to have your sidewalk and driveway shoveled in winter, you would sign up to be part of the Yard Work cluster. Your four hours of time could go to doing something else that was needed by Care Bank members — perhaps you could call a neighbor who needs reminding about the medications he or she is taking on a daily basis. And the Care Bank coordinator would make sure that someone was available to shovel your walk when needed.

At the *specialized* level, you make a higher commitment of time and money each month — eight hours of time and $15 per month for each service cluster you need. This level helps members have access to preventive care services and more highly specialized skills, like those of electricians and carpenters. The preventive services include things like massage therapy, chiropractic care, exercise and yoga classes, herbal therapy and other alternative and complementary healthcare services. The access to these services attracts a broad spectrum of the community to the system and provides the Care Bank with a solid foundation of people's time to continue to offer the assisted level of care to others.

The Japanese System

The Care Bank model shares a lot in common with the time exchange systems that have been in existence in Japan for over 15 years. The Japanese population is the second fastest aging population in the world. There are already 800,000 retired people needing daily help and another one million who have disabilities. The Japanese Ministry of Health forecasts a vast increase in these numbers in the foreseeable future.[8]

In order to address this rapidly rising problem, the Japanese have implemented several new time exchange currencies.[9] In these systems, the hours that a volunteer spends helping older or handicapped persons with their daily routine are credited to that volunteer's *time account*. Time accounts are managed like a savings account, except that the unit of account is hours of service instead of Yen. Time account credits are also available to complement normal health insurance programs. One of these time exchange systems is run on a national level by the Sawayaka Foundation in Japan. It's called the *Fureai Kippu* system and has a lot to teach us about how complementary currencies can address serious social issues.

In the *Fureai Kippu* system, different values apply to different kinds of tasks. For instance, a meal served between 9 AM and 5 PM can have a lower credit value than those served outside that time slot because they don't conflict with family dinners. Household chores and shopping have a lower credit value than personal body care.

These healthcare credits are guaranteed to be available to the volunteers themselves, or to someone else of their choice, within or outside of the family, whenever they may need similar help. Two electronic clearing houses ensure that if someone can provide help in Tokyo, the time credits become available to his or her parents anywhere else in the country. Many people just volunteer the work and hope they will never need it. Others not only volunteer, but also give their time credits away to people who they think need them. In these cases, it amounts to doubling their gifts of time: for every credit hour of service, the amount of care provided to society is two hours.

Most significantly, this type of service is also preferred by the elderly participants themselves because the caring quality of the service turns out to be higher than those obtained from Yen-paid social service workers. The meaning of *Fureai Kippu* (Caring Relationship Ticket) spells out its agenda. The system also provides a more comfortable emotional space for elders, who would otherwise be embarrassed to ask for free services.

The Japanese also report a significant increase in volunteer help, even by people who do not bother to open their own time accounts. The reason may be that in a community where this system is operational, volunteering is simply more acknowledged. The same effects were found in a US study by the University of Maryland Center of Aging.[10] These findings should put to rest concerns that paying volunteers with complementary currency might inhibit those not getting paid from volunteering.

As of end 2005 there were over 487 municipal level healthcare, time-credit systems in Japan, most run by private initiatives such as the Sawayaka Welfare Institute, the *Wac Ac* (Wonderful Aging Club, Active Club) and the Japan Care System (a nonprofit with some governmental funding). They range in size from a few families and small organizations of up to 50 people to large, nationwide programs that are run by labor unions. One estimate of the level of transactions that take place with this type of complementary currency stated:

As for the number of participants in each community currency system, the groups with 'less than 50 members' and '50 to 100 members' account for 60 percent of the total, indicating that small-scale systems are widely recognized in Japan. As for the extent of circulation of community currency related goods, circulation within the municipality accounts for about half of all transactions.[11]

If we in North America could build these caring, relational transactions so that they amounted to a higher percentage of the exchanges we made each day, this would certainly start to balance the effects of the competitive currency in our economy and our lives. In Bali, a very different society has emerged with about ⅓ of an adult Balinese's time spent in the cooperative economy. The same social change — one that captures ancient values like honoring elders and treasuring children while embracing a new level of consciousness to extend our idea of connectedness to the whole human and sentient family — is possible in our time.

CHAPTER 12

Eating Money

Food for all is a necessity. Food should not be a merchandise,
to be bought and sold as jewels are bought and sold by those
who have the money to buy. Food is a human necessity,
like water and air, it should be available.

PEARL BUCK

A Shared Meal

Among the !Kung people of Botswana, a successful hunt used to mean a shared community meal. When one family got a large kill, the expectation was that they would share it with the rest of the people in their circle of homes, which were arranged around a common central hearth, with the doors facing towards the center. Archeological research has revealed that this camp layout has been unchanged for over 10,000 years, earning the !Kungs the title of the most conservative people on Earth.

Because the !Kung maintained their traditional hunter-gatherer way of life until late in the 20th century, anthropologists were able to study them in depth and document what happened when this traditional culture was exposed to "modern" life. (This process inspired a popular movie called *The Gods Must Be Crazy*.) Before modern society arrived on their doorstep, even family living space was visible from the circle of homes through open doors. Everyone could see what everyone else was doing.

In the 1970s and 1980s, the government of Botswana started promoting trade among the villages in the Kalahari, and for the first time, money was introduced to the !Kung. This seemingly small change — the introduction of money — had an enormous impact on !Kung society and their social interactions. They began to use money to buy glass beads and other valuables, which they locked in new metal boxes in their homes. Within five years, people sought privacy rather than intimacy, and even the way they laid out their homes changed. No longer were doors open towards a common hearth; instead they faced away from the circle of homes. People started hoarding instead of depending on others, and the hunter-gatherer way of life that had shaped !Kung society over hundreds of generations gave way to totally different life patterns much closer to our own.[1]

This true story illustrates one of the links between the monetary exchange system we use, the economics of food and trade and the social practices that are shaped by both of them. In one culture, sharing is the norm; in another, hoarding is the norm. A way of life can be transformed and/or intentionally molded by the introduction of a new socially-constructed policy, program or monetary instrument.

Hunter-gatherer societies had to work together in order to have a successful hunt, and once the hunt was over, cooperation was required to drag dinner back to camp and skin, clean and cook or cure it. Sharing in the bounty made good sense, especially before refrigeration. The introduction of agriculture tended to change this, as food then became a product of private property. Food could be hoarded and stored, particularly by large landowners or those with the means to buy and store grain, including city-states, which sought to insure survival during drought and famine. In fact, some of the earliest forms of money can be traced to the storage of agricultural products.

Food and water are basic human needs, and depending upon the systems that drive our society, we see them either as critical for our individual survival or our collective survival. But, in truth, our individual survival is very much linked to the collective in the end. Until recently, water has been considered a public resource. Through our governance systems we have developed ways to share it with each other. Over the last 20 years, however, water is becoming increasingly privatized as companies purchase water supplies and systems and profit from the sale of water. What will the impact of this change be? We might ask, thinking about the !Kung people, whether the privatization of water might be the modern equivalent of the privatization of food? Perhaps in our distant history — too early for written documents to record — food was also a community product, shared for the common good?

From Subsistence to Surplus

As first mentioned in Chapter 4, there were two different kinds of money in Dynastic Egypt, the precious metals that were used for long-distance trade (including with other countries) and a different currency used for local exchange. The local currency was actually based on *ostraka* (singular *ostrakon*), shards of pottery used as inventory receipts, where dates and quantities were inscribed when farmers put their excess production in collective storage places attached to temples. The Egyptians charged a modest fee for the storage, and so the value of these shards of pottery declined over time.

This storage fee served as a negative interest rate, or demurrage fee, on the local money. Since the shards were used for local exchanges, it was in the best interest of the person holding it to spend it as quickly as possible (to avoid its inevitable penalty over time), which added more quantity and velocity to the local economic exchanges. The abundance of economic exchanges, driven in part by this money that did not serve as a store of value, helped make Dynastic Egyptian society a prosperous one for thousands of years.[2]

In the time since Dynastic Egypt, food has played many roles in society. Surplus has been stored and traded everywhere, in all agrarian societies throughout history. Yet regular and reliable food surpluses are for the most part historical anomaly. Until the 1950s, a majority of people on Earth did their own subsistence farming, which meant that at least on the family level, food was a shared resource.

Yet the dramatic reduction in family and subsistence farming, and subsequent urbanization brought on by an unprecedented migration to cities in the late 20th century, has changed all this. Today, over ½ the world's population lives in cities, compared with only 13% a century ago.[3] This has changed our relationship to food as dramatically as it has changed the landscape. Most people no longer grow or raise their own food and are forced instead to buy it from a market that is mediated by a single form of currency — national money. So when food prices go up, people go hungry because they no longer have the ability to stock their own larder.

In the US through the 1800s, over 80% of people lived on a farm. The farm may have been enough to feed their own family, or might have been large enough so that there were products to trade, but farm life was the country's core economic activity. Subsistence agriculture is fairly simple — people grow food based on the amount of land, labor, animals and seeds they have. The harvest reflects the inputs, with the vagaries of weather and pests added in to complicate things. When the food is harvested, the amount available to consume is somewhat dependent on the processing and storage capacity available. The health and welfare of the people who consume the food will also partly determine the inputs the following year. As shown in Figure 1, the whole process can be described as a simple positive feedback system.

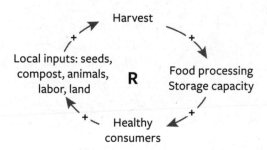

FIGURE 12.1. A Subsistence Agriculture Feedback System

There are problems when subsistence agriculture is the dominant form of agriculture. Food can spoil, and so finding ways to insure that the harvest can be preserved is an important strategy. Land is hard to obtain (unless you inherit it), and so good land is in high demand.

In the modern world we are no longer at the mercy of plague and famine, but we are at the mercy of the market. In the 1970s, inflation of the US dollar led to rising food prices, which led to a political crisis for the Nixon administration. Nixon responded by imposing wage and price controls in August 1971 at the same time he decoupled the dollar from the gold standard, which was designed to help check the inevitable rise in prices that resulted from the lower dollar value on the international market. He imposed price controls again in 1973, but they failed dramatically. Farmers drowned their chickens rather than selling them at the prevailing low prices.

But Nixon took further steps, appointing Earl Butz (who had until then been on boards of several agribusiness firms) as Secretary of Agriculture. Nixon told Butz to do everything in his power to increase food production, and Butz did. He dismantled the New Deal policies that were designed to protect farmers and consumers by regulating both price and the overuse of land—measures aimed at preventing another dust bowl. He provided generous new subsidies for large agribusiness concerns, whereas before this, the legacy of Franklin Delano Roosevelt protected small farmers from the consolidating force of corporate farms.

In addition to the subsidies provided by government for agribusiness, the large corporate farms found other allies in their expansive drive—the bankers themselves. Seeing it as a way to finally loosen the shackles of a system that limited the banks to specific states, big banks like Citicorp moved in to provide financing for the agribusiness firms. By 1985, the financial links between the big banks and corporate farms led to a landmark court case where interstate banking was declared constitutional by the US Supreme Court, overturning the limits which had been effectively imposed by Roosevelt-era restrictions. In his opinion on the case, Chief Justice Rehnquist specifically cited the fact that Citicorp was providing financing on a national scale. "Citicorp offers financial services to consumers and businesses nationally through its bank and nonbank subsidiaries."[4]

The Hidden Cost of Cheap Food

In the 1980s, a combination of the overproduction and lower prices brought on by these new policies and a spike in interest rates hit farmers like a one-two punch, and thousands of small farms went out of business. "Throughout the Grain Belt, abandoned farmhouses were burned to the ground, cleared, and incorporated into ever larger corn and soy fields."[5] Mass agricultural production by larger and larger corporations became the rule, rather than the exception, and the few remaining small farms had a hard time competing. Many of these farms were in areas where large-scale agriculture was almost impossible—rough terrain and poor soils in the Northeast meant that small farms either stayed small or sold out to subdivision developers.

Even in the Northeast, the federal government encouraged the consolidation and loss of family farms by instituting the dairy herd buy-out program in 1985. The Northeast farmers fought back and got the US Congress to pass the Northeast Dairy Compact, which imposed a surcharge on milk coming into the region, paying farmers in New England a new subsidy that helped keep them in business despite the competition from large farms out west. This program was eventually challenged by Canada, who threatened to challenge the Compact at the World Trade Organization. The Compact no longer exists.

Today, the cheap food policies of the last 40 years have created a globally integrated food system that routinely uses ten calories of fossil fuel to bring one calorie of food to supermarket shelves. By contrast, as recently as 1940, for every calorie of fossil fuel used in the US, 2.3 calories of food were produced. The unchecked overproduction of the agribusiness firms has led commodity prices on a race to the bottom worldwide, forcing 200 million of the world's 400 million farmers to live below the poverty line.

The subsidies driving the agribusiness expansion represent one of the largest corporate welfare programs in the world. In the years 2003, 2004 and 2005, subsidies for corn producers in the US were over $20.5 billion, fully 26% of their market revenue.[6] In the 2008 Farm Bill, corn, soy, wheat, rice and cotton were slated to receive $7.5 billion. Three cotton farms in California were promised the equivalent of the entire US budget for organic food research and extension. Five corn farmers in the Midwest were allocated the equivalent of the entire US budget for farmers' markets.[7]

Cheap commodities are routinely dumped on foreign countries in the name of international assistance, which is how the overproduction in the US affects poverty elsewhere. The US provides 60% of international food aid, spending billions of dollars on it every year. To a casual observer, this might seem generous and charitable, but a closer examination shows the self-serving nature of the aid. Virtually all of the money spent is used to purchase surplus commodities from US agribusiness firms. Rather than supporting the production of food in countries where food has become scarce, it undermines local production because farmers can't compete with food that is free. In contrast, Canada implemented a policy whereby at least 50% of its food aid would be used to purchase locally produced food because of their recognition that this is a more effective form of assistance.

> A September 2005 report, The Development Effectiveness of Food Aid, produced by the Paris-based Organization for Economic Cooperation and Development concluded that foreign assistance shipped in the form of food often arrives late, disrupts local markets, and costs up to 50% more to deliver than cash. Edward Clay, author of the report and a fellow at the Overseas Development Institute, points out that U.S. food aid being shipped to famine-struck Niger will likely coincide with a bumper harvest in the region, thereby competing directly with area farmers.[8]

This same phenomenon occurs within the United States as well. In the name of inexpensive school lunches, the Department of Agriculture ships commodities to schools around the country. In New Jersey alone, this program provides 30 million pounds of food, valued at nearly $20 million, to 700 participating school districts, adult daycare centers, summer food programs, camps and charitable institutions.[9] While this helps schools afford to serve free and reduced lunches to low-income students, it serves as an additional subsidy for unsustainable agricultural practices and makes it difficult for schools to cooperate with local farmers.

The glut of low quality calories has produced another unanticipated result for people across the United States — an obesity epidemic that brings with it an unprecedented burden of health problems. Adult onset, or type 2 diabetes, is now being found in children and adolescents, a problem which the US Centers for Disease Control has characterized as "sizable and growing," saying that "approval of oral hypoglycemic agents (to lower blood sugar) is urgently required for children and adolescents."[10] This recommendation appears to ignore the obvious link between diet and health — seeing the problem as something requiring more drugs rather than sweeping nutritional changes.

The global food industry provides clear examples of the problems that arise from the vortex of centralization and sole emphasis on efficiency. Where once food was a shared community resource, then a shared family resource, now it is primarily a commodity sold in markets which are systematically distorted by national subsidies and monopoly pricing. Food has traveled the distance from being produced in a primarily cooperative system to one that is competitive at the extreme and in which the largest and strongest actors eliminate their smaller and weaker opponents. The corner store is all but gone in most places, replaced by a corporate store that looks the same as the one 500 miles away.

Despite the overwhelming crush of big food, many people are trying to turn the tide. The *localvore* (after herbivore or omnivore) movement, which champions locally grown food as the main dietary staple, has taken on national significance in the US. In Europe, the Slow Food Movement, first championed by an Italian farmer named Carlo Petrini, has become popular. Slow Food found a financial champion in Woody Tasch, the Chairman of the Investors Circle, who has written a book about slow money, in which he acknowledges the role that finance plays in the food system, but stops short of looking at the structure of money itself.[11]

As we have seen, the nature of money, and particularly bank-debt money, played an important role in the consolidation of the modern food industry in the 1980s. It linked the shared interests of the banks and those of agribusiness, allowing their growth at the expense of the family farm, which faced the dual challenge of the bank's high interest rates and the undercutting of market prices by big agribusiness farms. Indebtedness and high interest rates were the direct cause of thousands of farms with traditional family ownership being lost during that same period. Not coincidentally, this was also the period in which the savings and loan crisis drove many local banks out of business, allowing the large interstate banks to consolidate their control of banking nationwide. The resulting control of land, food and money has given large corporations an inordinate amount of power and systematically robbed local communities of their ability to create their own food.

Although this discussion has touched on one aspect of the global food industry — food production on farms — it is only a part of the power puzzle. When you consider the comprehensive reach of vertically integrated food processing and distribution, the full impact of food consolidation overwhelms the imagination. The costs of this consolidation — to our health, our wealth and our future — have been incremental and largely hidden from public view. We are like the proverbial frog in the pot — the heat was turned up slowly over time so that we didn't notice the change. The brittleness of this hyper-efficient food system will become obvious with the first onslaughts of climate change. Then we may be fully cooked, like the processed food that lines the shelves of the supermarket and constitutes so much of our modern diet.

The Expanding Role of Debt

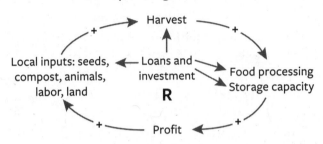

FIGURE 12.2 Debt's Place in Advanced Agriculture

As agriculture evolved over millennia, its variables — the inputs, the harvest, the processing and storage capacity — were subject to "improvements." People looked for ways to grow more food, harvest more, transport it further and make it last longer. On the small scale of subsistence agriculture, investing in improvements is fairly simple. Advanced agriculture, however, requires a sophisticated monetary system to fund its expansion of machinery and investment in technology.

Farmers borrowed money to buy machines to increase the planting and speed up the harvest. Companies developed products to control pests, to fertilize soil, to process and store food — to do all the hard work of farming. Agricultural production increased...and kept increasing. Food in some regions exceeded the demand for food, and prices fell. Falling prices meant that farmers had two choices — to reduce costs and/or to expand production — in order to stay profitable. So they bought larger machines, larger storage and processing capacities, resulting in even more production and lower prices. A major study done by the Sustainability Institute in 2003 characterized this trend in agricultural commodities as a "race to the bottom," documented by rising production and falling prices in every commodities market worldwide.[12]

In most production processes, falling prices and increased production force producers out of the market. Yet with improved transportation and standardization, the surpluses in one region could be exported to another region. Governments intervened in food pricing and production — curtailing production of some products, controlling prices, limiting entry into the food business, buying surplus, shipping food outside the country, subsidizing farm expansion, creating new markets for all the food being produced. All these "improvements" have created a colossal new system in which the Sustainability Institute identified three outcomes as "traps:" resource depletion, environmental pollution and community decline. Abundant food leaves most farmers impoverished, soils and water supplies are being depleted at alarming rates and the environmental impacts are too numerous to list here — one significant statistic is that, in the US, food production accounts for up to 40% of our carbon emissions.[13]

The role that money plays is pivotal. As mentioned earlier, it was no coincidence that banks and agriculture expanded dramatically during the 1970s in the United States. As Nixon changed the food production system, the banking system was modified to accommodate the enormous agribusiness firms that emerged from the consolidation. All of the investment in debt-based money drove agriculture out of a system that was largely dependent on local production capacity into a system that was truly global in scope and impact.

Food Currencies

Food-based currencies are obviously not new. We have already described dynastic Egypt's sophisticated Egyptian food currency earlier in this chapter. Similarly, at the beginning of the 17th century, Japan did a thorough inventory of all the rice it produced and measured it in *koku*, one koku being equal to the amount needed to feed one person for one year (which turns out to be approximately five bushels, or 48 gallons of rice). From this inventory, they determined that the country's wealth was equivalent to 28,000,000 kokus. Large landowners in Japan issued notes for the rice and maintained storehouses so that the note bearers could redeem the rice at harvest time. They soon discovered that all the rice wasn't being redeemed. Just as was the case with goldsmiths inventing the fractional reserve system, the landowners also started issuing notes above the amount of rice they actually had, causing inflation in the currency. By 1760, abuse of rice currency was widespread and the government banned the practice of issuing excess notes.[14]

Right around this same time, in 1739, the colony of South Carolina made it possible to pay taxes in rice. In 1740, they collected 1.2 million pounds of rice. People who were owed money by the colony were given *rice orders*, which were redeemable at a rate of 30 shillings per 100 pounds of rice. The rice orders circulated as a form of currency — people used the slips of paper for other purchases outside of the South Carolina government.[15]

Today, the idea of food as currency has been resurrected by the residents of the small, northern California town of Willits. Mendo Credits are backed by food — a stash of rice and beans in a local warehouse is the bank, for example. Mendo Credits can be purchased at several participating businesses, and the notes circulate just like national money in the local stores. Fully backed by commodity food, this is money you can eat. While Mendo Credits are not a true complementary currency, insofar as people use money to buy them in the first place, they do offer an alternative store of value for money that in turn supports the food system.[16]

Systemic Interventions

Food currencies can play an important role in reversing the effects of the global commodities market by providing local farmers with a source of income that is not reliant on the debt and investment cycle which has driven the global food industry to the brink of economic and ecological collapse. A local food currency can mobilize people and resources without using money and start to rebuild a system that relies more on local capacity and less on global supply chains.

To accomplish this goal, a complete circuit needs to be constructed, so that local food workers, farmers, grocers, restaurants and the processing, distribution and storage companies circulate the food currency among themselves as partial payment for the food they grow and use. The structure of the currency could be something like the Mendo Credits mentioned earlier, where food in storage serves as the store of value and the coupons circulate with the knowledge that they can always be redeemed for food. Or, a food currency could take on more of the characteristics of a commercial barter system, where businesses involved in food and related industries have a system of credits and debits among themselves that would be independent of national money — similar to the WIR system in Germany.

In either model, the addition of local food currency could mobilize local resources and build real wealth in the local food sector. Food workers would have additional income to supplement their wages. Farmers would have additional income to supplement the money they get for their crops. Perhaps most importantly, local grocers, processors and restaurants would be able to pay comparable prices in dollars for local produce to offset the competition of the cheap imported food from the global commodity system, paying the difference in a local currency.

The two systems would be complementary, insofar as they would exist together and work to maximize the income and wealth of the people in the food sector. By addressing one of the critical economic traps of the commodity food system, resources could also be more available to address resource depletion and environmental pollution. Most of the depletion and pollution can be addressed with more labor, and so the availability of a local currency to mobilize more of the labor pool to, for example, construct wetlands to manage agricultural runoff, to plant trees in areas which have been harvested, to compost food waste to rebuild depleted soils — none of the solutions to these problems needs to be capital intensive.

In every area of the world, there are people who need work. In every agricultural operation, there is endless work that needs to be done. The main cause of unemployment in the face of critical work tasks is a shortage of money to pay the workers. The shortage of money, as we have said before, is a function of the structure of the monetary system we have constructed, not an inherent lack of human ingenuity or motivation.

In this system, the national debt-based money plays its role, and the local currency supplements it and mobilizes more local workers to help offset the need for temporary immigrant labor on farms. A balance can be found between the two systems that benefits the agricultural producers, the communities that rely on their productivity and the environment we all rely on to continue to provide us with the food and water we need to survive.

Farm Stand: Vermont's Food Currency

The Central Vermont Food Systems Council was established by the City of Montpelier in 2008 to develop a plan for increased local food production and food security. The Council recruited representatives

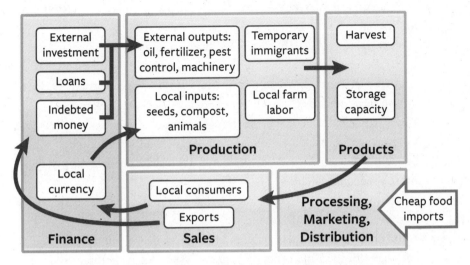

FIGURE 12.3. A Complementary Food Currency System

from all the different parts of the food system to form committees and research the needs and goals of each sector. Committees were formed on food production, food infrastructure (processing, storage and distribution), food policy, food justice, food education, consumers and households, and Gwendolyn chaired a food currency committee to explore what possibilities there might be for a local currency to help achieve the goals of the Council.

For any system, it takes time to discern how a currency might work to connect underutilized resources with unmet needs, and so the Food Currency committee didn't really get moving until late in 2009. The December meeting that year featured a presentation on a new statewide initiative to understand how to strengthen the food system's role in the economy, and at this meeting some of the local farms described how they currently had extra food storage capacity that was going unused. The light bulb went on, and the ideas for a local food currency started to gel. If there was underutilized food storage capacity in the region and if food storage in general was something we wanted to foster to develop better local food security, then this might provide the basis for a currency. Willits, California has shown that people were willing to invest in food storage as a backing for a local currency — Mendo Credits are based in food. If a similar system were used in Vermont, this might provide a local currency to circulate locally, but also could help build additional food storage capacity.

Several people who had attended the Food Systems Council meeting kept talking about the possibilities afterward. Another recurring theme that emerged was the need farmers have to understand their markets and to have dedicated customers in advance of their season every year. One farmer on the committee thought it would be a good idea to get people together to figure out how to organize a buying co-op, so that consumer demand could be aggregated for local farmers, giving them a more predictable market.

The two needs — food storage and aggregated consumer demand — gave rise to the idea of an online Farm Stand, a website where farmers could post products they have available, consumers could post the needs they have for food and other products and services that support the food economy could also participate, all facilitated by a local currency.

Local farmers are more open to using an alternative currency system as long as they are still able to have part of the costs paid in dollars. The Farm Stand website offers three alternatives for payment: dollars, food storage units and food credits. The food storage units are purchased with dollars, but then they can continue to circulate as currency — the buyers of the units know that their currency is ultimately backed by food that is in storage locally. The food credits are not purchased with dollars or backed by food storage — they are more of a pure complementary currency that is backed by the goods and services available in the system.

Farmers can post items for sale for dollars, or for a mix of dollars and the two types of food currency. Consumers can ask for different products and offer to pay dollars or a mix of currencies. One of the important features of the system is that people can offer farm labor for a mix of currencies. This helps farmers lower their real costs, which in turn can make it easier for them to accept the different forms of food currency for their products.[17]

Food is such a basic human need that it is imperative that we find ways to support the people who grow it so that they are not living below the poverty level. A food currency is not the whole answer to this question, but it's a start. Farming practices that are more decentralized, that use lower levels of non-renewable resources, that protect the resource base on which they depend need to be rewarded, and the destructive practices in place now need to end. One of the ways to intervene in this system is to change the way the rewards and penalties work. Changing the market — the mediator of rewards and penalties — needs to be done in both bank-debt money and complementary currencies.

PART III

MAKING
IT HAPPEN

CHAPTER 13

Intentional Cities

Ultimately, human intentionality
is the most powerful evolutionary force
on this planet.

Georgе B. Leonard

Cities can take a leadership role in creating wealth, but they need to find new ways to mobilize their residents around a common agenda. All of the currency strategies we have discussed so far require someone's vision, a plan, and specific strategic actions that bring them to fruition. The different solutions that have been proposed in the previous chapters will all be highly empowered and effective if a city decides to create an explicit shared vision: what we call an *intentional city*. Cities often undertake public planning projects that offer the opportunity to create these aspects of collective action, but most city plans have remained in the domain of experts, rather than engaging residents and other stakeholders. This chapter and the next tell the tales of four cities which took the initiative to create a long-term vision, to identify how needs are met in their community, and to articulate a sustainable strategy for the future. All of the cities described included complementary currency interventions in their plans.

Mobilizing Collective Action

What we are calling collective action — one aspect of which is political will — is based ultimately in what we hold dear, the things and values we care about as a people. If we value freedom, the legal and economic systems we create allow for it. If we value justice, there is a reliable rule of law, corrections for inequities, and fair, reciprocal checks and balances for the government. Values themselves contain a goal, or a vision, of an end result.

The challenge for society has always been to find enough common ground among competing values to exercise the political will needed to create systems and institutions that reflect and sustain the underlying ideals of the culture. A corollary challenge has been to hold true to our deepest values even when convenience, greed, fear, hardship and power threaten to derail the original intent of particular initiatives. This is the power of vision; communities need to come together to craft one that is compelling enough to have staying power, with strong shared values, so that it overcomes the usual bumps in the road.

In fact, businesses have long recognized the importance of creating and following a vision. There are thousands of high-level executive seminars on the topic, and the more successful enterprises are continuously refining and testing their actions against their vision. Since the vision approach to business came into fashion back in the 1980s, research has demonstrated that those companies who have managed their business around a vision are more successful than their competitors.

One example is Whole Foods Market, which is committed to a vision that goes beyond being just a grocery store. "They actually want to change a part of the world in which they operate. Even though they don't obsess over the bottom line, their earnings growth rate is triple that of the industry in which they operate. And their stock price over the past two years has more than doubled."[1]

Choice of the Methodology

A number of different ways are available to tackle the complexity of sustainability planning. Let us only briefly mention here well-known ones, such as the Natural Step, the Agenda 21, the Local Environmental Action Program (LEAP) and the World Health Organization's Healthy Cities program. The Natural Step was developed by Karl-Henrik

Robert, a physician in Sweden who was alarmed at the increasing rates of cancer in the country and worked backward to determine what the root causes were. He posed four system conditions that need to be met for a sustainable world, and offered a methodology for cities and companies to achieve these system conditions.

Local Agenda 21 was the local government response to the Earth Summit in Rio, which culminated in Agenda 21, a program for the planet to achieve environmental sustainability and community development. While its scope was originally broader than the environmental agenda, as it has been implemented over the past 20 years, the programs that have tended to be implemented as Local Agenda 21 in cities are local recycling campaigns and other environmental projects. Local Agenda 21 offers few tools for systematically considering the economy, the governance systems or the social development of a community.

LEAP uses a comparative risk assessment methodology to determine the impacts of different environmental threats, and then offers a program for addressing the problems. Healthy Cities encourages cities to study the health conditions of their populations as a way of making plans for environmental protection and social and human development.

Each of these programs have their specific strengths and advantages, but you will have noticed that they have in common the tendency to focus on only some of the dimensions involved in sustainable community development.

The approach described in *Creating Wealth* is original in that it attempts to be more comprehensive, to approach a long-term vision and integrated plan that deals with all dimensions needed to create an intentional city. While this may appear overly ambitious, some cities have managed to achieve this aim. Each of the four cities described here realized that they needed to take an integrated approach to planning rather than continuing to look for solutions to isolated problems.

The cities had leaders who appreciated the insights that system dynamics and the Earth Charter could offer city planning, and were inspired to take the approach Gwendolyn advocated in her previous book *The Key to Sustainable Cities*.[2] The four cities are very different, ranging from a very small state capital of 8,000 people to a small, impoverished city on the Hudson River, a regional center of commerce and one of the wealthiest cities in North America with over 1,000,000 people.

Visionary Cities—
Creating Excitement and Momentum

Unlike businesses, where the vision is often introduced by high-level management, the most effective city visioning processes engage a broad cross section of city residents, businesses, educational institutions and other stakeholders in an extended planning process that defines a vision and also includes specific actions that need to be taken to make the vision a reality. The four cities we use as examples have engaged in a vision process with a strong emphasis on long-term sustainability. They have asked their residents to imagine their city 30-100 years in the future. After this, they set intermediate goals and objectives, designed strategies to meet the goals and established ways to measure and report on progress toward the vision over time.

In a business, customers, clients, market and product lines limit the range of possibilities for a shared vision. In cities, where all dimensions of human life are expressed, there are a number of challenges when it comes to creating anything that could be called a "shared vision." One of the important questions to ask is *whose* vision is it? A statement that is issued unilaterally by people in power is not likely to capture the values of the whole community, and even less mobilize them to take the necessary initiatives to achieve it.

If the goal is to create a vision statement that does reflect the values of the whole community, how do you get the whole community involved? Most city leaders hold traditional public hearings on policy initiatives, to try to encourage public input. They draft the policy proposal, and they ask the public to comment on it before it becomes official. They complain of community apathy when only a small group of people show up for a hearing, typically at City Hall. Cities that have done a good job of community engagement have learned to attract more people to their policy discussions by structuring the possibilities for public input as the kind of activities that people normally like to attend, like sporting events, celebrations and cultural events. If you make the policy process fun instead of being wonkish and boring, you are more likely to have more people participate.

So in Calgary, the public outreach staff for the imagineCALGARY process showed up at a visit by the Queen—a crowd of 10,000—and handed out brightly colored surveys for people to complete. In Newburgh, the city named their long-term planning process "Plan-It Newburgh" and printed t-shirts and buttons for people who attended a festive kick-off event scheduled at the same time as the regular Arts Celebration on the first Saturday in September. In Burlington, balloons with "I'm part of the Legacy" were made for the kickoff ceremony, held on Church Street, a busy pedestrian mall in the heart of the downtown on a busy Saturday in September.

These cities sent a message to the public that city planning is fun and interesting, and in all cases, people responded by getting involved, either by simply filling out the visioning surveys or by joining stake-holder groups. Some took their interests a step further and stepped up to serve on the City Council or Planning Commissions.

A second challenge for cities trying to develop a shared vision for the future is the subject matter of the vision statement. Vague generalities about being a livable city aren't enough to carry more difficult policy agendas forward when priorities are set and trade-offs need to be made. An overarching view is important, but the vision needs to be detailed enough so that direction is clear. For this reason, the cities described in these chapters have used long-term sustainability as a methodology, a system that involves looking closely at the question of how human needs are met today without denying future generations the ability to meet their needs. The needs themselves can frame the vision and the goals, as assets are inventoried, systemic patterns uncovered and leverage points to change problematic behavior of meta-systems identified for strategic intervention. The balance of this chapter describes four case studies, different in their scale and means available, different also in terms of objectives pursued.

The Legacy Project: Burlington, Vermont

In 1998, Peter Clavelle, then mayor of Burlington, decided that it was time for the city to come together around a shared vision. The city was already a leader in a number of different areas — the arts, education, poverty alleviation, housing urban revitalization and energy efficiency — and could count on different groups who knew a lot about different aspects of urban sustainability. What the city lacked was a shared understanding of how all the parts fit together. Conflicts around a large affordable housing development planned for an open field, a planned expansion of a food co-op as the anchor grocery store in the downtown were skirmishes among different groups that illustrated a lack of understanding about all the various aspects of creating a sustainable future.

The city partnered with the Institute for Sustainable Communities and obtained funding from the US Environmental Protection Agency and private foundations to create a long-term sustainability plan for the city. Mayor Clavelle called it the Legacy Project, framing the process around what kind of city current residents would leave for their grandchildren. He defined his vision of an integrated plan as the Four Es of sustainability — Education, Equity, Economics and Environment.

To create a community-wide vision, the mayor convened a group of stakeholders that ranged from executives of the local banks, presidents of the University of Vermont and Champlain College (both located in the city), the CEO of the hospital, advocacy groups like the Peace and Justice Center and the Food Bank, local developers and ordinary citizens. The stakeholders agreed to meet on a monthly basis to discuss the planning initiative and make decisions about its overall direction.

The funding allowed the city and the Institute to hire several staff for the project, including two Americorps volunteers who would organize a lot of the public outreach activities; one staff person who worked for the City of Burlington; and another staff person — Gwendolyn — who worked for the Institute for Sustainable Communities at the time. Creating a vision was a goal, but an even more important goal was for the staff and stakeholders to draft an action plan that would help the city achieve the vision. In addition, the Institute for Sustainable Communities would compile a directory of best practices in use in Burlington, so other cities could learn from their example.

The project was scheduled to last 18 months — at the end a citywide vote was planned on any elements of the plan that required voter ratification. In addition, a large gathering was held — modeled after traditional New England Town Meetings — to get people in the community to help set the priorities for the action plan. In addition to the monthly stakeholder meetings, the Americorps volunteers participated in every public event they could fit on their calendars. They tabled at festivals, marched in parades, visited schools, organizations and anywhere people gathered to ask four simple questions:

1. What do you value about Burlington that you want to pass on to future generations?
2. What do you want to change?
3. What ideas do you have for the city's future?
4. How can you help make the city a better place?

The answers to the questions were compiled, and the vision statement for the city was written from the results of the survey and a series of neighborhood meetings, focus groups and other public events that were held as part of the engagement process.

The Legacy Vision

Five major themes emerged in the common vision that Burlington residents hold for the future of the city. These are:

+ Maintaining Burlington as a regional population, government, cultural and economic center with livable-wage jobs, full employment, social supports and housing that matches job growth and family incomes
+ Improving quality of life in neighborhoods
+ Increasing participation in community decision making
+ Providing youth with high-quality education and social supports, and lifelong learning opportunities for all
+ Preserving environmental health

In addition, the staff worked with four stakeholder committees to put together an action plan with goals, strategies and indicators that would be measured and reported by the University of Vermont, and an implementation plan to be monitored by the stakeholders with annual meetings into the future.

Committees and City Systems

Four committees were based on a modified version of the Four E approach to sustainability: Environment, Economy, Education, and Equity. As the feedback had come in from the surveys, it became obvious that the Four Es originally proposed were not enough to capture all the dimensions of community life that people valued. At first, the staff tried to add Es for things like Entertainment (the arts were a critical part of the community not expressed in the original formula), Eternity (people's spiritual life was also important to them) and Etcetera (for all those things that didn't lend themselves to an easy E).

From the chaos, an interesting order emerged that included and expanded on a basic truth the Es touched on — the key systems at work in every community. Education was an important part of the systems that provide social and human development. In addition to education, we have needs in this area that other activities have traditionally satisfied. Our need for aesthetic enjoyment and self-expression gives rise to the artistic and cultural life in any community. Our need for a sense of meaning, purpose and connectedness expresses itself in our wisdom traditions and spiritual practices. Our need for recreation, for safety, for caring relationships — all of these needs are met through the community's social and human development systems.

Equity is also an important need — for fairness, for justice. Our need for equity — for a level of self-determination, for systems that help us manage conflict — gives rise to the governance systems we have developed over time — the ways in which we use power. Power is another important systemic flow in communities. Understanding how to meet people's needs for empowerment in sustainable ways is a critical question for community leaders. Too often, the limited power that leadership brings makes people in positions of leadership blind to the need to share it widely, to cultivate leadership in neighborhoods, in civic organizations, in the faith community, so that the city itself is stronger and more resilient to the changes that the 21st Century brings.

So the four committees of the Legacy Project produced a plan for the Economy, Neighborhoods, Governance, Youth and Life Skills and the Natural Environment. Each section of the plan contained specific goals, a short list of priority actions, indicators that would be measured over time to track progress toward the goals and examples of some of the initiatives that have already been taken in the area. The final section of the plan outlined specific roles and responsibilities of the entire community, with stakeholders taking on particular elements of the plan as their institutional mission. The mayor was clear from the start that the city itself would not be the sole entity responsible for the plan's implementation. That was a big reason for convening a large stakeholder process to begin with — the mayor truly wanted the Legacy Plan to be a plan for the whole community, not just city government.

The Action Taken

Like any plan, some of the actions identified moved along faster than others. Some are more controversial, even with a broad based public planning process, and can get snarled in politics or funding issues. Several elements of the Legacy Plan were implemented in the first couple of years following its adoption by City Council, some failed to get off the ground and others are still in limbo. Still others took on a life of their own and have had success that goes far beyond what the stakeholders imagined when they drafted the plan.

Coming out of the gate, there were controversial elements of the plan. An issue that got a lot of ink for the first year after the plan was completed was the plan's orientation toward urban growth. The mayor and several stakeholders saw the sprawling growth patterns in Chittenden County and recognized that one way to change the pattern of the last 20 years was to take a more proactive orientation toward growth within the city limits. One of the first goals in the plan reflected this as a major theme inherent in creating a vibrant urban center, saying:

> In 2030, Burlington has absorbed the greater portion of the region's population growth, expanding to as much as 65,000. The city is the center of culture, commerce, education, health care, and government. Housing and job growth have kept pace with the population.[3]

Given that in 1999 when the plan was written, the population in Burlington was approximately 35,000, this was an audacious goal which would almost double the population. Also, unlike virtually every other goal in the plan, it did not come from the input received during the outreach process, but rather from the mayor. More could have been done during the public input process to have a discussion about growth; this might have reduced the challenges to the legitimacy of the goal that immediately surfaced and unfortunately became identified with the plan as it moved forward.

Two of the priority actions under the Governance goal could have been controversial, but didn't run into any real opposition as the mayor moved them forward. Since these actions involved changing the city's charter — the document that forms the constitution for the city — there were several legal protocols to follow, which also could have provided opponents with a place to stop them. Two of these were:

Increase diversity — including youths and minorities — on decision-making boards of all types and provide a regular "report card" on progress.

Reorganize city government to make it more responsive and accountable to the voters, with the mayor overseeing city departments while balancing strong input from commissioners and other committed citizen volunteers. Implement more effective and centralized management.[4]

The City Charter was changed and was approved by the Vermont State Legislature in 2001. The charter changes included adding youth representatives to city boards and commissions, such as the Planning Commission, City Council and Conservation Commission. It also included a provision that gave the mayor hiring and firing power over department heads. Prior to the charter change, individual commissions — the highway commission, the police commission — hired and fired department heads. This meant that the mayor did not have an important tool at his disposal to make the departments accountable to the citizens; he had been a lightening rod for complaints, but did not have the ultimate authority needed to solve problems. As a chief elected official, he was also accountable to the voters, whereas the appointed heads of the commissions were not.

Legacy Projects

In addition to the structural changes made to city government as a result of the Legacy Project, several projects have been undertaken since then to meet the goals. Each year, the stakeholders get together for a review of the progress toward the goals and to play a role in establishing projects that can be done in the current year. The projects to date include:

The Burlington Food Council

The Burlington Food Council (BFC) is an open community group exploring ways to ensure that Burlington creates and nurtures a healthy, equitable and sustainable food system for all members of the community. To accomplish this mission the Burlington Food Council provides networking, partnership building and educational opportunities around food issues and provides strategic recommendations for decision makers. The BFC also works to serve as a model and source of innovation for the many groups involved in creating and nurturing a healthy, sustainable and equitable food system for the City of Burlington.

One of the main projects of the BFC is the Burlington School Food Project (BSFP), a citywide collaborative formed to address the integration of local foods into school meals and food insecurity among school aged children in Burlington, Vermont. Partners in the BSFP include Shelburne Farms, VT FEED, NOFA VT, the Intervale Center, the Burlington School District Food Service, City Market/Onion River Co-op and Healthy City Youth Farm.[5]

The Food Council and the School Food Project worked closely with local schools to give the school meal programs access to locally grown organic food. This was more difficult than first imagined, partly because the food services in the schools did not have the staff or the time for the food preparation involved. Most school lunches come as prepared foods, not foods that need peeling, chopping and cooking. The students and parents helped design a system for food preparation, and the students helped the food service by designing recipes that would use the produce from local farms, to make the integration of the new food as easy and cost-effective as possible.

No Idling Campaign

Legacy launched its No Idling Campaign in April 2007 with public outreach, education and policy advocacy efforts to reduce unnecessary vehicle idling as a way to improve air quality and overall quality of life for everyone who lives, works and plays in Burlington.[6] The campaign worked with the city to enforce a city policy already on the books about city vehicles idling, and proposed an idling ordinance for the city to adopt. In March of 2008, the City Council passed a resolution directing the Public Works Commission to amend their parking ordinances to accommodate the anti-idling requirements.

Energy and Environment Coordinating Committee

The Mayor's Energy and Environmental Coordinating committee (E2C2) was formed in mid-2007 and is composed of citizen representatives, government officials and others concerned with and involved in environmental issues. It is charged with recommending projects, programs and ideas to the City Council that can improve air quality and significantly reduce the City's greenhouse gas emissions, the main culprit responsible for global warming.[7] In May of 2008, the E2C2 presented City Council with several recommendations about making the transportation sector of the city more sustainable over time. These recommendations included:

1. Increase accessibility to transit with 15-minute bus service on major roads into and out of downtown and free bus service within the downtown.
2. Establish a streetcar line from City outskirts to downtown points, possibly originating at Exit 14.
3. Design and build a park and public transit facility at Exit 14 with seamless transit connections to area employment centers, as recommended in the CCMPO Regional Park and Ride Plan (February 2004).
4. Design and build a surface parking lot using the existing Champlain Parkway right-of-way near the I-189/Route 7 intersection. Collaborate with City of South Burlington.
5. Investigate a garbage contracting system by allowing haulers to bid for exclusive service in districts of the City.
6. Investigate increasing the percentage of biodiesel blend in the City's summer fleet from 20% to 80% or higher.
7. Continue to strengthen and advance educational, outreach, incentive and recognition programs that promote walking, biking and car efficiency efforts.[8]

Social Equity Investment Project

The mission of the Social Equity Investment Project (SEIP) is to identify and support leadership in the Burlington community in order to facilitate sustainable and effective social change. SEIP does this through leadership development, social equity focus groups, the development of a coordination and influence network, financial development, and general education and awareness of social equity issues as Burlington moves beyond a crossroads of cultural and social shifting and growth.[9]

The Social Equity Investment Project does a lot through the coordinator working in the community to promote diversity. To do this, she works with a wide variety of community organizations to increase the representation in their leadership groups by people who are not traditionally in leadership positions—people of color, people who are physically challenged and people who have low incomes. Workshops are offered on subjects like "A Solution to Cultural Shifting," and the coordinator supports projects run by Burlington's Center for Community and Neighborhoods such as the Inclusive Community Initiative and the We All Belong Initiative.

A 2007–2008 report listed the following actions as the recommended next steps for the program:

1. Develop, extend and connect local community development capacity to ensure all the people have an opportunity to give voice to the future of their communities
2. Support increased capacity building efforts to improve the participation of marginalized groups in policy design
3. Support increased capacity building efforts to improve data collection, monitoring and evaluation of local, state and federal programs
4. Support increased capacity building to find, lift up and bring to scale programs that work
5. Identify and stabilize funding to support community leaders through access to leadership roles and opportunities
6. Local government leadership will contribute resources and participate in planning and action steps which support existing leadership to provide ongoing informed cultural dialogue, consultation and social resources
7. Identify methods to strengthen the city of Burlington collective work to more effectively achieve an equitable sustainable community
8. Maintain discussion and activity which foster awareness of and commitment to providing new emerging leadership the necessary tools to be effective

9. Continue to organize and facilitate discussion/gatherings with ethnic and culturally diverse and existing leadership at local government, business and non-profit sector to allow for greater opportunities to recognize commonality, valuable social connections and welcome strategies for successfully communicating and working with people across lines of different backgrounds

10. Encourage more social insight, short term vision planning and community based discussion from existing leadership within CEDO and local government

11. Establish the City of Burlington as a leader in the recruitment, retention and support for employment of ethnic and culturally diverse in leadership and other positions across all City departments

12. Increase direct participation and representation of ethnic and culturally diverse, and economically oppressed populations on City of Burlington boards and commissions

13. Increase and promote equal access to all City of Burlington services and programs with thoughtful and strategic outreach and educational activities

14. Encourage and support community-based organizing around ethnic and culturally diverse barriers, racism and immigrant issues

15. Visibly, technically and financially support diversity initiatives and curriculum throughout the Burlington School District and other educational outlets in the City of Burlington, including alternative schools, early education programs, and colleges and universities

16. Work with UVM and business community on offering customer service training to retail/restaurant staff to better serve a diverse customer base

17. Work with Stakeholders, local government and existing leadership about sharing power, restructuring racial equity lens "who gets to decide", being a learning community of leadership "not a binding community" and support ethnic and culturally diverse leadership participation in their own decision making.[10]

The Social Equity Investment Project, and all the goals and targets the city set for governance and social well-being, represent a significant contribution by the city to ongoing discussions about sustainability. Burlington was the first city to address issues of equity and justice in a planning project that otherwise would have been seen as having only an environmental and economic focus. Sustainability had traditionally been presented as a three-legged stool, with legs of environment, economy and a broad category of subjects lumped under a "social" heading. With the emphasis on equity and governance issues, Burlington added a fourth leg to the stool, effectively dividing the broad social category into two — social well-being and governance.

On March 16, 2009 in Washington DC, the City of Burlington was honored with the runner-up 2009 City Cultural Diversity Award by the National Black Caucus of Local Elected Officials and National League of Cities. Burlington was honored for implementing the innovative program, the Social Equity Investment Project, and promoting the necessary cultural diversity leadership in community governance to make the program a success.

Burlington Bread

The local currency that the Burlington community created, called Burlington Bread, was not a direct result of the Legacy Project; it was already in circulation when the Legacy Project began. Modeled after Ithaca Hours, Burlington Bread was a *fiat currency* — a form of currency that is issued in notes and accepted in stores and service businesses around the city.

The currency was reinvigorated in the years immediately following the conclusion of the Legacy Project, when Gwendolyn organized an international conference on Sustainable Communities in Burlington in 2004. A new note design was created, and student interns at the Gund Institute for Ecological Economics, founded by Robert Costanza, fanned out across the city to encourage new businesses to accept it. The conference provided a marketing tool for the currency — participants in the conference were provided with Burlington Bread as part of their conference materials and encouraged to find stores to spend it in while they were in town.

Ultimately, the administrative burden and cost of maintaining a paper currency spelled the demise of Burlington Bread, and it doesn't exist today. It was replaced in Burlington with a Time Bank system that serves the North end of town, a traditionally low-income area, and a new commercial barter system called the Vermont Sustainable

Exchange. Since both of these systems are structured as mutual credit systems, they are easier to manage and have promise for long life.

The Earth Charter

At the same time that Burlington was completing their plan, another global project was underway that had come to the same conclusion about the need to include social justice, equity and democratic practice in any discussion about long-term environmental sustainability: the Earth Charter. Back in 1992, the first global Earth Summit held in Rio de Janeiro, Brazil, was convened, and the hope was that a Charter would be drafted to capture the compelling interest all nations had in protecting the global environment. The Rio Earth Summit marked the first time that world leaders — presidents, premiers, prime ministers, kings, queens, despots, dictators and other heads of nation states — got together with the express purpose of discussing the degradation of the global environment.

During the summit, no consensus about the Charter was reached, and so the summit created a new Commission to study the subject, draft a Charter and report back to the United Nations. The Commission was chaired by Maurice Strong — a former under-secretary general of the UN who had chaired the Earth Summit, Michael Gorbachev, former head of the Soviet Union and Steven Rockefeller, a college professor and philanthropist from the United States. In the first seven years following the summit, an ambitious and massive global dialogue was undertaken, with representative committees in 52 different countries engaging people from all walks of life to ask the fundamental questions about what is required to create a just and sustainable future for the Earth and for future generations.

This effort was completed in 1997, and all the input was sent on to a drafting committee that had been created by the Earth Charter Commission in 1996. Professor Rockefeller was appointed by the Commission to chair the drafting committee, and the committee held meetings with groups of experts, including scientists, international lawyers and religious leaders and then circulated numerous drafts back to all the national committees, focal points and organizations in the countries that had engaged in the dialogue for comment. At the Rio +5 Forum in 1997, a benchmark draft of the Earth Charter was released for circulation and comment. In 2000, the Earth Charter Commission came to consensus on the document in a meeting held at the UNESCO Headquarters in Paris. A formal launch of the Earth Charter was held in the Peace Palace in The Hague.

Cities and Towns Support the Charter

The launch kicked off another large-scale global effort to endorse and adopt the Earth Charter, and one of the first groups of people identified by the Commission as important partners were cities and local governments. The Earth Charter was presented to the ICLEI World Congress in 2000, which is a coalition of local governments all over the world who have been implementing Local Agenda 21, another major agreement that came out of the Earth Summit in Rio. ICLEI endorsed the Earth Charter and made a commitment to use its resources to move the Charter toward adoption at the Summit on Sustainable Development in Johannesburg in 2002.

Gwendolyn attended the ICLEI World Congress in 2000, and was inspired by the connection between what she had seen on the grassroots level in Burlington and on the global level with the Earth Charter — the similarities between the two processes were a clear indication that there was something universal in the aspirations shared by people all over the world that transcended all political, religious, national and cultural boundaries. When she got back to Vermont, she immediately started work to bring the Earth Charter to people and local governments there.

Part of this effort was working in cooperation with some Vermont artists who had been inspired by the Earth Charter to organize a celebration event in 2001. Another part of the work was through a campaign to ask Vermont Town Meetings to demonstrate to the world grassroots support for the Earth Charter by endorsing it at their annual meetings in March of 2002. Vermont Town Meetings are pure democracy in action; in those towns, the citizens themselves voted for the endorsement.

In March of 2002, 23 cities and towns in Vermont voted to endorse the Earth Charter, and Gwendolyn was invited to speak at the World Summit on Sustainable Development in Johannesburg to talk about this campaign. The Local Government Summit that was held as part of the World Summit included a reference to the Earth Charter in their political statement presented to the leaders of the World Summit, and

ICLEI also went on to adopt the Earth Charter as guiding principles at the following World Congress they held in Athens in 2003.

The Town Meeting campaign and the Local Government Summit made it obvious that if local governments supported the Charter, they would need tools to turn their support into concrete action plans. It is one thing to endorse a set of principles; it is another thing altogether to use the principles to shape local government policy and implementation efforts. Working with Steven Rockefeller and the World Resources Institute, this idea about a tool for local governments gave birth to a project called the Earth Charter Community Action Tool (EarthCAT). Steven Rockefeller convened a committee of Earth Charter supporters from all over the world to develop the tool, and over the next two years GCI and WRI formed a partnership to develop both a workbook and a web-based management support system.

A Community Action Tool

EarthCAT combined the principles of the Earth Charter and the insights from the Burlington Legacy project about the importance of using a broad spectrum of human needs and their corresponding city systems as a starting point for long-term sustainability planning. The work in Burlington had explored and articulated the sustainability of five critical systems in cities — social and human development, governance, economics and livelihoods, the built environment and infrastructure and the natural environment. The Earth Charter provides a set of global principles that can form the ethical and sustainable guidelines for all these systems as well as hope that they will to continue to provide for our needs and the needs of all life on Earth into the future.

Cities can easily see the link between the key themes which form the categories of principles of the Earth Charter and their city systems:
+ Respect and care for the community of life
+ Social and economic justice
+ Environmental integrity
+ Democracy, non-violence and peace.

The daily work of cities involves all of these themes, and our municipal systems reflect the way we address all of these issues as a human community. This makes a link between the Earth Charter and city planning conceptually coherent, but the politics were far from easy. Some of the advocates of the Earth Charter in the United States were targeted by the John Birch Society and other right-wing ideologues. The artwork created by the artists celebrating the Earth Charter—a beautiful Ark of Hope—was defaced while it was on exhibit in the Midwest. In Vermont, Gwendolyn received hundreds of letters and messages of hate mail during the campaign she ran to get local towns to endorse the Charter. A slick, magazine-quality piece of John Birch propaganda was distributed that likened the artists and advocates of the Earth Charter to the anti-Christ, and in Vermont the members of the society toured communities to alert them to the "dangers" of the document.

To avoid other city planners and local leaders being targeted in a similar way, the EarthCAT methodology does not make the links to the Earth Charter obvious enough to attract this kind of negative attention. Rather than structuring the planning process principle by principle, the principles are embedded in the methodology itself. References in the margins alert planners to the key links, and the entire approach is designed to emphasize the integration and connection among the actions taken to insure environmental integrity, democratic practice, social and economic justice and the underlying respect and care for the community of life. This whole system approach pioneered an important alternative to the dominant practice of considering each area of work separately, dividing government into silos of expertise that cannot understand other imperatives.

After the preparation of the EarthCAT workbook and management support system, the next step was to make cities and towns aware of the importance of sustainability planning. To this end, Gwendolyn and an organization that she founded in 2001 called Global Community Initiatives organized an international conference called *Sustainable Communities* in July of 2004 in Burlington, Vermont. Over 500 people from 48 different countries attended the conference, where workshops and conference structure mirrored the EarthCAT materials and methodology and included an official launch of the workbook and website as a session at the conference.

Since that time, more than 50 cities, towns, regions and other organizations around the world have used the EarthCAT workbook and website to complete their long-term sustainability plans. In Chapter 14, we describe three cities who used EarthCAT to complete their plans, along with the links between the unmet needs they identified as part of the planning methodology and the possibilities these needs offer for new complementary currencies.

CHAPTER 14

A Tale of Three Cities

*The axis of the earth sticks out visibly
through the centre of each and every town or city.*

OLIVER WENDELL HOLMES, SR.

Among the 50 cities that have already used the EarthCAT approach, the following three were chosen as case studies because they are very different from one another — different in size, different in means, different in the objectives pursued. They are respectively Calgary in Canada; Newburg in New York state and Montpelier, Vermont. A detailed account of these three initiatives is also possible because Gwendolyn worked with each of them to carry out their planning projects. Many of the other cities using EarthCAT do it on their own — the workbook is detailed enough for cities to use without the help of a consultant.

Calgary's 100 Year Plan

In 2004, the Mayor of Calgary, Alberta played a pivotal role in reaching further than was typical of city planning anywhere in the world at the time: he challenged the city to create a 100 year plan. He might have been challenged by a healthy sense of competition with the nearby city of Vancouver, BC, that had just prepared a similar plan, and he certainly saw synchronicity in the fact that Calgary was about to turn 100 years old. Taking a look forward 100 years into the future at the same time the city would be celebrating its centennial had a symmetry that was irresistible.

The initiative was pursued at the outset by the city's environmental department, but was quickly transferred to the planning department as the links between the sustainability orientation of a 100 year plan and the city's other planning responsibilities became clear. As they started to contemplate how to execute such an outlandish program as a 100 year city plan, Calgary's planners looked around for resources that could help. Gwendolyn had spoken earlier that year about the Earth Charter and the Burlington Legacy project at Globe 2004, a large conference held biennially in Vancouver, and the staff of the mayor and the environmental department attended the talk and had bought her book.

Later that year, she was sitting in a parking lot in Burlington, having just left a meeting about the Sustainable Communities conference, when she got a call from Calgary, asking questions about how they might proceed with the planning exercise. The multi-stakeholder approach Burlington had taken was all well and good for a city of 35,000, but could it work for a city of a million people? How would they insure broad representation? How would they reach the different neighborhoods? Gwendolyn spoke of breaking the public outreach part of the project down into manageable parts, and mentioned the EarthCAT workbook as a resource, offering to come to Calgary and train the staff at some point in the future. Over the wavering signal of a patchy cellphone, a partnership was born.

The challenges of an effective public outreach campaign in a city of a million people were not the only issue the planning team in Calgary had to face. It's a lot more complicated to achieve political buy-in and ongoing support in the multi-dimensional city that is home to the Canadian oil industry than it is in a small, politically progressive college town like Burlington. Even the project methodology had to be carefully considered, and the city convened a peer review session to insure that all the different possibilities for how to proceed were effectively integrated into the planning process. Several consultants were invited from all over Canada. Gwendolyn came from the US, and out of all the input, an approach and peer concurrence on the methodology emerged.

The EarthCAT workbook was the primary material to be used in the planning process, but Calgary added some activities and perspectives from other experiences as well—a charrette from the Vancouver project and a few other enhancements. This made the approach uniquely Calgary's, which gave the city a greater sense of ownership of the methodology.

In Calgary, the relationship of principles to planning methodology was clarified in a way that hadn't occurred before. The city considered adopting the Earth Charter, but since there were so many elements of the document that didn't directly apply to cities—it called for a ban on space weapons, for example—they opted for the more city-oriented Melbourne Principles instead.[1] The city saw the principles as guardrails—as the framework within which the planning and action would take place. But more than principles were needed to effectively address all the complex issues cities face. The integration of both a principled approach and the rigorous methodology based in systems dynamics that was offered by EarthCAT gave Calgary a new and relevant way to proceed.

Integration and Whole Systems

A couple of flawed habits of thought have led us to our current unsustainable trajectory. The first is our obsessive prioritization of short-term results over long-term outcomes. While this flaw largely defines the standard operating procedure for corporations, governments are not immune to *short-termism* either (the politician's version of NIMBY is NIMTO—Not In My Term Of Office). The EarthCAT method calls for a long-term time horizon for planning, looking out 30–100 years instead of the usual 3–5 year time frame.

This longer-term approach has two key advantages. First, it asks city leaders to think beyond the life of their current infrastructure, which helps focus the question on more sustainable alternatives. Second, when stakeholders are asked about the kind of world they want for their grandchildren, it doesn't matter if they are Democrats, Republicans, Progressives, Socialists, Communists, Conservatives, Liberals, NDPs or Greens; it turns out that they all want the same thing. They want a healthy environment and good job opportunities. They want their grandchildren to have a voice in their own destiny, to have safe, high quality housing, clean water, friendly neighborhoods and good health. So when you start a planning process with questions about longer-term outcomes instead of the usual short-term problem solving, you tend to start from a place of agreement rather than conflict.

The second flaw traces its origins back to the scientific revolution and the advent of empirical, analytical thinking. The gift of rigorous analysis has led to a *fragmentation of knowledge* that now forms a significant obstacle to a more complete understanding of integrated, complex systems. We have lost the forest for the trees. At the same time our PhDs know more and more about less and less, our government departments have been organized in silos where one team of bureaucrats works directly against the interests of other teams, and there is no one who understands the whole system well enough to help it become more than the sum of its parts. When the parts are working at cross-purposes, the synergy that would otherwise be possible is seriously compromised.

Integration and whole systems understanding are the antidotes to fragmentation, but given the culture of specialization promoted by our educational system and the increasing complexity of the world we inhabit, these are not easy to achieve. It's hard to know enough about the wide variety of issues cities face every day to see the links and tie the strands together so that they support each other. How does wastewater treatment relate to chronic, intergenerational poverty? Do property rights have an impact on biodiversity? Do some strategies we use to solve problems make them worse? Principles alone don't help answer these questions, but learning something about whole system dynamics, complexity and even chaos theory can help.

The EarthCAT workbook walks city leaders through a process of considering all the issues they face as part of a larger system. Some rudimentary exercises and tools help them make the connections, although it is difficult to teach a short course in systems dynamics in a workbook format — it really requires more intensive, hands-on training. Calgary had allocated $2.5 million to the planning process, and so Gwendolyn provided the imagineCALGARY planning staff a set of training sessions on city system dynamics and technical assistance in applying the insights from system dynamics to the issues in Calgary.

Roundtables, Stakeholders and Working Groups

In a city of a million people, the organization of the planning project was in itself a complex system. There were a wide variety of constituencies to involve, all with their own agendas and degrees of influence on the outcome. As a starting point, the mayor convened a group of people who would serve as his advisory team — the Mayor's Panel on Long-Term Sustainability. The panel members advised the mayor on stakeholder selection, the measures of success and the contributions of their own organizations to the project. The panel also provided feedback on the question on how imagineCALGARY would be sustained after the planning project was complete.

The mayor's panel helped identify some of the key constituents who were then invited to be part of the Round Table, a stakeholder group that served as the steering committee for the project. Members were chosen from all walks of life and also from key organizations that would need to partner with the city to implement the plan. The members of the Round Table didn't necessarily represent the groups and organizations they were part of, but their affiliation with the constituencies helped them bring that perspective to the dialogue. This Round Table made a commitment to meet at least monthly throughout the project and oversaw the work on the vision statement, the goals, targets and strategies for the plan.

The third key set of participants were members of the Working Groups. These were formed around each of the key city systems — social, economic, governance and the natural and built environments. Here, experts were invited to participate with the Round Table members, and in an exemplary effort to insure that integration was part of each dialogue, specialists from each system were also part of every other working group. So the governance committee had representation from the natural environment, built environment, economic and social systems groups, and the other committees had representation from governance.

Stakeholder Training

The groups started their work with training on the way the imagineCALGARY process was going to work. The training included a timeline and a detailed schedule of meetings, with preliminary agendas for all of the meetings included. This provided both the staff and the stakeholders with a sense of certainty; even when they were moving into uncharted waters, they at least had a map. It also gave people a lot of food for thought, because the questions to be answered in the meetings were not so easy. The training also included some background information about Calgary and an overview of how systems dynamics would apply to their planning process.

It became clear at the beginning that there were different levels of training needed for different participants, at least in terms of the ways in which lessons from systems dynamics would be used. Three levels emerged — the advanced, intermediate and beginner level — that guided the content of the training that was offered. Systems dynamics is a vast subject area, with many possible schools of thought ranging from what is characterized as hard systems dynamics (the world of computer modelers and mathematical formulas) to soft systems thinking (where diagrams and stories are used to convey the ideas and hard data is not used). Calgary was unusual insofar as it already was using hard systems models to manage its traffic planning, so they had experts on staff. The imagineCALGARY project, on the other hand, was primarily using soft systems thinking, where causal loop diagrams were used to convey the interrelationship of different variables to each other both within and between city systems.

The beginner level training in systems thinking was given to the Round Table and working group participants. At this level, participants needed to understand that systems dynamics was part of the methodology being used, and if systems diagrams were presented to them by the staff or consultants, they needed to understand the diagrams. If they had more understanding than this — and some of them did — it was fine, but the majority of them would not. Gwendolyn provided some of the training to this group, but the city also invited in local experts to demonstrate why systems dynamics were important — one of the first Round Table meetings featured a speaker from a local institute that made connections through a discussion of locally grown food.

The intermediate level training was given to the consulting team that Calgary hired to manage the Working Groups. Two facilitators were assigned to each group, one to lead the discussion and one to keep a record of their work. In addition, the team members from the planning office also attended each meeting. At this level, the facilitators and re- cord keepers needed to be able to not only understand the diagrams and the logic of systems dynamics that was presented to the group, but they needed to be able to explain it to other people. The workshops for this group were designed as more hands-on training, so they worked with different systems diagrams and were given more practice applying the ideas to real life situations.

Finally, the advanced level training was provided to the core staff of the imagineCalgary team. For this group, it was important that they be able to use an understanding of systems to both describe the existing situation and to identify possible interventions that could be made to improve things. This team was provided a lot of material on systems archetypes, and they used the different archetypes to analyze trends over time and describe the causal patterns for different situations in Calgary.[2] Then they were also given instruction on how to identify leverage points in the systems that were causing problems. Leverage points are a seductive idea for planners—they offer the hope that small changes can lead to big results. The challenge of leverage is that often the "small" changes needed are quite countercultural or expensive, even if in the larger scheme of things they aren't significant.

The training helped make a challenging project—developing a 100 year plan for a city—something that people from many different disciplines, from all political stripes could understand. It established a common language to use, defined a set of goals and created a map to follow through a long series of meetings where controversial issues would be discussed. In many ways, the training and early project organization created a safe space to discuss difficult issues, and the new language of systems also provided some tools to diagnose intractable problems in new ways.

For example, some of the more difficult issues in Calgary and in other cities are those associated with economics and livelihoods, since any discussion about poverty and wealth can immediately turn into a politically charged debate. Yet there are systemic patterns of behavior within the economy that can be described with systems diagrams to give participants a new way of looking at a story which otherwise might be layered with ideological misinformation. The staff and working group on the economy in Calgary came up with a diagram to describe a problematic pattern that leads to a high level of economic inequity; this diagram also opened up a good discussion about ways in which different interventions might help reduce the resulting systematic impoverishment.

The story they outlined is simple, really, describing how money and power interact to keep more resources flowing to people who already have money and to deny income potential to people who don't already have it. In a society where the myth of upward mobility and individual success is powerful, this story is often hard to discuss in a group of people who don't share the same political orientation. A discussion of the need for more economic equity quickly devolves into labeling and ideological positions that tend to obscure real issues. While diagramming the systems does not completely eliminate this tendency, the patterns of behavior and feedback loops do provide a new lens with which to view the story.

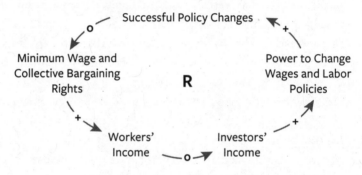

FIGURE 14.1. Flows of Money and Power

In Figure 1, the feedback loops describe a common system archetype known as Success to the Successful. This pattern of behavior occurs in many places in society, including bright children in school getting more attention from teachers or people moving up the ladder within a corporation. There is no denying that it is easier to be successful when you already have some advantages. What the archetypical diagram demonstrates, however, is that when people who are already successful are gaining the resources their success allocates to them, this can turn into a zero sum game where others are denied the same resources. So, in this case of money flow, the systemic economic imperatives work in a reinforcing feedback loop that makes the situation go more and more in the direction of the accumulation of wealth on one side and impoverishment on the other.

If you start at the bottom of the diagram, people who have income from their investments tend to have more power to influence the rules of a given society. Moving upward in the diagram, since wages are a cost for enterprises, and since profit depends on the revenue from sales being more than the costs of production, there is a lot of pressure within our system to reduce costs and keep wages low. The lower wages are, the more income people can make from investments. So policy changes are made to reduce or eliminate minimum wages and restrict collective bargaining rights by people who have more influence. As this book goes to print, the state of Wisconsin has been making headlines for several months where the Republican leadership there is trying to strip public employees of their collective bargaining rights. So the pressure exists in both the public and private sectors to keep wages low.

It follows, therefore, that more income from existing investments directly influences the level of wages paid to workers. The more income going to the investors, the lower the wages are for the workers. Lower wages mean lower possibilities for workers to invest themselves so that they can benefit from a profitable enterprise. The lower the investment possibilities there are for the workers, the more income from investments flow to the people who are already benefiting from the system. This pattern forms a vicious cycle where the rich get richer and the poor get poorer.

Figure 1 also suggests ways that the system might be fixed. In this particular system, if there were a way to allow workers to have access to investment income that would supplement their wages, it would help break the cycle of impoverishment. There are many ways to do this — through Employee Stock Ownership Programs (ESOPs), cooperative ownership structures, small business loans and entrepreneurial training. This also illustrates the idea of leverage — one of the leverage points in any system may slow or reverse the positive reinforcing feedback loops. Finding ways to intervene in this system might involve adding a variable that changes the feedback. If more income from existing investments, for example, meant an increase in profit sharing plans for workers, the system could be changed so that the increasing inequity could be reversed. This could be facilitated with complementary currencies within businesses or governmental agencies that rewarded innovation and cost-cutting.

Training in how systems work provides planners and stakeholders with a new way to look at strategy development and sustainability planning. It isn't a panacea, but combined with: 1) the integrated principles of the Earth Charter, 2) a comprehensive framework of human needs so that city issues can be considered as a whole system and 3) a long-term time horizon for a vision and goals, these four methodological elements can put city plans on a more sustainable path than the current planning paradigm.

Principles serve as the guardrails, the guidelines for action within the constraints of ecosystems and social justice. The systems orientation and human needs framework provide the vehicle that gives the planning initiative focus and structure to move forward — a series of important questions to ask and an integrated way for the questions to be answered. The long-term vision and goals give the vehicle both its drive and its destination. Bob Miller, a strategic planner in the City Manager's office in Calgary, summarized it this way: "The systems view creates connected pathways; the focus on human needs energizes and grounds the 'why we are doing this planning initiative at all' — providing the urgency and momentum to move forward."[3]

Calgary's Vision

While the stakeholders and working groups were starting their work considering the existing condition of the different city systems and setting goals for the future, another major effort was underway to involve as many of Calgary's citizens as possible in creating a vision for the future. As happened in Burlington, the city staff asked people to answer five open-ended questions designed to elicit people's values — the things they cared about that make Calgary special. These questions were:

+ What do you value about Calgary?
+ What is it like for you to live here?
+ What changes would you most like to see?
+ What are your hopes and dreams for the next 100 years?
+ How can you help make this happen?[4]

Posing the questions is relatively easy; finding ways to make people aware that the questions are being asked and getting them to answer is a lot more difficult, especially in a city of a million people. It's a challenge faced by more than city leadership — each day billions of dollars in marketing campaigns try to do the same thing, to get people to pay attention to a product or service that is offered and respond to it. City leaders can learn from these marketing campaigns at the same time as all the commercial messages occupy the space that more important questions might have. City leaders can also learn from other activities that engage people — after all, people turn out in large crowds for events like the Calgary Stampede, for the arts, for celebrations, to practice their spiritual and faith traditions and for competitions and contests. Even the name of the initiative — imagineCalgary — was designed to be a way to interest people in the effort.

A special team on the Calgary staff was tasked with reaching out to the community. This team spent a lot of time developing materials, going to events and dreaming up new ways to reach people. One of the principles for public outreach and engagement that was included in the training session on the methodology at the outset was that cities need to go where people are, not simply to expect people to come to them. So the special team set up lemonade stands on the pedestrian mall and had a local team mascot there to entice people to come over and fill out the survey. They developed a special guidebook for Imagineering Sessions that neighborhood groups could use to have coffee table discussions about their collective future. They sponsored a photo contest, turned up at the cross-country solar car race and found lots of new and innovative ways to reach out to people who normally wouldn't be involved in anything as specialized as city planning.

In the end, over 18,000 people participated in creating the vision statement, one of the largest public outreach campaigns by a city in history. Even the effort made in New York City to solicit citizen input into the redesign of downtown Manhattan after the World Trade Center attacks only managed to reach 5,000 people in the end. The way the city summarized all of this outreach in their final plan provides a flavor of the enormity of the effort.

Developing the vision was a celebration of community participation and imagination! It was an adventure in exploring values, building on assets and incorporating citizens' hopes and dreams for the next 100 years. Based upon the success of Imagine Chicago and other community movements around the world, imagineCALGARY reached out to Calgarians using a variety of strategies. Over 18,000 responded via:

+ the imagineCALGARY Web site (including the opportunity to complete the questions online in nine languages)

+ imagineCALGARY booths at more than a dozen festivals and approximately 364 events
+ over 40 youth volunteers spent approximately 425 hours interviewing 150 community leaders
+ focused visioning sessions with over 60 groups from a range of diversity communities (ethno-cultural, seniors, low-income, urban aboriginals, disability groups)
+ focused visioning sessions with 70 youth groups
+ about 30 sessions with City of Calgary internal groups; and
+ over 40 CalgaryQuest sessions (scenario exploration tool).[5]

Once all the responses were in, the next challenge was to compile them and translate all the input into a coherent, inspirational and above all concise vision statement. The city used a couple of different tools to do this. One was a computerized database of all the answers that could be searched by keyword so that themes in all the answers could be identified.[6] People were able to enter their answers directly into an on-line survey, but one of the lessons learned from the project was how few participants actually did it this way. The city's consultants worked to compile the themes and produced a report on the collective vision for the Round Table and the staff.

The next step was to craft a statement that reflected the themes and was inspirational enough to serve as a collective value statement for the city. A small committee from the Round Table was convened, and a local poet was hired to help do this. Many drafts went back and forth; there was much wordsmithing and revision to arrive at the final result.

Our vision for Calgary
For thousands of years, people have met at the confluence of two vital rivers to imagine and realize their futures. Together, we have built a city of energy, born of a powerful convergence of people, ideas and place. Together, we continue to imagine Calgary, making a community in which

+ We are each connected to one another. Our diverse skills and heritage interweave to create a resilient communal fabric, while our collective spirit generates opportunity, prosperity and choice for us all.

+ We are each connected to our places. We treasure and protect our natural environment. Magnificent mountain vistas and boundless prairie skies inspire each of us to build spaces worthy of their surroundings.
+ We are each connected to our communities. Whether social, cultural or physical, these communities are mixed, safe and just. They welcome meaningful participation from everyone and people move freely between them.
+ We are each connected beyond our boundaries. We understand our impacts upon and responsibilities to others. Our talent and caring, combined with a truly Canadian sense of citizenship, make positive change across Alberta, throughout Canada and around the world.

We can make it happen!

With purpose, drive and passion, Calgary will be a model city, one that looks after the needs of today's citizens and those to come. We make imagination real; it's the Calgary way. It's what we've always done and will always do.

Calgary: a great place to make a living, a great place to make a life.[7]

The vision statement was further elaborated by goals, which were organized around each of the human needs within the different city systems. The goals articulated the *end state* that Calgary wanted to achieve in 100 years. Each of the goals was then put into action through a series of 10, 20 and 30 year targets, which were measurable steps to the goal, and these in turn each had a set of strategies to be used to achieve the targets. All of this was written up in the ImagineCALGARY Long Range Plan for Urban Sustainability, along with a plan to institutionalize the process, both within city government and in the community. To launch the plan, Calgary attended the World Urban Forum in Vancouver in the spring of 2006, where it was featured as a leader for urban sustainability for cities all over the world.

Award Winning Plan

Since the adoption of the plan, Calgary has won several awards for its work in this area. The Canadian Urban Institute presented imagine-CALGARY with its 2009 Natural City Award to recognize the role the plan has played in creating a sustainable future for the community. Other awards the city received include the Municipal Sustainability Innovator Community Award from the Alberta Urban Municipalities Association and the CH2M Hill Sustainable Communities Award from the Federation of Canadian Municipalities.

At the time of this writing, it is too early to say much about the implementation of the plan, although work has been done to institutionalize it into city government by creating a Sustainability Coordinator in the City Manager's office and to establish a formal organization outside of city government that will keep community efforts going. The new coordinator's job is intentionally low-key; the goal was not to develop a new department for sustainability, which has the unfortunate unintended consequence of allowing other departments to assume that the job is being taken care of without their involvement. The position will instead continue to integrate the work of the broad range of city departments and to hold their feet to the fire with respect to the targets that were set and refined by the City Council into a shorter term work plan for the city.

Calgary Dollars

As was the case in Burlington, the City of Calgary already had a complementary currency when imagineCALGARY began. Called Calgary Dollars, the currency is a taxable currency that exists both in printed and in electronic form. The project is supported by the Arusha Center, an organization dedicated to social justice, the United Way of Calgary, and the City of Calgary Family and Community Support Services.[8]

One of the benefits to Calgary Dollars of the imagineCALGARY project was that its importance to the different goals and objectives the city established was articulated in the long-term plan the city developed. This raised awareness among a broader range of stakeholders about the currency and linked it to city objectives.

Plan-It Newburgh

At the same time Calgary was moving forward with its 100 year plan, another small city on the Hudson River in New York State — Newburgh — hired a new City Manager. Jean-Ann McGrane had been a professor who taught sustainable development before she worked in

Newburgh. She was interested to hear what a local organization called Sustainable Hudson Valley, led by Melissa Everett, had to say about the possibility of producing the state's first sustainable Master Plan. Gwendolyn was invited to speak to department heads in the city about the work that Burlington had done, and a new partnership was formed to begin work on a stakeholder process in Newburgh.

The story of the two planning initiatives in Calgary and Newburgh could be a tale of two cities, because they couldn't be more different. It was the best of times in Calgary, it was the worst of times in Newburgh. Calgary was a wealthy city and could budget $2.4 million simply to produce the plan itself. They had a worker shortage and were looking for immigrants to fill over 16,000 jobs that were available. Newburgh was an impoverished, boarded up, crime ridden pocket of urban blight — the construction of an interstate highway bypassed its downtown in the 1970s, and the city had been in decline ever since. Newburgh suffered from high unemployment, double digit teenage pregnancy rates, a long history of corruption and almost feudal governance that allowed a small handful of elites to use the city's resources to enrich themselves. An urban renewal program in the 1960s had been the flagship of this effort; it displaced the African American population without ever completing the projects that were promised, creating an open wound in the city that still festered 40 years later.

The population of Newburgh was split three ways — ⅓ African American, over ⅓ Hispanic (undocumented illegal immigrants made this statistic a bit slippery) and a little less than ⅓ white. The city had a total population of about 32,000, so it was similar in size to Burlington. There was enormous tension among the different groups, everything from serious gang warfare in the streets to a take-no-prisoners approach to local politics that dominated City Council meetings. Convening a group of stakeholders that were truly representative of the different parts of the community and creating a shared vision was going to be difficult. Gwendolyn figured that if she could do it in Newburgh, it could be done anywhere.

Stakeholder Recruitment

Following the instructions in the EarthCAT book, the first step in Newburgh was to recruit a Core Team of people who represented the various constituencies in the city. In Calgary, this group had been the advisory panel to the Mayor; in Newburgh this group represented trusted members from each of the ethnic groups who managed to rise above ongoing strife. Nuns from the Catholic Church had already heard of the Earth Charter and were eager to help. The daughter of a prominent pastor in the African American community and a few other key citizens volunteered to help recruit stakeholders.

The city planned a two-day training for the stakeholders, which was led by Gwendolyn and Melissa. The training covered the methodology for the process, but also included an important section on conflict management, listening skills, facilitation skills and dialogue. It also gave all the participants a lot of opportunity to interact with each other and to get to know everyone there — plenty of small group work and hands-on exercises demonstrating everything from cooperation and teamwork to systems dynamics.

The first group of stakeholders met for the training on a sunny day in the spring of 2005. The local bank, which had a meeting room that offered a beautiful view of the Hudson River, made the training space available — it was to become the main meeting room for the stakeholders for the entire process. There were about 50 people there, representing everyone from the local police department to the leaders of a local group of street poets and rappers who were known for being vocal opponents of city policies.

Every training started with introductions, despite objections from the staff in Newburgh that it would take too long for 50 people to say a few words about themselves. An important principle of adult education is that people need to identify themselves to the group; they can't be anonymous. Given the volatile political situation in the city, this was more important than ever. People stood in a circle and were asked to give their names, either where they worked or lived and to say one thing about Newburgh that they thought was hopeful for the future. We also asked them to think about who was missing from the training and the planning process that should be there and to make suggestions to us before the end of the training.

This method of recruiting stakeholders came to be named the *concentric circle process*, because it turned out to be so successful in Newburgh. The trainees at the first session did suggest other people to the city staff person, Betsy McKean, who was the backbone of the project as it moved forward. So after the first training, 50 more trainees were invited to the second, who in turn were asked to suggest people for the training. A third training was held, and a fourth. Finally, during the fourth training the stakeholders suggested that more youth be involved, and a special youth training was scheduled — by this time it was summer and so a local youth group could be recruited to accomplish this.

In hindsight, while it was a great idea to have more youth involved, it was a real challenge to manage an entire training session filled with inner city teenagers. At first, it was like pulling teeth to get them engaged — the training was so dependent on hands-on, small group work that engagement was not optional. Gwendolyn finally figured out that several kids thought that they were in this session as some kind of punishment. This called for a change in the approach. She reassured them that, to the contrary, they were taking the training because someone in the city thought they might make good leaders. She abandoned one of the modules scheduled for the first morning and walked them all over to City Hall where she gave them a chance to sit in the seats occupied by the City Council and let them pretend to be the mayor. This impressed them, and helped them be a little more cooperative for the rest of the two days they spent with the trainers.

Lesson learned: it is critically important to involve youth in the training, but do it when a whole room of adults can help keep them on task by having them participate in the same training as the adults. The fact that the adults were required to take the same training was one of the important pieces of information Gwendolyn gave the youth group — this raised eyebrows and got them to sit up a bit straighter. Of course, being in the same training as the adults would accomplish this same goal.

Visioning Questions

Newburgh found that the questions Calgary asked were relevant to their community, so they began a public outreach process to ask citizens to answer them:

- What do you value about Newburgh?
- What is it like for you to live here?
- What changes would you most like to see?
- What are your hopes and dreams for the next 100 years?
- How can you help make this happen?

It was a challenge to find ways to reach out in Newburgh's rough inner city context. The local team assembled to manage the project included Sarah Pasti, a local advocate from across the river in Beacon and a couple of local residents who could devote time to outreach and committee attendance. The Special Projects coordinator from the city was a contact person to help coordinate the group, along with the hardworking City Clerk.

Creative ideas about how to do the outreach included a kickoff event during the annual fall arts festival, using a bus to visit the neighborhoods and do some canvassing, visiting local community groups and asking all of the stakeholders to participate by bringing the surveys to the people they knew. A basketball game was held between the police and the school team, and the city printed buttons and t-shirts with the Plan-It Newburgh logo. (Plan-It being a homonym for Planet — it was a mild joke about the city). A local team of activists was hired to help with the outreach efforts, and they pulled together an outreach plan to reach all the diverse and often dangerously competitive sectors of the community. Community outreach can be very challenging in a city where gang violence is high; truces have to be declared before weddings that involve people from different neighborhoods can be held peacefully.

The School Surprise

Despite all these efforts, several months passed in the fall, and not a lot of surveys had been returned. People were busy, some of the initial enthusiasm for the project had faded and the stakeholders hadn't really taken ownership of the visioning process. The December meeting arrived, and the staff of the project were getting nervous that there wouldn't be enough surveys to be credible as a statement by the people of the city about their values and aspirations.

What we didn't know was that while the rest of the stakeholders were procrastinating, one young student named Vinny Gaetano took on the project of getting student input into the plan quite seriously. He had gone to his principal, who in turn directed him to the school board to obtain permission to distribute the surveys to all the children in the schools. The school board had given him the OK, and he had personally visited a lot of the schools with the surveys in hand.

He got up to speak at the meeting, holding hundreds of completed surveys from the schools. The stakeholders spontaneously broke into

applause — you could feel the mixture of excitement and embarrass-
ment as everyone realized that Vinny, age 14, had done more work than
any of the adults to find answers to the questions. From this moment
on, things changed. The surveys began to come in from all quarters as
people found new ways to circulate them to their peers and in their
workplaces. The city decided to extend the period of time to collect the
answers, to allow more of them to be returned, and in the end they had
answers from more than 2% of the population — a level that indicates
that just about everyone had been given an opportunity to participate.

The Vision

A small committee of stakeholders was formed to review all the surveys
and draft a vision statement for the city. It was a diverse committee, and
the statement went through many drafts, some which had wording that
spoke more powerfully about the need for economic justice than the
one finally ratified by the group. But given the challenges and divisions
that continued to run through city relations, the simple fact that such a
diverse group of people settled on a shared vision was a real accomplish-
ment in Newburgh.

> Newburgh, Queen City of the Hudson River Valley, offers spec-
> tacular views, historic architecture, and a vibrant cultural blend. We
> share a vision of justice and prosperity for all, health and vitality for
> our people, and our own distinctive place in the world.
>
> Established by immigrants seeking liberty and opportunity,
> the city is a natural transportation hub — the river, rails, highways
> and airport continue to shape our economy and our lives. Built on
> accomplishments of the past 300 years, Newburgh will foster the
> achievements of many future generations.
>
> Our city continues to renew itself as a clean, safe and caring city,
> where community thrives and individuals flourish. A respected en-
> vironment, an enterprising spirit, and the diversity of our citizens
> will shape our future. Newburgh and its people will be known for
> creativity, compassion, prosperity and peace.[9]

Even as the vision was being drafted, changes in the dynamics of local
government were underway. When interviewed by a local cable station
during one of the events sponsored by the project, the City Manager

described how the stakeholder training had changed the tenor of dia-logue at City Council meetings. She said that while a take-no-prisoners approach had been the rule in the past, the level of respectful listening and dialogue "changed the political culture of the city."[10]

She wasn't as happy about the changes a few months later, when the newly empowered stakeholders organized in opposition to a decision the city had made about the location of a new courthouse. One of the inevitable (and even desired) outcomes of a process where people from a city work together on a shared vision over time is a renewed sense of cohesion that empowers people to take action and hold city leadership's feet to the fire when it comes to implementing the goals of the plan. For the first time, a diverse group of people got together and successfully challenged a decision by the city that was seen as contrary to their vision. An outside mediator was brought in to facilitate a dialogue between the stakeholders and the officials from the city, and the decision was reversed.

The Power of Culture

Nothing short of cultural change was required in Newburgh to make a lasting difference in the way the city worked, and cultural change does not happen overnight. The planning project left a legacy of improved social capital that continued to serve the city as it moved forward with major plans to redevelop the waterfront. Yet at the same time, the cor-rosive force of corruption and inequitable power relationships under-mined the legitimacy and credibility of city government.

One of the clear recommendations from the process, for example, was a city charter change that would eliminate at-large city council rep-resentation and realign councilors with the old ward system. This would almost certainly increase the diversity of the council, since the city was segregated into ethnic areas. The at-large system continued to mean that the percentage of relatively wealthy, white councilors was higher than their proportional population in the city. Since it is a rare moment when people voluntarily give up their power base, this idea failed in Newburgh, and the Council refused to move forward with this change.

On another front, a scandal erupted when one of the key staff people in the Code Enforcement department was accused of sexual harassment by a city employee who had been active in the stakeholder group. The evidence against him was compelling, and yet when presented with all the information, the City Manager chose to defend the supervisor rather than taking appropriate disciplinary action. Perhaps more than any other misstep, this undermined her credibility among those involved in the project. The Code Enforcement employee left the city within a few months of the accusations, but not before the damage had been done.

Newburgh went on to draft a Sustainable Master Plan that was adopted by the City Council in December of 2008. One month later, the City Manager was fired; the scandals and broken promises of the past combined with an unfavorable audit on grants the city managed from the US Department of Housing and Urban Development (HUD) ultimately led to her demise. A quote from one of the councilors illustrates the dilemma many leaders face when moving forward with a substantial change agenda:

McGrane is "a person of tremendous vision," Bell said Tuesday. But Bell and others had complained the ex-city manager tried to force her vision forward, even if that meant circumventing the council. "Impose her will — that was Jean-Ann McGrane," Bello said.[11]

It is not sufficient to have a vision as a leader. Leaders must know how to mobilize the whole community to establish a sense of collective vision, and then they must be willing to move *with* the community toward a common goal. This is necessarily a longer process than simply moving forward with an agenda of your own; it can't be forced. It is possible to patiently rest assured that the final outcome will be consistent with a sustainability agenda providing that at the outset, people agree to frame the process as a long-term plan, looking ahead 20–100 years. This, combined with a reliance on collective knowledge and aspirations — the wisdom of the crowd — should be enough to moderate hidden agendas and unsustainable habits that tend to drive city planning in the wrong direction.

Newburgh's Complementary Currencies

During the time of the Plan-It Newburgh project, two different complementary currencies were introduced. Edgar Cahn, the founder of the Time Bank system, worked with the city social services department to start a Time Bank. Gwendolyn and Bernard also worked with the city to develop a housing currency of a kind described in Chapter 5. Unfortunately, the corruption scandals that dominated the city made it very difficult if not impossible to actually implement these projects. One lesson we learned from this experience is that, no matter how effectively you bring people together, if the city government cannot be trusted, no innovative initiatives will work.

enVisioning Montpelier

In July of 2006, Gwendolyn had returned from the World Urban Forum where Calgary had unveiled their 100 year plan. Newburgh's planning process was drawing to a close as well, with the action plan due before the end of the year. She picked up the paper one morning and noticed that the planning director in Montpelier, which is where she lives, was leaving. Montpelier is the capital of Vermont, a small city of 8,000 people. Unlike larger cities, Montpelier was unlikely to call in consultants to help them with long-range planning — there just wasn't the money for it. An attempt to do this a couple years earlier had resulted in a scandal as the price of consulting time flashed in the headlines and contracts were cancelled.

Yet over the past five years, Gwendolyn had noticed that the city would benefit from a different approach to long-range planning. A proposal for housing in an open field to the east of the city had created an enormous public outcry as the neighborhood around the field clamored to save the open space for parkland. To stop the proposed development, interim zoning was adopted and the master plan was amended — all symptoms of an underlying planning process that might not reflect the aspirations of the people. As a resident of the city since 2004, Gwendolyn hadn't been aware of any real outreach on the part of the planning office or the city to get residents involved. So she applied for the job and started work as the Director of Planning and Community Development in Montpelier in November of 2006.

As it happened, Montpelier's Master Plan was long overdue for a major rewrite. The last time the plan had been updated with any level of public engagement was in 1995. The Planning Commission welcomed the introduction of a planning process that brought in a high level of stakeholder involvement, and the enVision Montpelier project began in the early part of 2007. At the same time the Planning Commission proposed a new way of doing the Master Plan, the city was threatened with flooding as an unusual ice jam in the downtown formed — the result of increasingly erratic climate patterns. The need to approach city government differently in changing times resonated with city leaders in ways it might not have before.

From the beginning, enVision Montpelier was framed as a learning process rather than a traditional planning process, a new approach that resulted from reflection about the work Gwendolyn had done in the other cities and towns where she had worked. Rapid change in the 21st century is already the rule, and so taking the traditional approach to planning — relying on experts to provide short-term strategies based on what worked in the past — will be increasingly irrelevant as the level of chaotic change increases. Old solutions won't work in the new world we find ourselves in, and so the most important dimension of any sustainability planning process is to make all the stakeholders conscious of learning. Adults don't particularly like to be learners — we like to be knowers and teachers. Taking a learning posture to city planning is much more challenging than it might seem on the surface — city planning has traditionally been left to experts.

Learning our Way to the Future

As in Burlington, Calgary and Newburgh, stakeholders were recruited and organized into subcommittees. The recruitment process was opened up to the public, and immediately over 100 people signed up to participate. Some targeted recruitment was done to try and involve minority voices, elders, youth and key organizational stakeholders, but even here a wide net was cast. Two VISTA volunteers were hired through the Vermont Youth Bureau, and their main charge was youth involvement, so there was a special focus on recruiting people in high school and college.

The subcommittees each had a member of the Planning Commission as a co-chair, and then the committees elected another co-chair using the *Sociocratic* method for elections.[12] All of the elected co-chairs, two representatives from the Planning Commission and three representatives from the City Council formed the Steering Committee for the enVision process, which was chaired by the Mayor (as one of the City Council representatives).

Each of the committees started their work by creating a set of learning objectives, a list of things they wanted to learn about the area of city life they had as a subject area. The six committees for the first phase of the process included Social Systems, Human Development, Governance, Economics and Livelihoods, Built Environment and Infrastructure and Natural Environment. As time went on, the Social Systems and Human Development committees merged, partly due to the overlap in their subject areas and partly due to the new initiative to create a Time Bank led by the Social Systems committee that took all the members onto its new Board of Directors.

The learning objectives each committee developed framed the early part of their work, as they identified different ways to learn what they needed to know about the assets and issues in the Social Systems in Montpelier, for example, and to set goals for the different needs that were identified. The committees invited professionals to come to their meetings and talk about their work; they read material that was developed for them by the VISTA volunteers; they sponsored community forums on topics such as how the faith community could work together or what the democratic town meeting tradition was like in Switzerland.

Each committee took responsibility for the monthly stakeholder meeting agendas as well, which were opportunities to invite speakers to give presentations or conduct exercises with the stakeholders to learn more about a topic. So at the first stakeholder meeting about Economics and Livelihoods, the local director of the Chamber of Commerce and a state expert on economic development were invited to talk about their views of the economy in the future. This resulted in the Chamber director becoming an active stakeholder in the process, which helped insure a balanced viewpoint in the discussions.

By the end of the first year of the project, each subcommittee had drafted a set of goals for each of the human needs included in their area, and the goals reflected both the work they had done learning about the topics and the vision that had been generated for the city by the massive public outreach campaign that was done during the same period. During the second year of the project, the committees took the goals and drafted targets and strategies that would enable the city to achieve the goals. Once this was complete, and the descriptive work was compiled to describe current conditions, the Master Plan moved forward into the adoption process.

Montpelier's Complementary Currencies

The three currencies that Montpelier designed and implemented as a direct result of the enVision Montpelier project were described in Chapters 10 and 11 — two different projects based on the Time Bank model and a food currency. Businesses in Montpelier were also made aware of the new Vermont Sustainable Exchange that is being developed in Burlington, so it's possible for businesses to join a commercial barter system as well. There is no question in Montpelier's case that the shared vision for the future and the collective action that was mobilized as a result was key to the success of these currency interventions.

Moving From Vision to Action

All of the cities discussed in this chapter have followed a pattern of activity that facilitates taking a long-term vision and turning it into concrete actions to move a community toward the vision. The vision often sounds too ideal for more practical people. One City Councilor in Montpelier was always shaking his head at the "utopian" ideal that the Master Plan was presenting to the city. Yet once clear goals are defined and then further refined into measurable targets and achievable strategies, the vision comes into focus.

Planning Phase	Time Frame	Stakeholders
Visioning	6 months–1 year	Broad cross section of the public
Goal Setting	6 months–1 year	Committees, with public input
Targets	6 months–1 year	Committees, with public input
Strategies	6 months–1 year	Committees and key partners

FIGURE 14.1 Planning—Activities and Timelines

The involvement of key partners in the strategy phase is one of the first steps to mobilizing the resources needed to implement the plan. The plan needs to account for activities that are already underway — it can be a resource that describes the overall level of effort in a community toward the goals.. There is no need to reinvent the wheel. If the local college is already pulling an arts calendar together, this can be one of the strategies described in the plan under the appropriate target. If the local homeless shelter is working to find transitional housing for people in its care, be sure to mention it in the overall plan. Recognition by the city of all the diverse efforts being undertaken is actually a goal in itself, because a compendium of strategies citywide can also be a resource that makes it easier to identify where gaps exist.

One result of these efforts was a Montpelier City Master Plan, with a horizon of 100 years, that was formally approved by the City Council in September 2010 and ratified by the Central Vermont Regional Planning Commision in November of 2010.

Community and Resource Mobilization

Making real change takes time and money. The types of strategies we describe in Creating Wealth mobilize underutilized resources to meet unmet needs through the use of complementary currencies, which can make the limited funds you have go a lot further. There is never enough money to do everything we want to do, but there often are hidden resources that can take the place of money to implement important strategies.

If cities are going to play a role in wealth creation for their residents, establishing the policy framework that supports this role and clearly identifying strategies that incorporate complementary currencies sets the stage for successful city action. The planning processes described in this chapter obviously address more than the issues complementary currencies can help address, but these processes are very important — they create a context where innovative strategies which rely heavily on collective action are possible.

Toward a Monetary Democracy

It is not the creation of wealth that is wrong,
but the love of money for its own sake.

MARGARET THATCHER

Local governments all over the world are struggling to promote economic development to provide better jobs for their citizens, to create a more valuable tax base and to improve municipal services. Yet the ways in which local governments pursue economic development often inadvertently undermines the long-term security of their community. The money and time spent recruiting large, outside companies (in the hope of driving economic growth) often backfires, leading instead to the closure of locally owned businesses, while at the same time redirecting profits from the local community to those of large corporations.

The resulting trends are well-known — large, big-box stores undermine small, downtown shops. The pressure of higher insurance rates, labor costs and regulations, increased shipping costs and the lack of economies of scale push more and more small businesses into the "failed" column every year. When this happens, local municipalities are left with a lower revenue base, which in turn drives up taxes, the costs of water and sewer fees and road maintenance for the local population. When

207

their low-income residents can't pay, municipal officials have few alternatives except to discontinue services or initiate tax sales on properties.

Other troubling trends exacerbate the problem. Fewer people are joining civic and religious organizations, traditionally the glue that holds communities together. The pervasiveness of television and isolating entertainments like video games and computers undermine the social structures that supported community life in the past. New ideas and new institutions are needed to reinvigorate the social system and get people back out into the community, connecting with each other and creating networks of support for everyone.

Local governments need ways to increase employment and to pay for local services like education, child care, healthcare, waste management, fire and police protection, infrastructure and administration. Even after all exchanges facilitated through conventional money have been completed, there remain clearly a variety of unmet needs in our communities, and at the same time there are underutilized resources available that could meet those needs. As we have explained earlier in *Creating Wealth*, complementary currencies allow localities and regions to link such unmet needs with unused resources and thereby create additional wealth in the local economy. They also provide a mechanism that ensures that this wealth will benefit local people, rather than being siphoned off to distant headquarters.

We have all been trained to believe that an economy requires a monopoly of a single currency, and that bank-debt money is the only type of currency that is appropriate for a modern economy. Furthermore, anybody who has taken a course in economic theory is convinced that money is a passive medium that simply facilitates exchanges that would have happened otherwise anyway. In other words, the implicit hypothesis underlying the entire economic theory from Adam Smith to today is that different kinds of money wouldn't encourage different types of exchanges, don't affect the relationships among their users or motivate different types of investments. In short, for a conventional economist, using another type of money doesn't make any sense. That is of course true when one compares the use of different national currencies: they are all generated through bank-debt with interest, i.e., they are all of the same type. But there is plenty of empirical evidence from the thousands of complementary currency systems in existence today that using different types of currencies does encourage different kinds of exchanges, and/or significantly changes the relationships among their users.[1] Many complementary currency systems are in fact introduced with the specific aim of changing relationships in a community, and these systems have demonstrated such behavior changes in practice as well.

There are two ways to deal with this blind spot that afflicts our collective perception of money. The first way is to deal with it explicitly by providing empirical evidence; and the second is to bypass this entire issue by selective use of vocabulary. There are two classical arguments to justify the existing monopoly of bank-debt money. The first is efficiency; and the second is that complementary currencies have remained invariably marginal compared to the use of "real" money.

The Efficiency Argument

The first argument runs as follows: having a single currency is more efficient in terms of price formation and of market exchanges. It's easier and faster if everyone uses the same exchange unit. This argument appears to be valid when first considered, because the benefits of efficiency are easily understood. However, it ignores the problems that excessive emphasis on efficiency brings. We can now prove that too much efficiency brings a hidden cost in the form of the structural instability of the entire financial system, of which the 2008 crash is only one recent and spectacular example. As stated earlier, the World Bank has identified no less than 97 banking crashes previous to that one, and 178 monetary crises over a recent 25 year period![2]

Let us imagine that we introduce a law to enforce global monoculture of a specific type of tree. For instance, because pines are considered the most efficient trees in terms of growth, we ban any other type of tree worldwide. We intuitively can feel that such a ban would be a recipe for disaster. Predictably, there would be a fire, an insect epidemic, a new disease — something would happen that would counteract this unnatural strategy. Such monoculture is nevertheless what we impose in the monetary domain.

Let us emphasize that comparing an economy and a natural ecosystem is not just a metaphor or a reductionist comparison of two very different systems. There is one important characteristic that a financial system, an economy and a natural ecosystem have in common: they are all complex flow networks. A breakthrough research finding published in peer-reviewed literature has demonstrated that we can now measure with a single metric the sustainability of any complex flow network independently of the nature of what flows through the system — be it biomass in a natural ecosystem, information in an immune system, electrons in a power distribution network or money in an economy.[3] The reason is that sustainability requires an appropriate balance between two emergent properties of such networks:

+ Efficiency (the capacity for a system to process volumes of whatever flows through the network)
+ Resilience (the capacity for a system to survive a shock or disease, or adapt to a changing environment)

This framework has been tested using 25 years of quantitative data collected about how biomass flows through natural ecosystems. Natural ecosystems happen to be our best examples of large-scale complex flow networks that have proven their sustainability over millions of years. It turns out that both efficiency and resilience depend in turn on two *structural* variables of a complex flow network: diversity and interconnectivity. Increasing efficiencies typically involve streamlining the process, i.e., reducing diversity and interconnectivity.

In the opposite direction, higher diversity and interconnectivity tend to increase resilience. As a consequence of this push-pull in opposite directions, a complex flow network will be sustainable if and only if its diversity and interconnectivity lie within a fairly narrow range, a *window of vitality*. In other words, if there is too little diversity and interconnectivity, the network will collapse in a crash; if too much it will become stagnant. Because these key variables of diversity and interconnectivity are both structural, any complex flow network with the same structure will exhibit the same characteristics of (un)sustainability.

These network properties explain why the behavior of natural ecosystems is not a simple metaphor of our money or economic system. The fact that our current money system is a monoculture is therefore a predictable structural cause for its instability.[4] This analysis also turns the efficiency argument on its head, as it is precisely the excessive emphasis on efficiency that causes lack of resilience. Similarly, blind emphasis on greater economic efficiencies — which favor largest companies at the expense of the smaller local ones — explains the problems that local econo-mies experience today.[5] These articles provide scientific evidence for the claim that the stability of our financial and monetary systems requires the introduction of complementary currencies.

Marginal Role of Complementary Currencies

It is a fact that for more than a century, complementary currencies have been playing only a marginal role. However, this is not due to an in-trinsic flaw of these media of exchange, but a direct result of policies actively pursued by central banks to enforce the monopoly of bank-debt money. Whenever complementary currency systems become success-ful, political and ideological strings are pulled in order to eliminate this "competition" by making them illegal. This happened on a large scale, for instance, in the 1930s in the US, Germany and Austria.[6] And the same attitude is still present today. For instance, a detailed study of the regional currency movement in Germany was performed by the depart-ment of economics of the Bundesbank, the German central bank. In it, Dr. Rösl showed that current regional currencies represent only a fraction of 1% of the total money supply in the country and therefore weren't worth eliminating. In other words, if they ever were to grow beyond marginality, the assumption was that action should be taken to get rid of them.[7]

There is, however, another more permanent mechanism to main-tain the monopoly of bank-debt money as legal tender. Economist John Maynard Keynes made the point that bank-debt money would have disappeared a long time ago if it weren't for the fact that govern-ments require all taxes and fees to be payable only in that particular currency. The irony of course is that this rule can cripple governments as they need to borrow any funds from the financial system in order to obtain the money that they can't raise in taxes. There is a whole school of economic thinking — the Chartalist School — that proposes that the monopoly of creating money should be exclusively a governmental prerogative.[8]

Although we can sympathize with the Chartalist criticism that it is an anomaly that the creation of money — something that should clearly be considered as a commons — has been privatized in favor of the bank-ing system, their solution of creating a monetary monopoly in favor of the government doesn't address our finding that we need a diversity of currency systems. We claim that replacing a private monopoly with a governmentally controlled monopoly would not resolve the structural instability of our monetary system. Instead, a structural solution requires a democratic monetary ecology, where a diversity of currency systems of different scales and functions would thrive.

Therefore, our recommendation is to keep the bank-debt money system in place, with whatever reforms that are judged useful. But there is no reason that governments, including city governments, couldn't require some taxes to be payable only in a currency that it issues itself, without interest, to address specific needs. That is also why the most effective way for a governmental entity at any level to encourage the acceptance of any complementary currency is to require that it be used for payment of a tax. As shown in Chapter 9 with the example of the C3 business-to-business complementary currency, the first country to have followed this strategy was Uruguay.

The Bypass Approach

There is another approach which avoids the entire theoretical debate about complementary currencies, and thereby does not draw the attention of the institutions in charge of guarding the monetary monopoly. After all, the airline industry has successfully launched and managed for decades the frequent flyer miles systems and without ever using the words "money" or "currency." These loyalty currencies are now the largest complementary currency systems in the world and have grown without any interference by monetary authorities.[9]

In retrospect, it might be better to describe complementary currency systems as "information systems," "social incentive schemes" or something else that doesn't include the words money or currency. As everybody agrees that we are moving towards an information society, doesn't it make sense for us to equip ourselves with some additional information gathering mechanisms that go beyond the old industrial age bank-debt money system?

A Vision for a Vibrant Local Economy

We finished writing this book in Reykjavik, Iceland, in a country which had recently experienced one of the first 21st century monetary system crashes in the wake of the 2008 stock market disaster. As a result, a new political party and many informal ad hoc groups had started to ask questions about the financial system and to propose ways in which it might be changed. There was talk about organizing a symbolic *Althingi* — the world's oldest continuously operating Parliament which took place as a huge annual gathering at Thingvelleir for more than a thousand years — to declare the world's first Monetary Democracy. One group had the idea that the City of Reykjavik could establish its own bank so that the city could take advantage of the low interest rates offered to the regular banks by the central bank. A city owned bank would secure the city a line of credit from the central bank. The city then could use the credit to pay back its loans that have higher interest rates than the central bank and save the difference. Just a drop of 1% in interest rate could mean significant savings for the city and its inhabitants. Still another group was taking a look at the country's constitution, to try to restructure the way the financial system worked. There were lots of questions being asked as people struggled with higher mortgage and tax payments and higher unemployment than the country had known in human memory.

In the land of ice and fire, perhaps people will achieve their vision of a more democratic monetary system. Given how accustomed we are to the current system, it's hard to imagine what a new one might look like, especially in light of all the questions which would challenge it as it tries to be born. Yet even in Iceland, there are deep memories of earlier days when money didn't dominate people's idea of wealth. We heard stories of *bread money*, where people would bring their corn to the baker and receive tokens they could exchange for bread later on. The tokens circulated like regular currency, as people traded them for other things they needed. The time when government had set the barter rates for the exchange of agricultural products and fish — how many fish were the equivalent of a lamb, for example — wasn't too distant a memory. Money as we know it was seen in the not-too-distant past as another product of trade — people needed it to buy things from overseas, but they didn't need it to live in their own communities. So they "bought" money from people who traded overseas with the products that served as the currency in Iceland — fish, wool, mutton and lamb.

Perhaps the next time we visit Reykjavik, they will have recreated their own democratic ecology of currencies, instead of the monoculture/

monopoly of bank-debt money that has brought them so much hardship. To reduce unemployment and revalue all of their residents, the city may have introduced a mandatory time contribution, not paid in bank-debt money, but rather using an electronic time currency similar to the Japanese *Fureai Kippu*, as a way to simultaneously reduce taxes and give people work to do. A time currency reduces taxes because people spend their time doing things government pays money for — education, senior care, child care, healthcare, keeping the parks and the streets clean, community justice systems where mediation reduces the load in the courts. Time currency reduces unemployment because not everyone can spend time on these things. People who are willing and able to work above and beyond the time requirement could be paid for their time by those who are not. An e-Bay type electronic market could emerge where the city's time currency could be sold for bank-debt money or whatever else people are interested in exchanging.

Meanwhile, the time exchange system could also include many goods and services that people need in their lives. It wouldn't be limited to tasks the local government needed to perform. So if Leifur enjoys giving piano lessons but doesn't enjoy weeding his garden, he could offer lessons in exchange for garden work. Or perhaps Bjork makes very beautiful handcrafts — she could offer the handcrafts for a mix of time and money. Bjork could then spend the time portion on work she needed to have done repairing her house, and the money could pay for the materials.

As we walk down Reykjavik's main shopping streets during this hypothetical future visit, we can see that the merchants are prospering, and there are no obviously unemployed people hanging around, looking as if they had too much to drink the night before. This is because the businesses have come together to form a commercial barter system like the one in Switzerland, where instead of taking bank loans to meet their cash flow needs, they exchange debits and credits with each other at minimal or no interest, knowing that the system will balance out in the end. Their new commercial barter bank, named after Sigridur, the woman who steadfastly refused to cooperate with foreign investors who wanted to turn Gulfoss (a spectacular waterfall in the southern part of the country) into a hydroelectric dam, offers loans to help businesses get started and for the purchase of real estate. Businesses are no longer burdened with high interest debt, so their owners are much more pros-perous as a result and have more time to enjoy the scenic beauty of the spectacular island.

Another reason that people in Reykjavik look healthy — we notice that there are a lot fewer people smoking cigarettes than the last time we were here — is because of the wellness token system that was intro-duced by the national health insurance system back after the declara-tion of monetary democracy. People who engage in healthy habits get tokens they can cash in for reduced taxes. So many people quit smoking, exercise regularly, bicycle to work, eat healthy food and follow doctor's orders on health regimes.

Greenhouses heated by the abundant geothermal energy available here are everywhere, and food that is grown in these greenhouses has replaced food that the country used to import. A food currency system similar to the bread money of old makes it possible for all the people who work in the food industry to make a good living and makes the cost of food for people in Iceland much lower in monetary terms.

The local currencies have also made it possible for the island state to dramatically reduce their dependence on foreign oil, as local renewable energy has increased in value. This is a result of the carbon credits and energy credit trading system that was introduced on a national scale, which pays people for doing things with a low carbon impact. The new fund created with this energy currency has made it possible for innova-tors and inventors to come up with new ways to use the natural energy on the island for transportation (electric cars and bikes are everywhere, and there is a thriving cottage industry converting normal cars and bikes to electric vehicles), for electricity and for heat.

This vision is within reach, not only in Iceland. All it takes is a group of people with enough energy and courage to start something new and keep at it despite the obstacles that arise. We must remember what Mar-garet Mead said:

Never doubt that a small group of committed people can change the world. Indeed, it is the only thing that ever has.

The Community Currency
How-to Manual

To create a community currency, you need to:

1. Do an assessment of your community in which you identify the priorities for matching unmet needs with underutilized resources — this will determine the *objective* of the complementary currency project you do.
2. Build local support for the community currency system, which means finding a group of people at the outset who can help with different aspects of the project.
3. Review the different complementary currencies mechanisms that are available, and choose the type or types that best suit your needs.
4. Establish a system for managing transactions in your community — this system can take many forms, depending on the local resources available and the type of currency you select.

As described in earlier chapters, complementary currencies can have a social or business purpose. Identifying the needs you have, the purpose for the currencies you plan to introduce and the systems you need to have in place to make them work are the first steps in establishing these currencies in your local community.

Evaluating Currencies to Meet Your Needs

There are a wide variety of *unmet needs*:

+ Social needs such as elder care or youth mentoring
+ Economic needs like unemployment and underemployment
+ Commercial needs like helping the locally owned businesses to better compete against the multinational chains
+ Ecological, cultural or educational needs like supporting local nonprofit organizations, community or regional identity building.

Similarly, *underutilized resources* can be found in the most unexpected places:
+ Any unemployed person who is willing and able to do something has some unused capacities
+ The next time you go to your neighborhood restaurant or movie house, count the tables and chairs that are empty: these are all unused resources that could be mobilized for your purposes
+ Schools or other buildings that are empty during part of the week or the year
+ College, university or vocational courses
+ Youth organizations and other nonprofits that have people ready to do things if supplies are provided

The idea is to design complementary currencies that use the underutilized resources and mobilize to meet the unmet needs of your community.

Remember, the starting point for complementary currencies is to meet needs that remain unfulfilled after transactions facilitated with conventional money have taken place. Similarly, unused resources are those that haven't been used in economic transactions mediated by conventional money.

Beginning Currency Design

There is not one "ideal" design for a complementary currency. Almost every design characteristic has advantages under certain circumstances that can become disadvantages in others. The best design for your community depends on what the objectives you have set for the medium of exchange and the conditions under which it has to operate. Various objectives can be relevant to implement a currency system, such as the functions the currency is supposed to serve, the type of concern it addresses or the people it aims to involve in exchanges.

Legal Tender

Legal tender is the currency that the government of a country accepts as payment in taxes.[1] For example: "This note is legal tender for all debts public and private" is printed on every US dollar bill. What this means is that if you owe someone money in the US and she refuses your offer to pay with US dollar bills, you can walk away and simply declare your debt void. If needed, the courts will back you in such a declaration. One particularly important type of debt that almost everybody incurs is taxes, and therefore *legal tender* means in this context that the government of the country in question accepts only this type of currency in payment for taxes. Normally, only conventional national currencies are defined as legal tender.[2]

The principal coercive feature of legal tender is that no matter how much exchange value you earn in various types of complementary currencies, if you can't pay your taxes in them, you have to find a way to earn legal tender. It gets worse, of course, if transactions in complementary currency incur taxes in legal tender. In the United States, both commercial barter and informal barter systems generate what is considered taxable income, so this taxation has served as a disincentive to their use.

Commercial Purpose Currencies

There are a wide variety of commercial purpose currencies that are defined by the kind of exchange relationships they are designed to encourage. The four main categories are:

- Business to Business (B2B)
- Business to Consumer (B2C)
- Consumer to Consumer (C2C)
- Consumer to Business (C2B)

They typically take electronic forms (see classification by support medium below), offering dramatic cost reductions due to data processing technologies over the past decades.

B2B

These complementary currencies usually are exchange units created by businesses to facilitate exchanges with suppliers and wholesale customers. For instance all the contemporary *commercial barter currencies* fall into this category. There are well over 500 such commercial barter systems, particularly in the US, regrouped under two trade associations: the International Reciprocal Trade Association (IRTA) and the Corporate Barter Council (CBC).

B2C

The most widespread category of complementary currencies today is *loyalty currency* issued by a business or a group of businesses to encourage clients to return to them. Frequent flyer miles are the largest such system today, with 1.5 trillion miles issued yearly worldwide by five major airline alliances. One older and still very common paper-based variety of such system is the ubiquitous discount voucher redeemable for goods or services in retail shops and supermarkets.

C2C

At some level, one can describe an important part of the conventional payment system managed by the banks (i.e., checks, cash payments) as a commercial C2C system. Outside of the banking sector, the PayPal™ payment system is a successful example of this approach extensively used by the e-Bay online auction system, although it exchanges only conventional money at this point.

C2B

An interesting innovation by Strohalm Foundation introduced in Amsterdam, the Netherlands, El Salvador, Uruguay and in the South Brazil is called *Consumer and Commerce Circuits* or C3.[3] It is an Internet-based system in which some basic rules guarantee sound performance and inter-C3-exchange, but most of the details in any system are decided locally. Consumers buy vouchers with a locally established premium (varying between zero and 10% to encourage consumers to join) with conventional money from the C3 network. The vouchers are used to pay for goods and services provided by member businesses. The businesses can use the vouchers to pay other businesses members of the network or can cash them in at C3 against a small fee (similar to the Save Australia project).

Using this system, businesses obtain customers they wouldn't get otherwise and improve customer loyalty in general. The float (in conventional money) accumulated in the system is handled by a local bank which uses it to offer low-cost financing for member businesses or projects. Consumers get loyalty discounts and help make decisions about the way their money is being invested in the community because consumers and businesses all get an equal vote in the management of the system; and there are more consumers than businesses. This, and the fact that consumers are initiating the creation of the complementary currency by buying the vouchers, justify labeling this approach as a new type of commercial application: a Consumer to Business (C2B) financial product.

Combinations of the Above

There are also successful combinations of the above like currencies issued by businesses that are used among individuals as well. For instance, the WIR system in Switzerland or the WAT system in Japan fall in this category.[4]

Social Purpose Currencies

The bulk of social purpose currencies are highly focused on specific problems or social classes, ranging from elder care to employment or education. Here are some examples.

Elder Care

The very first post World War II complementary currency systems were conceived in 1950 by and for women[5] in Japan for the care of elderly, children and disabled persons. These women also created the first Volunteer Labor Bank in 1978, a prototype that was later reinvented in the West (in the US and the UK in particular) as Time Banks. In Japan, the *Fureai Kippu* system is today the direct descendant of those earlier pioneering systems.

Retirees

Some of the first Time Bank applications in the US were implemented by Edgar Cahn in retirement homes and encouraged self-help activities among retirees. The time currency also created stronger community ties.

Employment

The first LETS systems originated in Canada in 1982 aiming specifically at currency scarcity in areas with high unemployment. Still today, most LETS systems tend to flourish in areas with high unemployment.

Education

The Brazilian Saber described in Chapter 6 is a complementary currency designed to stimulate learning and teaching by youngsters among each other.

Child Care (Baby-sitting)

There is a long tradition of more or less formal but small scale local baby-sitting groups constituted by families who in turn take care of each other's children. A large, national-scale Internet-based system is being designed now in Holland, under the name of "Care Miles." Its aim is to help the 2.3 million families who have trouble finding access to care centers, particularly for the 0-4 year olds.[6]

Community Building

Community healing and rebuilding are the most popular reasons for starting complementary currency systems in neighborhoods where there are no major unemployment or economic stress situations. Various designs have been used for such purpose, including Time Bank systems, LETS and Ithaca HOURS. The Balinese time currency described in Chapter 4 could also be considered a well-established system of this nature, operational for more than 1,000 years.

Identity Reinforcement
Reinforcing the feeling of belonging to a particular community or area is one of the secondary reasons that some complementary currencies were introduced. For example, the logos on Ithaca HOURS proudly claims "In Ithaca we trust," and most paper-based complementary currencies prominently feature local landmarks, plants or history as a means to reinforce local identity.

Ecology
Applications of complementary currencies specifically for ecological purposes have remained surprisingly rare so far. One example is the NU smart card system used in Rotterdam, Netherlands to reward ecological behavior (using public transport, buying more energy efficient devices, buying a bicycle) Green-points are charged on a smartcard, and these points can be used to get discounts in the same type of activities, thereby creating a double incentive to behave in an ecologically responsible way. A less successful model is the Earthdaymoney project in the Shibuya neighborhood of Tokyo in Japan, started by a major advertising firm to honor people who are contributing to the ecological sustainability of the area. A Japanese currency called *"eco-money"*[7] has played an important role in the acceptance and use of complementary currencies in Japan, because its originator, Kato-san, was originally working for the MITI (Ministry of International Trade and Industry), and thereby obtained substantial multi-year funding from the government. Over 40 substantial projects were launched in this way, that had in common to be operated for 3 years as experimental projects. As far as we know, there has not been a publicly available analysis of the results of all these experiments. However, despite its name, the purposes of the currencies vary, and only a few of them are specifically for ecological purposes. One exception of an ecological project was the use of eco-money to give an incentive and track the reduction of the use plastic bags during the big 2005 international exhibition in Aichi Prefecture.

Other Social Purpose
One could theoretically continue almost ad infinitum a list of specialized social functions for which complementary currencies could be implemented. Indeed, the whole field of complementary currencies is sometimes labeled as "social money." So the above list is mostly indicative of projects that already do exist somewhere in the world, rather than what could be designed in the future.

Mixed Social Purpose

One could of course easily combine several social objectives, such as having the possibility to earn credits through ecological support activities, and use them for obtaining baby-sitting hours or other combinations of the above list.

Critical Organization, Skills and Practices

Once you have chosen your objective, you need to recruit a team of people who can help implement the project. The team will be suggested by the objective itself, since the people you will need for implementation must have connections with the needs and resources identified in the objective. Here are some examples:

Social Purpose Currencies

Elder Care

The team you will need includes organizations that:

+ are currently involved with care for the elderly
+ recruit and deploy volunteers
+ have other underutilized resources related to the elderly — fitness facilities, restaurants, beauty parlors, educational programs
+ have older people as members or clients

Employment

The team should include:

+ state service providers for the unemployed
+ unemployed people
+ organizations that recruit and deploy volunteers
+ businesses and government employers

Commercial Purpose Currencies

Business to Business (B2B)

The team you will need includes:

+ business leaders
+ business organizations — the Chamber of Commerce, industry associations
+ local government,
+ business support centers — incubators, industrial parks
+ businesses that specialize in business services — temp agencies, accounting firms

Business to Consumer (B2C)
The team you will need includes:
+ business organizations
+ civic groups — Rotary Clubs, churches, hobby clubs
+ retail businesses
+ local government

The team is needed because one of the critical elements of success for a community currency is direct contact with and involvement of the target audience. If your objective is to have a real impact on the social or commercial sector you have identified, the stakeholders in that sector need to be actively involved in the design and implementation of the currency. As ideas come to fruition, you will discover other people you need on the team, like bankers, printers or other companies. Don't hesitate to expand the group — the more people who have a voice in how the system will ultimately work, the more likely it is that it will be successful.

Working with a team, especially a team with diverse backgrounds and perspectives, can be a challenge — there are many skills that can make the work more effective. A lot has been written about leadership, listening, conflict management, meeting facilitation and introducing innovation, and there is no need to repeat it all here. Global Community Initiatives offers a free resource guide to all of these community organizing skills.[8]

Selecting Mechanisms for Complementary Currencies

Once you have convened the Community Currency Team, there are several aspects of the currency you need to consider to design the system you need:
1. Support Medium   3. Issuing Process
2. Function   4. Cost Recovery Mechanism

Each of these considerations will first be defined, and then we'll identify the choices available within each category. We will also briefly identify advantages and disadvantages of each one of these choices. In the conclusion of this appendix, we will map some real-life currency systems according to their characteristics.

The starting point for a general typology of complementary currencies systems is our working definition of currency as "an agreement within a community to use something as a medium of exchange." On the basis of this definition, one can identify as currencies a wide range of social tools that had been, are currently or could be used as medium of exchange in the world.

Support Medium

The support(s) used for issuing or handling a currency is one of the easiest features to grasp — we are familiar with the various forms that currency comes in — notes, coins and plastic cards, given that conventional money uses practically all of them today. These supports fall into the following types:

Commodity Money

Commodity money in history took an extraordinary wide variety of forms. For centuries, societies have successfully used salt, eggs, cattle, textiles, various handicrafts, ingots of various metals and dozens of other items as currencies. In modern times, during World War II cigarettes were used as currency in prison camps in many places. Today, the charcoal currency of Osaka, Japan is a contemporary example of that tradition.

Paper and Coins

Paper and coins are the most familiar form of money today. Paper is the most popular form for contemporary complementary currencies because it is both easy to carry and handle and comparatively cheap to produce (e.g., Ithaca HOURS, WAT bills of exchange, LETS account booklets).

Electronic Media

Electronic media include smartcards, a central computer running the accounts or Internet networks — or for large systems, mainframe computer systems. Over the past four to five decades, most conventional money has taken the form of computer bites, and complementary currency systems have been following this path as well.

Mixed Media

When several media are used for the same currency, this provides maximum flexibility. The historical evolution of conventional money has traced a logical sequence towards more convenience: currency started with physical commodity money (such as precious metal coins), but now it is more convenient to handle paper receipts with promises to pay that physical commodity ("I will pay to the bearer the sum of one Pound Sterling" is still written on the English currency bills). And of course, if the appropriate technological infrastructure is available, electronic bits are even cheaper to move around than paper currency. The same currency can and often does take different forms depending on the media that supports it. National currency takes many forms: electronic bits, paper or coins.

The advantages and disadvantages of each of these media are relatively straightforward.

Commodity currencies have an advantage that one doesn't need a lot of social or legal infrastructure to make them work — it is the only currency that can operate in extreme circumstances such as civil war, social or economic chaos. Such currency can be literally consumed directly by the recipient as a last resort, and it is also most impervious to counterfeiting. Its inconveniences are also clear: it may not be easy to create, and it can be inconvenient to store, handle and transport as well.

Paper currencies, in contrast, are among the easiest to handle and are cheap to produce. But they have as downside — they can also more easily be counterfeited. With high quality photocopying equipment available to almost anybody today, security is a perpetual issue for paper currencies. Even for complementary currencies, this issue needs to be addressed as soon as a currency become successful enough to make it worthwhile for someone to counterfeit.

Electronic media are fairly familiar by now. PCs are the most common support for small to medium-sized complementary currency systems, and are satisfactory if one has access to phones and other communication means to convey the information to the person handling the PC. The downside of these media is that processing the transactions can be labor intensive. Internet connections in which the users update their own transactions reduce the cost of overhead but create additional risks for fraud, and not everybody has an easy access to a computer. Smartcards combine the advantages of both, but require readers that are both expensive and not commonly found anywhere but in Europe at this point. The best electronic solution would be to have the complementary currency piggyback on another smartcard application, such as a public transport or a bank smartcard. That way the marginal cost of adding the complementary currency application becomes very reasonable.

Mixed media is of course ideal, because one can tailor the advantages of each form to whatever the specific application of the currency. But as a downside one should remember that, particularly from a security viewpoint, the weakest media will end up as the weakest link in the entire chain.

Functional Considerations

The three most important functions of money according to classical economics are standard of value, medium of exchange and store of value. In most of history these three functions were not played by the same currencies. For instance, many cultures have had standards of value different from the medium of exchange. One important unit of value in ancient Europe used to be cattle—Homer (8th century BC) would invariably express values in oxen. However, payments were often made in a more practical media such as standardized bronze ingots, gold or silver bars and later coins.

All currencies can therefore be classified in terms of the number and kinds of functions they are designed to fulfill: Standard of Value, Medium of Exchange, and Store of Value.

Standard of Value

The first classical function of money is as a standard of value that enables one to compare prices of the proverbial apples and oranges. The majority of complementary currencies actually don't attempt to set standards of value at all; their unit of account is denominated in terms of conventional money, leaving the standard of value function entirely to conventional national currency. There are of course exceptions, examples of which will be listed below. Since the end of Bretton Woods system in 1971, there is no longer a single international standard of value.

All currencies can be classified as follows in terms of their function as a standard of value.

Reference to Conventional Money

Many local complementary currencies use as unit of account a conventional national currency. Most systems use logically the currency of their own country as reference, but in case of trouble with the national currency some other country's can also be used. The former is the case for instance for most LETS-type systems (e.g., Green Dollars in Canada or Australia, or Bobbins in Manchester) and also for the majority of the systems where local businesses participate. Examples of the latter include the dollar being used in South America or the Euro in the former Yugoslavia.

Time Denomination

Currencies denominated in time (hours, minutes) are the second most popular unit of account. Its system is the one used by Time Bank systems and by the Japanese *Fureai Kippu*.

Physical Unit Denomination

Currencies can be denominated in some physical unit. In the best known commercial loyalty currency, the airline mile system, the unit of account is a flight of the distance of one mile. Among other contemporary examples let us mention some Japanese models: the WAT (whose unit is equivalent to the value of 1 kWh of electrical current generated by citizens' cooperatives through renewable energies such as wind, water, sun), the gram of charcoal used as bio-regional unit in Osaka or the crop denominated currencies of the "leaf" unit in Yokohama or Kobe. Historically, the *Wara* currency in Germany in the 1920s and early 1930s was similarly denominated in kg of coal.[9]

Comparative Advantages of Different Standards of Value

Currencies which refer to *conventional national currencies* have familiarity as their main advantage. They also avoid forcing shops and businesses to deal with multiple pricing systems — one in dollars, one in local units. Particularly when the national currency is a stable one, such a choice makes a lot of sense (e.g., the WIR currency in Switzerland equivalent to one Swiss Franc). The downside is of course that if the national currency gets into a major crisis (e.g., the Russian Ruble in 1998), the complementary currency risks going down with the national currency.

Currencies using *time as unit of account* make most sense when services are the most typical use of the complementary currency. Sometimes there is a misunderstanding that "everybody's time is supposed to be of the same value" for such a unit to work well. This isn't actually true: nothing impedes a dentist to ask customers for instance five hour units for one hour of work as her or his activity requires longer training and expensive equipment compared to one hour of "unskilled" labor.

Time currencies also automatically avoid being caught up in a crash of the national currency and can make it easier to make exchanges with other time-based systems. Their downside is that it may require multiple pricing (how many hours for a dozen eggs?), something that businesses in particular don't like. One easy way to solve this problem is to ensure that the time unit is roughly equivalent to a round value in conventional money (that is why one Ithaca Hour is equivalent to US$10 or one WAT in Japan to 100 Yen).

Currencies using a *physical unit of account* such as miles, grams or kilos of something have advantages similar to the time currencies. Often such units provide a "real physical connection," and if the product involved is widely used and produced in an area, it makes the currency logically bioregional. While physical unit currencies have the same issues with pricing as time currencies, the potential solution is also the same.

Medium of Exchange

For currencies that are not playing the role of standard of value (i.e., the majority of the complementary currency systems), the function of medium of exchange is the most important one. The ease and costs of their use as medium of exchange depends predominantly on the support medium used in the currency. Hence, this aspect has already been dealt with above, when we described different supports.

Store of Value

The last classical function of money is as store of value. As noted before, it may be desirable to have as complementary currency one that is not used as a store of value. Currency was indeed not the preferred store of value in most civilizations. For example, the word capital derives from the Latin *capus* which means head. This word referred to heads of cattle and is still used today in Texas or among the Watutsi in Africa: "He is worth 1,000 head." In the Western world, from Egyptian times through the Middle Ages and until the late 18th century, wealth was stored mainly in land and improvements, that's why it's called *Real Estate* (irrigations, plantations).

Specifically, if one desires to encourage circulation of a currency, one good way to do so is to discourage the hoarding of that currency through various mechanisms such as demurrage or expiration deadlines. Therefore, classifying currencies in terms of their function of store of value is in fact the same as analyzing the way they relate to time.

Interest Bearing Currencies

One way to encourage people to save in the form of a currency is to pay interest. This is the typical situation with all conventional currencies because they are created by bank debt. Interest is a charge that is proportional to the length of time involved in the transaction. In this type of currency, one receives interest by making a deposit in that currency; and one can borrow money by paying interest.

Zero-Interest

The vast majority of complementary currencies simply operate without interest. For example, loyalty currencies or mutual credit systems don't accrue interest, and for those systems where one can borrow complementary currency typically no interest is charged either.

Demurrage Charged Currencies

The opposite of an interest bearing currency is a demurrage-charged currency. Demurrage is a time related charge on outstanding balances of a currency. It operates exactly like a negative interest rate and is used as a disincentive to hoard the currency. John Maynard Keynes, Silvio Gesell, Irving Fisher and Dieter Suhr provided a strong theoretical foundation for this approach, and it was extensively implemented in the form of *stamp scrip* in the 1930s. Today, the most successful grassroots complementary currency in Japan, the Peanuts, charges a demurrage of 1% per month.

Currencies with Time-Related Step Function Valuations
There are also currencies that are characterized by *step functions* triggered by time, a crude form of demurrage. For instance, during the Central Middle Ages, the practice of *renovatio monetae* was widespread. It meant that (for instance) every five years, the old currency would be withdrawn and three new pennies would be given in exchange for four old ones, implying a tax of 25% on the value of the currency. This process produced income for the local currency authority (typically a local lord, bishop or monastery) and gave an incentive not to hoard this type of currency. Stamp scrip systems — whereby a periodic stamp has to be purchased and applied on the currency for it to keep its value — are modern applications of this principle.

Currencies with Expiration Dates
The most radical step function is for a currency to have an expiration date. This process is equivalent to a 100% tax on the date of the expiration.

Trade-offs Available Between Functions
If one desires to encourage the circulation of a currency as medium of exchange, one can achieve this most effectively by charging a "parking fee" of demurrage, or the simpler forms of step functions or expiration dates.

The advantage of interest bearing currencies is that they provide an income to those who create the currency (called *seigniorage*). Its disadvantage is that it implies a systematic money transfer from people who don't have money to those who do, so that it tends to concentrate wealth. It also gives an incentive to save in the form of currency as opposed to real assets. Finally, it provides a systematic incentive to think only short-term, as income generated in the distant future is discounted to irrelevance with positive interest-rate currencies.

In contrast, demurrage-charged currencies provide an incentive to circulate currency as opposed to accumulating it. It also motivates holders to be concerned about long-term implications, particularly for investments. The Terra currency is a currency proposal specifically designed with this latter objective in mind.[10]

The currencies with time-related step functions or expiration dates can be seen as cruder and more radical forms of demurrage-charged currencies.

General Purpose

General purpose currencies are designed to fulfill all three classical functions of money (standard of value, medium of exchange and store of value). Historically, many traditional currencies used locally would fall into this category.[11] Today, conventional national currency is by far the most important general currency.

However, there exists an implicit contradiction between the function of store of value and medium of exchange: notionally when someone accumulates money he or she also deprives others from using it as a medium of exchange.[12] This is why some currencies are actually designed purposely to separate those functions.

In general, complementary currencies are typically designed with a narrow and specific purpose in mind. Although a successful complementary currency system tends to gradually expand its applicability over time, today no complementary currency has reached the point where it can truly be considered a "general purpose" local or regional currency. But this could happen in the future.

Issuing Procedures

This is perhaps the least familiar of all four dimensions of this classification system, but is nevertheless also one of the most important. Errors in designing the issuing process are the most common reason for dramatic failures of complementary currency systems (consider the fate of the Argentinian *creditos* for instance). There are seven major ways of issuing a currency.

Backed Currencies

The strongest currencies are those that are fully backed by a good or service, and are directly and legally redeemable for them. Historically, many currencies were inventory receipts, with 100% backing secured by a physical inventory of a good (e.g., the wheat currency in Dynastic Egypt). Some contemporary complementary currencies use conventional money as backing, others some specific goods or services.

Borrowing with Legal Collateral

This is the way the bulk of the conventional currency is created: through bank loan backed by collateral such as a mortgage on a house or inventories for businesses. Loan-created currency can be considered as a form of a backed currency, but its redemption requires legal action (seizure of the collateral) which is normally an exception rather than the rule. Some complementary currencies, most notoriously the WIR in Switzerland, exactly reproduce the conventional banking model in this sense.

Purchased and Redeemable Vouchers

Vouchers that are purchased directly with national currency, and that are circulating as a medium of exchange, and are redeemable at some pre-determined conditions into national currency again. Current examples of this include Save Australia vouchers, Berkshares in Great Barrington, MA, Capital Cash in Montpelier, VT, the Swiss Chiemgauer and Toronto dollars.

Commercial Vouchers

These are similar to purchased vouchers, except that they are not redeemable back into conventional money. They may be given for free (for example as coupons in newspaper ads) or can be purchased at a discount. They are not redeemable for cash, but typically are redeemable into some good or service instead. They tend to be used only between the issuer and the customer, and rarely circulate as payment device among customers. A typical example is the supermarket discount token.

Loyalty Currencies

Loyalty currencies are commercial complementary currencies that are issued by businesses to customers in proportion to their purchases in conventional money. It is a form of corporate scrip typically redeemable for goods or services in the same corporation or in a consortium of participating businesses. Frequent flyer miles issued by airlines created the first large-scale system; Tesco's loyalty currency in the UK is probably one of the most successful of such systems.

Mutual Credit

Money issued by a simultaneous debit and credit between participants in a transaction create mutual credit currency. Examples of Mutual Credit Systems include LETS and TimeBanks. For instance, in TimeBanking if Julia renders a service of one hour to James, she gets a credit for one hour, and James gets a debit for one hour. They have therefore created the currency necessary for their transaction by agreeing on the transaction itself. The main advantage of mutual credit systems is that they self-regulate to always have sufficient currency available.

Borrowing Without Collateral

A currency can be issued as a credit, but without formal collateral of any sort (other than perhaps an informal promise to provide a good or service in the future). In fact, mutual credit can be seen as a form of borrowing among the participants themselves without collateral. There are also systems which permit borrowing without collateral from a central office which plays a role similar to a complementary currency bank (e.g., *Bia Kud Kum* in Thailand).

Central Distribution

One of the simplest ways to issue a currency is to have a central office distributing it to everybody or to everybody who qualifies. This is the way major currency reforms are typically introduced when a radical departure is necessary (e.g., the German *Währungsreform* after World War II, the *credito* system in Argentina or the purchase coupon experiment used in Japan in 1999).

Mixed Processes

Some systems combine features of various issuing approaches described above. For example WIR is issued both as mutual credit and from a central office with legal collateral. Some social purpose complementary currencies are also accepted in partial payment by local businesses as a loyalty currency.

Advantages and Disadvantages of Issuing Procedures

Here again, one can identify some advantages and disadvantages for each system. There tends to be a systematic trade-off between the ease of creating a currency and the effort needed to gain and maintain its credibility. Finding an appropriate balance between these two objectives is key for a robust currency design. All things being equal, as one goes down the above list of the different ways to issue the currency (from backed currencies to central distribution), it becomes easier for participants to create the currency; but it simultaneously requires more discipline to maintain the currency's credibility.

Currencies that have a legally enforceable collateral (as is supposed to be the case for the majority of the national currencies issued), currencies that are fully backed by a good or service that is in broad demand or that are purchased and backed with national currency logically have an easier time gaining credibility. But on the downside, often the very people who don't have the necessary collateral or cash would benefit most from a complementary currency.

Loyalty currencies have the reputation of the businesses that issue them as their main backing. Mutual credit has as significant advantage: the quantity of money created by definition always perfectly matches need. There are also no risks of inflation in mutual credit systems. By contrast, overissuing is the biggest risk run by currencies that are created by borrowing without collateral or by central issue. It is important with these latter models to cautiously control the quantity of currency issued, otherwise its depreciation and loss of credibility is a predictable outcome.

Cost Recovery Mechanisms

All payment systems cost some human effort to be kept in operation; there are typically also infrastructure expenses. While some costs may be covered in the complementary currency itself (typically labor), there is often a hard currency component (computers, internet service or telephone expenses) that need to be covered one way or the other. When that aspect hasn't been thought through, the operation and maintenance of the currency system tend to gradually deteriorate, service is provided in a haphazard way and users become more and more unhappy with the system. In short, unless some income is generated to pay for work performed, the complementary currency system is probably not going to be sustainable in the long run.

The first step is to clearly separate what costs need to be covered in conventional money from costs which can be covered with the complementary currency. There are two types of budgets to be made in each of these currencies: a start-up and an ongoing operational budget.

Next, choose options to generate income for each type of currency involved. These options are limited; what follows is an exhaustive list.

No Recovery

The first option is not to recover any of the costs. For the complementary currency component of the costs, most mutual credit systems simply open an account for "general overhead," people doing work for the system are credited and this overhead account is debited.

For other systems, or for the conventional currency component, not recovering any costs is sustainable only if the system is designed so that no such costs are incurred in the first place — or if there is a sugar-daddy organization that is willing to either provide or raise funds to make the system operational and keep it going. Some peer-to-peer systems are actually designed to incur no costs, and therefore do not need membership or recovery mechanism either. That is the case, for instance, with the WAT system in Japan, based on bills of trade issued by businesses among each other.

Flat Fee

The second classical option is to have a flat fee. That can be a periodical membership fee (typically yearly or quarterly) or an entry fee that participants pay to the central operation to be able to participate. In some cases, there are higher membership fees for businesses than for individuals. This is usually done to cover the conventional money component of costs.

Transaction Fee

Transaction fees fall in two categories: those that are based on a small percentage of the amount involved, and those that are a flat amount for each transaction. They are typically levied at the moment of the transaction, although some systems compile a monthly total instead. Transaction fees are normally levied in the same currency as the transaction itself.

Interest, Demurrage and Other Time-related Charges

In the section on store of value we discussed the issues around interest, demurrage, step functions or expiration deadline currencies. Of course, such time-related charges produce an income — although only in the type of currency involved in the transaction — and that income is a perfect candidate to cover the running expenses.

Combination

Many complementary currency systems use a combination of the above ways to cover costs. Typical examples of such combinations include:

+ Charges on both positive and negative balances beyond a certain level (i.e., demurrage and interest).
+ Membership fees used to cover conventional money expenses, while other mechanisms dealing with the complementary currency costs.

Advantages and Disadvantages of Cost Recovery Mechanisms

Of course, keeping costs as low as possible is the best approach of all. Particularly if costs in conventional currency are high, a complementary currency system is predictably going to have difficulties over time. Costs in complementary currencies are easier to deal with because, particularly with mutual credit systems, the recovery problem can be dealt with easily within the system itself.

Whenever cost recovery mechanisms are needed, there are some advantages and disadvantages in the different solutions listed above. Try to use cost recovery as an incentive that is lined up with the objectives of the system. In this sense, the worst recovery mechanism is a transaction fee, as it provides

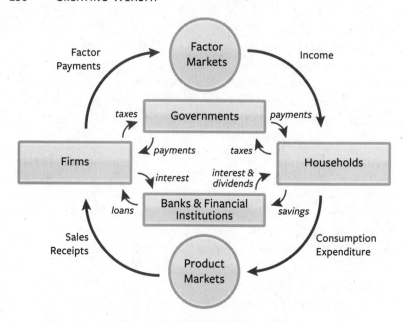

FIGURE A.1. Cycles of Economic Activity

an incentive *not* to trade with the currency. In contrast, membership fees and demurrage fees both give incentive to trade and are therefore preferable.

Establishing a System for Circulation

At this point, you have chosen an objective, recruited a Community Currency Team and selected the various mechanisms that the currency will need. The last step in designing a community currency is to make sure that you have a complete system in place for circulation.

Circulation — the word itself implies a key consideration for this phase. To be successful as a medium of exchange, currency needs to travel through the community in circles — closed loops, complete cycles. If you were an electrical engineer, you'd be looking for a "complete circuit." A simple concept, but yet this is where a lot of community currencies have failed in the past. They have neglected to establish complete circulation patterns, and as a result, there are some people who start using it, a few businesses perhaps, but the currency tends to *pool* in different parts of town, people who are using it get frustrated and it tends to deteriorate.

Our money systems functions in cycles, and these cycles are partly responsible for the multiplier effect that is so well known in economics. When money circulates through a community, is stored in banks for future use and the banks lend the money out to homeowners and businesses, then the total value that is in use in the community is greater than the absolute value that people feel they have — and the economy expands. Within these cycles, there are several important points which involve different people and organizations:

Households: Consumers, Employees, Savers, Investors

Firms: Businesses, Organizations, Producers, Service Providers, Employers, Investors

Government: Taxes and Fees, Service Delivery, Employment Support

Banks and Financial Institutions: Savings, Investment, Loans

Factor Markets: Labor Rates — Wages and Salary Levels

Product Markets: Raw Materials and Finished Products

If you show all the circulation of currency that occurs between these different points, it might look like Figure 1.

When you are designing the system for circulation of a community currency, you want to make sure that *all* of the points in this figure are involved in some way, so that the currency can circulate successfully.

Currency Design Questions

1. What are the unmet needs you would like to address?
2. Are there underutilized resources that offer themselves as a possible resource?
3. What is the objective of the currency you would like to design?
4. What support medium will you use to circulate the currency?
5. What function(s) will the currency serve?
6. What issuing procedures will you use?
7. What will your cost recovery mechanisms be?
8. Draw a circulation diagram for the currency you propose.

Case Histories

Katadhin Time Dollar Exchange

Ken Anderson grew up in a rural community in Michigan during the 1950s and 1960s. Ken grew up watching his father, a full-time farmer, barter skills to accomplish daily activities, leaving the flow of cash in the community to be maintained by those who wouldn't participate in the system of exchange. For example, instead of paying the butcher to cut up his venison after hunting season, Ken's father might shoe the butcher's horses. No money was exchanged.

While the example above was not very formalized or part of any community-wide program, Ken now participates in the Katahdin Time Dollar

Exchange. In this more formal bartering system, one time dollar is credited for each hour of service performed. Whether the service is a professional service, mowing a lawn, helping to clean a stream or playing cards with seniors at a local nursing home, for every hour you give, you get an hour back. These time dollars can be redeemed later in the form of services that you may need from someone else.

In the spirit of helping a neighbor in need, the KTDE brings people together for mutual benefit. In addition, its members perform community services for the greater benefit of the Katahdin, Maine region.[13]

Barter Systems Inc.

Barter Systems, Inc. is a commercial barter organization which aims to offers business owners and professionals other means of meeting many of their ongoing business and personal needs without using cash. BSI clients have the ability to exchange trade dollars earned by selling their products or services to other BSI client companies or to member companies belonging to other barter exchanges located throughout North America, the Caribbean, Europe, Australia and South America.

Satisfied members report that they have gained new customers and new income, but also used trade dollars to host company parties, purchase medical services and reward employees.[14]

Local Exchange Trading System (LETS)

Prior to the early 1980s, the small town of Courtenay, British Columbia was heavily dependent on a local air force base and a timber mill. Unfortunately for local residents, when some staff at the base relocated and the mill closed, the local economy plummeted. As a result, unemployment was high and people were experiencing significant financial hardship.

The LETS program was established around 1983, introducing the *green dollar* (the LETS currency). This system allowed people to exchange goods and services with one another even when they didn't have access a lot of official Canadian dollars. The LETS network allowed members to participate in the economy without needing an employer or having money to spend. An additional positive aspect of LETS in Courtenay was that the use of green dollars freed up more Canadian dollars for other uses. It was also an efficient and inexpensive way for local businesses to advertise, since participating businesses were listed in a local directory.

Resources

General Framework

Global Community Initiatives. global-community.org.
Currency Solutions for a Wiser World. lietaer.com.

Commercial Barter Systems

Barter Systems, Inc website. [online]. [cited December 28, 2010]. bartersys
.com/index.asp. A leader in the commercial barter industry which of-
fers exchange by way of goods and services and no cash.
Colin Harrison. *Project Proposal: CyberTroc — A Barter System for the
Information Society.* [online]. [cited December 28, 2010]. ict-21.ch/ICT
.SATW.CH/IMG/doc/ProjectProposalCyberTroc_c.doc. An article
about CyberTroc, a type of internet-based barter system.
Hazel, Henderson. *Paradigms in Progress: Life Beyond Economics*
(Indianapolis: Knowledge Systems Inc. 1991)
Hazel, Henderson. *Ethical Markets: Growing the Green Economy* (Vermont:
Chelsea Green Publishing. 2006)

Mutual Credit Systems

Thomas H. Greco, Jr. "Chapter 12: Community Empowerment through
Mutual Credit Systems." *New Money for Healthy Communities.* [online].
[cited December 28, 2010]. ratical.org/many_worlds/cc/NMfHC/chp
12.html.
Complementary Currency Resource Center website. [online]. [cited December 28, 2010]. complementarycurrency.org.

LETS Systems

LETSystems — The Home Page. [online]. [cited December 28, 2010]. www
.gmlets.u-net.com. An excellent source, providing several links to sites
with information about issues, administration software, organization
and user materials.
LETS-Linkup International LETS Directory. [online]. [cited December 28,
2010]. lets-linkup.com. An international LETS groups directory with a
guide to over 1,500 LETS groups from 39 countries.

Transaction Net: Local Exchange Trading Systems — LETS. [online]. [cited December 28, 2010]. transaction.net/money/lets. A complete description and glossary of terms related to LETS and other currency systems.

John "The Anti-Poverty Engineer" Turmel website. [online]. [cited December 28, 2010]. cyberclass.net/turmel. Links to many LETS currency press reports and articles.

Time Banks

The TimeKeeper Organization. What is the Time Dollar Network? [online]. [cited December 28, 2010]. www.timekeeper.org/whatis.html. Information about what drives the Time Dollar and how it can benefit the economy.

Time Banks USA website. [online]. [cited December 28, 2010]. timebanks .org/. An organization which works towards building local economies and communities that reward decency, caring and a passion for justice through its Time Banks system.

Time Dollar Tutoring. [online]. [cited December 28, 2010]. timedollartutor ing.blogspot.com. An organization which works with students using a Time Banking system to track the time they give as tutors.

San Antonio Time Dollar Community Connections website. [online]. [cited December 28, 2010]. mc-sa.org/partners/neighborhood/time dollar.asp.

Local Currencies

E. F. Schumacher Society. *Local Currencies.* [online]. [cited December 28, 2010]. smallisbeautiful.org/local_currencies.html.

Transaction Net. Complementary Community Currency Systems and Local Exchange Networks. [online]. [cited December 28, 2010]. trans action.net/money/community/index.html.

Roy Davies. "Alternative Currency Systems: Local and Interest-Free Currencies, Social Credit, Social Lending and Microcredit etc." *Money — Past, Present & Future.* [online]. [cited December 28, 2010]. projects .exeter.ac.uk/RDavies/arian/local.html.

Ithaca Hours — Local Currency — Ithaca, New York. [online]. [cited December 28, 2010]. ithacahours.com/.

Economic Development and Community Currency

Creating a community currency is not the only way to strengthen your local economy and build real wealth. There are many other aspects of community life that need to be addressed as well.

Global Community Initiatives has worked in partnership with Natural Capitalism Solutions and the America's Development Foundation to create a new workbook for local communities to revitalize and develop their local economies in ways that build real wealth, enhance the quality of life and protect and restore the natural environment. The workbook is called *LASER — Local Action for Sustainable Economic Renewal*.

LASER is designed to help you initiate economic renewal activities in your local community. Each idea in the workbook is accompanied by a step-by-step tool that helps you put the ideas into practice. The Guide is based on the idea that we can satisfy our common human needs by building on our strengths, intervening at the system level and integrating all the different parts of community life into a whole package, rather than trying to tinker with different problems in isolation.

The principles and activities outlined in *LASER* are relevant whether you live in a rural village in Afghanistan or a neighborhood in a modern western city. The details will obviously differ, but the broad opportunities exist everywhere. All it takes is you. *LASER* describes how you can take control of your own future and begin to create the sort of economy that will bring real jobs, real prosperity and a high quality of life to you and your family.

Please visit our website at global-community.org or the *LASER* website at global-laser.org for more information.

Notes

Chapter 1

1. *Collins English Dictionary*, Complete and Unabridged. HarperCollins, 2003, s.v. "wealth."
2. United Nations General Assembly. *Report of the World Commission on Environment and Development.* A/RES/42/187, 11 December, 1987. [online]. [cited October 15, 2010]. un.org/documents/ga/res/42/ares42 -187.htm.
3. Jane Jacobs. *Cities and the Wealth of Nations: Principles of Economic Life.* Random House, 1984.
4. *ICLEI: Local Governments for Sustainability.* [online]. [cited October 19, 2010]. iclei.org/.
5. *United Cities and Local Governments* official website. [online]. [cited October 19, 2010]. cities-localgovernments.org/.

Chapter 2

1. G. Caprio and D. Klingelbiel. "Bank Insolvencies: Cross Country Experience." *Policy Research Working Papers #1620.* World Bank, Policy and Research Department, 1996; J. Frankel and A. Rose. "Currency Crashes in Emerging Markets: an Empirical Treatment." *Journal of International Economics* (1996), Vol. 4, pp. 351–366; G. Kaminsky and C. Reinhart. "The Twin Crisis: the Causes of Banking and Balance of Payment Problems." *American Economic Review,* Vol. 89 #3 (1999), pp. 473–500.
2. Henry Ford. *My Life and Work.* Doubleday, Page & Company, 1922, p. 179.
3. Bernard Lietaer. *The Future of Money: Creating New Wealth, Work and a Wiser World.* Century, 2002, pp. 50–51.
4. Herman E. Daly and John B. Cobb. *For the Common Good: Revitalizing the Economy Toward Community, the Environment, and a Sustainable Future,* 2nd ed. Beacon Press, 1994.
5. Marjorie Deane and Robert Pringle. *The Central Banks.* Viking, 1995.
6. Quoting a speech made by Michael Schuman in Vermont in the winter of 2007.
7. Amory Lovins. "Natural Capitalism." *Resurgence* #198 (January/February

2000). [online]. [cited October 23, 2010]. resurgence.org/magazine /article1806-natural-capitalism.html.

8. The environmental crises in the region prompted Eastern European governments to request assistance from the US EPA. The Institute for Sustainable Communities (ISC) worked with the EPA to establish Environmental Management Training Centers in several countries — Poland, Bulgaria, Hungary, Ukraine and Russia — so that the regulators in these countries could learn from their western counterparts. One of us worked for ISC at the time.

9. US Bureau of Labor Statistics website: bls.gov/.

10. Merriam-Webster Dictionary. [online]. [cited January 17, 2011]. merriam -webster.com/dictionary/system.

11. For more information about all the system archetypes, there are many good resources. One helpful source is: *Mental Model Musings*. [online]. [cited October 24, 2010]. systems-thinking.org. To see how the archetypes apply to community development: "Conducting and Understanding a Trend Analysis." *Local Action for Sustainable Economic Renewal (LASER)*. [online]. [cited October 24, 2010]. global-laser.org/resources /trend_analysis.pdf.

12. In systems diagrams, the feedback between variables, represented by the arrows, is either positive or negative. *Positive feedback* (marked as a +) means that the next variable changes in the same direction as the previous one, so if you're talking about healthcare, *lower* access to treatment leading to *lower* individual health is positive feedback. *Negative feedback* (marked as a o) means the next variable changes in the opposite direction as the previous one, so *lower* health leading to a *higher* demand for treatment is negative feedback. The important thing is the effect of the feedback — the words higher and lower are used here for illustration. Another important symbol illustrates when there is a delay in the feedback; in these diagrams, delay is indicated by two lines: /o/.

When the combination of feedback in a system is positive, this creates a *reinforcing feedback loop*, symbolized here with an R. Reinforcing feedback is a vicious or virtuous cycle — things are getting worse and worse, or better and better. When the combination of feedback in the system is negative, this creates a *balancing feedback loop*, symbolized here with a B. In these systems, there is equilibrium — the system behaves as if it were seeking a goal of staying in balance. When there is delay in the timing of feedback between variables, systems can change from being reinforcing to balancing and vice versa over time; when there is a number next to the B or the R, it means that after delay, the system dynamic has changed. Sometimes there are several changes in the system, which would be illustrated by R1, B2, R3 and so on.

13. Dennis and Donella Meadows, Jorgen Randers and William Behrens. *The Limits to Growth.* Signet, 1972; Donella H. Meadows, Jorgen Randers and Dennis L. Meadows. *Limits to Growth: The 30-Year Update.* Chelsea Green, 2004.

14. R2 calculation courtesy of Chris Martenson, from a presentation he made in Reykjavik, Iceland for the Balaton Group in September of 2010.

15. John Maynard Keynes. *Economic Consequences of the Peace.* Harcourt Brace, 1920, chapter 6.

16. *Blackwater Lodge and Training Center, Inc. v. Broughton et al.,* and *City of San Diego v. Blackwater Lodge and Training Center, Inc.* [online]. [cited January 17, 2011]. dockets.justia.com/docket/california/casdce /3:2008cv00926/271052/.

17. Stephen A. Zarlenga. *The Lost Science of Money: The Mythology of Money, The Story of Power.* American Monetary Institute, 2002.

18. Personal conversations with city leaders over the past 20 years.

19. Calculated by the authors from the Milennium Development Goals.

Chapter 3

1. Merriam Webster dictionary, s.v. "capitalism" [online]. [cited October 25, 2010]. merriam-webster.com/dictionary/capitalism.

2. See Figure 1 in Chapter 7 for details.

3. See a full development of this approach in: Bernard A. Lietaer. *The Future of Money: Creating New Wealth, Work and a Wiser World.* Random House, 2001.

4. Total volume of outstanding Frequent Flyer Miles is estimated at 14 trillion, worth about US$700 billion: Jenni Roth. "Die schlummernde Weltwährung: Fluggäste haben 14 Billionen Bonusmeilen angesammelt." *Der Tagesspiegel* (17 Januar 2005).

5. Time Bank is a trademarked term of Time Banks USA and will be capitalized throughout this book.

Chapter 4

1. Bernard Lietaer. *The Mystery of Money.* Riemann Verlag, 2000, p. 182.

2. M.I. Finley. *The Ancient Economy,* Sather Classical Lectures Volume 43. University of California Press, 1985. Cited in Lietaer, p. 166.

3. Lietaer, p. 209.

4. Lietaer, p. 173.

5. Bernard Lietaer and Stephen Belgin. *Of Human Wealth: Beyond Greed and Scarcity.* Human Wealth Books and Talks, 2005.

6. See L. Randall Wray. *Understanding Modern Money: the Key to Full Employment and Price Stability.* Edward Elgar Publishing, 2006.

7. See Bernard Lietaer and Stephen De Meulenaere. "Sustaining cultural vitality in a globalizing world: the Balinese example." *International Journal of Social Economics*, Vol 30#9 (September 2003).

8. The term comes from renowned economist Neva Goodwin, who felt it important to give a positive name to that portion of the "non-market" economy.

9. In 1981, the value of the economic production by households was estimated by Robert Eisner and his colleagues at Northwestern to total $1,709 billion. That amounted to 37.5% of the "extended GNP" of $4,560 billion. In 1998, Redefining Progress, a nonprofit organization based in San Francisco, pegged the value of household work in 1998 at a total of $1.911 trillion — about ¼ the size of the US gross domestic product (GDP) that year.

10. Edgar Cahn. *It's the Core Economy stupid: An Open Letter to the Non-Profit Community.* [online]. [cited October 27, 2010]. timebanks.org /documents/CoreEconomyOp-Ed_000.pdf.

Chapter 5

1. RealtyTrac.® *US Foreclosure Market Report,* November 13, 2008. [online]. realtytrac.com.

2. Lynn Adler. "US 2009 Foreclosures Shatter Record Despite Aid." *Reuters News Service,* January 14, 2010. [online]. [cited September 6, 2010]. reuters.com/article/idUSTRE60D0LZ20100114.

3. RealtyTrac.® *US Foreclosure Market Report,* August, 2010. [online]. [cited September 6, 2010]. browse.realtytrac.com/2010/foreclosures/.

4. United States Department of Labor. Bureau of Labor Statistics website: bls.gov.

5. Ross Colvin. "Family Homelessness Rising in the United States." *Reuters News,* November 12, 2008.

6. US HUD, Community Planning and Development. *Neighborhood Stabilization Program Grants.* [online]. [cited October 28, 2010]. hud.gov /offices/cpd/communitydevelopment/programs/neighborhoodspg/.

Chapter 6

1. A Native American and African American poet from Hartford, CT. Born in 1820, she is the first woman to have published a book of poems and essays in the United States.
2. US Census Bureau News. "College Degree Nearly Doubles Annual Earnings." *Census Bureau Reports*, March 28, 2005.
3. US Census data.
4. 2000 US Census.
5. Grace E. Merritt. "College-Loan Ploys Probed." *Hartford Courant*, June 25, 2007.
6. Steve Kroft. "For-Profit Colleges: Costly Lesson." *60 Minutes*. CBS News, January 30, 2005.
7. With gratitude to David Orr for contributing this component. See also: Beyond Bells and Whistles. *Retention Rate Model*. [online]. [cited November 2, 2010]. cofc.edu/bellsandwhistles/research/retentionmodel .html; The National Learning Laboratory. [online]. [cited November 2, 2010]. know.org.
8. The original funding source was finally not used for this purpose. See Bernard Lietaer. "A Proposal for a Brazilian Education Complementary Currency." Paper presented for publication in the *International Journal for Community Currency Research*, Vol. 10 (2006). [online]. [cited November 2, 2010]. www.uea.ac.uk/env/ijccr/abstracts/vol10(3) lietaer.html.
9. Such an expiration penalty is a form of demurrage. See Chapter 4 and Bernard Lietaer and Stephen Belgin. *Of Human Wealth: Beyond Greed and Scarcity*. Human Wealth Books and Talks, 2005, pp. 104–110.
10. *Encyclopaedia Britannica*.

Chapter 7

1. National Endowment for the Arts. *Artists in the Workforce: 1990–2005*. Research Report #48 (May 2008).
2. CollegeGrad.com. *Career Information — Artists and Related Workers*. [online]. [cited April 15, 2009]. collegegrad.com/careers/prof21.shtml.
3. Murray Whyte. "'Starving Artist' Image Only Too True." *Toronto Star*, March 31, 2009.
4. International Average Salary Income Database. *United States Average Salaries and Expenditures*. [online]. [cited April 15, 2009]. worldsalaries .org/usa.shtml.

5. United Artists Reserve Note. [online]. [cited August 30, 2010]. artist reservenote.com.
6. US Bailout. *Fluxus Bucks the Next Currency?* March 14, 2009. [online]. [cited August 30, 2010]. usabailout.blogspot.com/2009/03/fluxus -bucks-next-currency.html.

Chapter 8

1. Martin Cohen. "Beyond Debate?" *The Times Higher Education*, December 10, 2009. [online]. [cited December 17, 2010]. timeshighereducation .co.uk/story.asp?storycode=409454.
2. Alan Durning with Anna Fahey, Eric de Place, Lisa Stiffler and Clark Williams-Derry. *Cap and Trade 101: A Climate Policy Primer*, July 2009 Federal Policy edition. Sightline Institute. [online]. [cited November 4, 2010]. sightline.org/research/energy/res_pubs/cap-and-trade-101.
3. Ibid., pp. 27–28.
4. This carbon currency system was developed with substantial input from David Johnston, founder and President of What's Working (whatsworking.com).
5. See their website: builditgreen.org.
6. Fiona Harvey and Stephen Fidler. "Industry caught in carbon 'smoke-screen.'" *Financial Times*, April 25, 2007. [online]. [cited January 10, 2011]. ft.com/cms/s/0/48e334ce-f355-11db-9845-000b5df10621.html #ixzz19jbUUwWe.
7. Ibid.
8. See Lietaer, *The Future of Money*, note on page 71: "See Kobayashi, Kazunori Community Currency (Unpublished Senior Thesis, May 9, 1999)...."

Chapter 9

1. Clive Humby, Terry Hunt and Tim Phillips. *Scoring Points: How Tesco Continues to Win Customer Loyalty*, 2nd ed. Kogan Page, 2008.
2. LoyaltyMatch website. [online]. [cited November 5, 2010]. loyaltymatch .com.
3. Patent application title: Point Of Interaction Loyalty Currency Redemption in a Transaction. [online]. [cited November 5, 2010]. faqs .org/patents/app/20100211469.
4. Swissinfo.ch. *Cash substitute greases business wheels*. October 21, 2009. [online]. [cited December 12, 2010]. swissinfo.ch/eng/business/Cash _substitute_greases_business_wheels.html?cid=7613810.

5. Cyclos Project. [online]. [cited November 8, 2010]. project.cyclos.org/.
6. Chartered Banker. "Complementary Currencies: Hands Up for a Money Revolution." [online]. [cited January 22, 2011]. www.chartered banker.com/Home/Member_and_Students/Chartered_Banker_ Magazine/December_2010_January_2011/Dec_Jan_Features/Dec_ Jan_Money_Revolution/.

Chapter 10

1. David Schab and Nhi-Ha T. Trinh. "Do Artificial Food Colors Promote Hyperactivity in Children with Hyperactive Syndromes? A Meta-Analysis of Double-Blind Placebo-Controlled Trials." *Journal of Developmental and Behavioral Pediatrics*, Vol. 25#6 (December 2004), pp. 423–434.
2. Stephen Daniells. "FDA urged to ban artificial colors linked to hyper-activity." Foodnavigator — USA website, June 4, 2008. [online]. [cited December 8, 2010].
3. OECD Directorate for Employment, Labour and Social Affairs. *Health at a Glance 2003 — OECD Countries Struggle with Rising Demand for Health Spending.* [online]. [cited December 8, 2010]. oecd.org/doc ument/6/0,2340,en_2649_34631_16560422_1_1_1_1,00.html.
4. Ernst & Young. *Gesundheitsversorgung 2020.* Frankfurt, 2005. [online]. [cited December 8, 2010]. rsf.uni-greifswald.de/fileadmin/mediapool /lehrstuehle/flessa/Gesundheitsversorgung_202020.pdf.
5. *OECD Health Data 2006: How Does the United States Compare.* [online]. [cited October 16, 2009. oecd.org/dataoecd/29/52/36960035.pdf.
6. All data on bankruptcy through medical bills comes from Elizabeth Warren. "Sick and Broke." *The Washington Post*, Wednesday, February 9, 2005, p. A23. [online]. [cited December 8, 2010]. washingtonpost.com/ wp-dyn/articles/A9447-2005Feb8.html.
7. B.D. Smedley and S.L. Syme, eds. *Promoting Health: Intervention Strat-egies from Social and Behavioral Research.* Institute of Medicine, 2000.
8. J.E. Fielding. "Getting Smarter and Maybe Wiser." *American Journal of Health Promotion*, Vol. 11#2 (November–December 1996), pp. 109–111.
9. IRSA, Association of Quality Clubs. "The Economic Benefits of Em-ployee Fitness." 1992. fitresource.com.
10. Michael Murphy. *The Future of the Body: Explorations Into the Further Evolution Of Human Nature.* Tarcher, 1992.
11. The benefit is mainly manifesting in such programs after the second or third year. So 100 dollars or Euros spent in an preventive care program

for employees each year will have a return after the third year of 300 dollars or euros. R. Z. Goetzel et al. "What is ROI? A Systematic Review of Return on Investment Studies of Corporate Health and Productivity Management Initiatives." AWHP's *Worksite Health*, Vol. 6, 1999; J. C. Erfurt, A. Foote, M. A. Heirich. "The cost effectiveness of worksite wellness programs for hypertension control, weight loss, smoking cessation and exercise." *Personnel Psychology*, Vol. 45#1, March 1992, pp. 5–27; L. Chapman. *Proof Positive: An Analysis of the Cost Effectiveness of Worksite Wellness*, 6th ed. Chapman Institute, 2008; Don R. Powell. "Characteristics of Successful Wellness Programs." *Employee Benefits Journal*, September 1999, pp. 15–21; S. G. Aldana. "Financial Impact of Worksite Health Promotion and Methodological Quality of the Evidence." *The Art of Health Promotion*, Vol. 2#1, March–April, 1998; L. Chapman. "Methods for Determining Economic Return." *The Art of Health Promotion*, Vol 4#6, January–February 2001; L. Chapman. "Meta Evaluation of Worksite Health Promotion Economic Return Studies." *The Art of Health Promotion*, Vol. 6#6, January–February, 2003.

12. Time Bank Models — Elder Care. [online]. [cited January 22, 2011]. besttimebank.org/Links/Time%Dollar/Elder%Care.htm; David Boyle. "The Co-Production Principle and Time Dollars." [online]. [cited January 22, 2011]. timebanks.org/documents/Co-ProductionPrinciple .pdf.

13. This cash-in option deserves more explanation. Businesses providing goods or services that are supporting preventive healthcare could become certified through a formal evaluation process that determines the economic impact on future medical costs. Basically, any thing or service that has been able to convincingly demonstrate an impact on reducing future medical care costs could qualify for this process.

 The discount and conditions for cashing-in should be designed to be covered by a reduction in medical costs made possible by the preventive programs and by home care activities (which reduce the length of a hospital stay for example). Furthermore, there should be some discount in cashing in the Tokens to encourage business owners and preventive healthcare providers to use them rather than always cashing them in. The cost of the cashing-in program should be paid by those entities that derive the direct financial benefits (reduction in costs) from a healthy society (e.g., HMOs, businesses, insurance companies and governments).

14. Laura Petreccca. "Cost conscious companies re-evaluate wellness programs." *USA Today*, June 19, 2009.

15. Ibid.

16. "Should Smoker's Pay a Surcharge?" HR.BLR.com. April 7, 2006. [online]. [cited October 26, 2009]. hr.blr.com/news.aspx?id=17927.

17. Petrecca, "Cost Conscious."

Chapter 11

1. Recent archaeological discoveries have found the remains of Ur; it's called Tell-y-Mukayyar and is located near the city of Nasiriyah, south of Baghdad in modern Iraq.

2. All data in this paragraph from US Censuses from 2002 and 2005.

3. National Research Council Panel to Review Risk and Prevalence of Elder Abuse and Neglect. *Elder Mistreatment: Abuse, Neglect, and Exploitation in an Aging America*. National Academies Press, 2002.

4. *Child Maltreatment 2003*. Administration for Children and Families, US Department of Health and Human Services, 2005.

5. Time Bank® is a trademark of TimeBanks USA. Instead of putting the little ® next to all the references, we have capitalized the words instead.

6. TimeBanks website. "The Five Core Values of Time Banking." [online]. [cited December 7, 2010]. timebanks.org/five-core-values.htm.

7. Care Bank® is also a trademark of TimeBanks USA.

8. National Institute of Population and Social Security Research. *Selected Demographic Indicators for Japan*. [online]. [cited January 22, 2011]. ipss .go.jp/p-info/e/S_D_I/Indip.html.

9. *A l'écoute du Japon* — Information Bulletin of the Japanese Mission to the European Union. July 3, 1995, pp. 7–8.

10. Robert Wood Johnson Foundation. *Service Credit Banking Project Site Summaries*. University of Maryland Center of Aging, 1990.

11. Junko Edahiro. "Locally Sustainable Economy Supported by Community Currency." Via3Net website. [online]. [cited November 30, 2009]. via3.net/pooled/articles/BF_DOCART/view.asp?Q=BF_DOCART _137159.

Chapter 12

1. J.E. Yellen. "The Transformation of the Kalahari !Kung." *Scientific American*, Vol. 262#4. 1990, pp. 96–105.

2. Bernard Lietaer and Steven Belgin. *Of Human Wealth: Beyond Greed and Scarcity*. Human Wealth Books and Talks, 2005.

3. United Nations Department of Economic and Social Affairs, Population Division. *World Urbanization Prospects: The 2005 Revision.*[online]. [cited November 13, 2008]. un.org/esa/population/publications/WUP 2005/2005wup.htm.

4. *Northeast Bankcorp, Inc. v. Governors, FRS,* 472 U.S. 159 (1985) at 165.

5. Tom Philpott."A reflection on the lasting legacy of 1970s USDA Secretary Earl Butz." *Grist: Environmental News and Commentary,* February 7, 2008. [online]. [cited November 13, 2008]. grist.org/comments/food /2008/02/07/.

6. Bruce A. Babcock."Cheap Food and Farm Subsidies: Policy Impacts of a Mythical Connection." *Iowa Ag Review* (Spring, 2006).

7. Institute for Food and Development Policy."Food, Fuel, and Green Revolutions: The U.S. 2007 Farm Bill Slogs Forward." *Food First: News and Views,* October 5, 2007. [online]. [cited November 11, 2008]. food first.org/en/node/1777.

8. International Relations Center."Congress Rejects Food Aid for Local Development." *Global Policy Forum,* [online]. [cited November 14, 2008]. globalpolicy.org/socecon/hunger/relief/2005/1021congr.htm.

9. State of New Jersey Department of Agriculture."School Lunch Commodity Distribution Program." [online]. [cited November 14, 2008]. www.state.nj.us/agriculture/divisions/fn/fooddistrib/slcd.html.

10. Centers for Disease Control and Prevention. *Children and Diabetes— More Information.* [online]. [cited December 10, 2010]. cdc.gov/diabetes /projects/cda2.htm.

11. Woody Tasch. *Inquiries Into the Nature of Slow Money: Investing as if Food, Farms, and Fertility Mattered.* Chelsea Green, 2010.

12. Elizabeth Sawin et al. *Commodity System Challenges: Moving Sustainability into the Mainstream of Natural Resource Economies.* Sustainability Institute Report, 2003. [online]. [cited December 13, 2010]. sustainer. org/pubs/SustainableCommoditySys.2.1.pdf.

13. Michael Pollan."Why Bother." *New York Times Magazine,* April 20, 2008.

14. Leesa Woodhouse. *Rice as Currency.* October 2006. [online]. [cited December 11, 2009]. e-articles.info/e/a/title/Rice-Currency/.

15. Ibid.

16. Jason Bradford."Food-backed Local Money." *The Oil Drum:Campfire* website, March 4, 2009. [online]. [cited January 11, 2011]. campfire.the oildrum.com/node/5158.

17. Farm Stand website: vtfarmstand.org.

Chapter 13

1. Mark Lipton (*Guiding Growth: How Vision Keeps Companies On Course*. Harvard Business Press, 2003) in an interview with Martha Lagace. Harvard Business School Working Knowledge for Business Leaders, February 24, 2003. [online]. [cited December 14, 2010]. wiki .aalto.fi/download/attachments/44302349/Lagace+(2003)+Why+Vision+Matters+More+Than+Ever.pdf?version=1&modificationDate =1272361748000.

2. Gwendolyn Hallsmith. *The Key to Sustainable Cities: Meeting Human Needs, Transforming Community Systems*. New Society, 2003.

3. *Burlington Legacy Plan*, p. 10. [online]. [cited December 13, 2010]. cedo .ci.burlington.vt.us/legacy/Burlington%Legacy%Plan.pdf.

4. Ibid, p. 26.

5. Burlington Legacy Project. *Projects and Activities*. [online]. [cited December 13, 2010]. cedo.ci.burlington.vt.us/legacy/projects.html.

6. Ibid.

7. City of Burlington Energy and Environment Coordinating Committee. *Suggestions to Advance Sustainable Transportation in Burlington*. [online]. [cited December 13, 2010]. cedo.ci.burlington.vt.us/legacy/City %Council%Recs%Update%May%12.pdf.

8. Ibid.

9. Burlington Legacy Project. *Projects and Activities*.

10. Wanda Hines. *Social Equity Investment Project Annual Report 2007–2008*. City of Burlington. [online]. [cited May 19, 2009]. cedo.ci.burling ton.vt.us/legacy/SEIP2008AnnualReport.pdf.

Chapter 14

1. The Melbourne Principles had a link to the Earth Charter in their embryonic stages — even though the principles were named after the City of Melbourne, Australia they had their genesis in Toronto, Ontario in 2002, where UNEP sponsored a meeting about sustainable city planning. Gwendolyn was invited to this meeting and presented the Earth Charter's history and how it inspired the cities and towns in Vermont to endorse it, along with information about the Burlington project. The idea of a set of principles to guide city planning caught on, but instead of simply adopting the Earth Charter, the team from UNEP decided to create something new. The Melbourne Principles hold a lot in common with the Earth Charter, and were going to reference the document in the second and final draft, but the final draft

never got printed as the personalities involved went off in different directions. Unlike the Earth Charter, the Melbourne Principles do not have a broad base of support from a global audience, nor do they have an ongoing educational effort to keep them relevant. ICLEI Oceania. *Melbourne Principles for Sustainable Cities.* [online]. [cited December 14, 2010]. www.iclei.org/index.php?id=4490.

2. Through all this work, a rich set of resources on how to apply systems thinking to cities was created. This material is all available now on the LASER website (more about LASER in Chapter 3), which you can read by going directly to: global-laser.org/resources/trend_analysis.pdf.

3. Noted down by Gwendolyn during a joint lecture for the Cities PLUS Network at the World Urban Forum in June of 2006.

4. ImagineCALGARY Plan for Long Range Urban Sustainability. June 2006, p. 192. [online]. [cited December 16, 2010]. imaginecalgary.ca /imagineCALGARY_long_range_plan.pdf.

5. Ibid. p. 194.

6. Calgary had enough funding for the project to develop their own, but a free version of it is available on the EarthCAT website: earthcat.org.

7. ImagineCALGARY Plan for Long Range Urban Sustainability, p. 1.

8. More information about the currency can be found on the website calgarydollars.ca.

9. *Plan-It Newburgh: Sustainable Master Plan,* Adopted December 8, 2008, p. 8 [online]. [cited December 17, 2010]. cityofnewburgh-ny.gov/master plan/docs/MasterPlan2006-9-10.pdf.

10. Jean-Ann McGrane in a video interview at the kickoff event for Plan-It Newburgh.

11. Doyle Murphy. "Newburgh Begins Search for New City Manager." *Times Herald-Record,* January 14, 2009.

12. *Sociocracy: The Organization of Decision-Making* is the title of a book by Gerard Endenburg (Eburon, 1998), about a unique model of group process he developed for his manufacturing business in the Netherlands. It has been further articulated and developed by many social change professionals. The structure of enVision Montpelier — with two interlinking chairs for each committee, one appointed from the main decision making body and one elected from the group — reflects one of the principles Endenburg advocates. The election process is a particularly good one for sustainability planning (and other public purposes). To conduct an election, everyone nominates someone, writing their nominee on a piece of paper with their own name on it too. The election is facilitated

by either a neutral party or by someone who volunteers from the group, and the facilitator collects the nominations and reads them out loud. After this, each person talks about why they nominated the person they offered. Then each of the nominees have a chance to say a few words (including whether or not they are willing to serve). After this, a decision making round is held, where each person states whether they have changed their mind, and if they have, whom they would like to lead the group. It is an excellent way to bring people forward into leadership who might not be ones who usually volunteer for these positions.

Conclusion

1. See various examples of such evidence, for instance, in any issue of the *International Journal of Community Currency Research*. [online]. [cited December 20, 2010]. uea.ac.uk/env/ijccr/.

2. See Chapter 2.

3. Robert Ulanowicz, Sally Goerner, Bernard Lietaer, Rocio Gomez. "Quantifying Sustainability: Resilience, Efficiency and the Return of Information Theory." *Ecological Complexity* Vol 6 #1 (March 2009), pp. 27–36.

4. Bernard Lietaer, Robert Ulanowicz and Sally Goerner. "Is Our Monetary Structure a Systemic Cause for Financial Instability? Evidence and Remedies from Nature." *Journal of Future Studies* (April 2010); Bernard Lietaer, Robert Ulanowicz and Sally Goerner. "Options for Managing Systemic Financial Crisis." *Sapiens* Vol 2 #1 (March 2009).

5. Sally Goerner, Bernard Lietaer, Robert Ulanowicz. "Quantifying Economic Sustainability: Implications for Free Enterprise Theory, Policy and Practice." *Ecological Economics* Vol 69 #1 (October 2009), pp. 76–81.

6. See Chapter 7.

7. Gerhard Rösl. *Regional Currencies in Germany: Local Competition for the Euro?* Deutsche Bundesbank Discussion Paper Series 1: Economic Studies, No. 43/2006. [online]. [cited December 20, 2010]. bundesbank .de/download/volkswirtschaft/dkp/2006/200643dkp_en.pdf.

8. Chartalism was developed by economist G. F. Knapp into the 1920s. It was influential on the 1930 *Treatise on Money* by John Maynard Keynes — Knapp and Chartalism are cited approvingly in its opening pages. Chartalism experienced a revival under Abba P. Lerner in *The Economics of Control* (1944) and later in *The Economics of Employment* (1951). It also has a number of modern proponents who largely identify as post-Keynesian economists. A good recent synthesis is provided

by L. Randall Wray in *Understanding Modern Money: The Key to Full Employment and Price Stability*. Edward Elgar, 2006.

9. See Chapter 9.

10. See Chapter 11.

Appendix

1. It was Chartalist Georg Friedrich Knapp who defined money as anything that the government declares as acceptable in payment for taxes. See Georg Friedrich Knapp. *The State Theory of Money*. Augustus M. Kelley, 1924 and L. Randall Wray. *Understanding Modern Money: The Key to Full Employment and Price Stability*. Edward Edgar, 2006.

2. There are nevertheless exceptions, but they tend to be temporary in today's world: for instance, in Russia the government accepted commodities and goods from corporations in payment of taxes after the collapse of the Ruble in 1998.

3. See Chapter 9.

4. Ibid.

5. The first (in chronological order) post-war complementary currency pioneer was Teruko Mizushima, who was born in 1920 in Osaka. In 1950 she wrote a visionary article about a "Labor Bank," a paper that was honored at that time with the Newspaper Companies' Prize.

6. The organization involved is called Regeltante: see regeltante.nl.

7. For more information on all the Japanese currency projects, see Bernard Lietaer. "Complementary Currencies in Japan Today: History, Originality and Relevance." *International Journal of Community Currency Research*, Vol. 8 (2004), pp.1-23 [online]. [cited December 21, 2010]. uea.ac.uk/env/ijccr/abstracts/vol8(1)lietaer.html.

8. Global Community Initiatives. [online]. [cited December 20, 2010]. global-community.org/.

9. *History of Money: 1930-1933.* [online]. [cited January 16, 2011]. mind contagion.org/money/hm1930.html.

10. The Terra (TRC) Trade Reference Currency. [online]. [cited December 22, 2010]. terratrc.org/.

11. The Department of Economic History of Bocconi University in Milan, Italy, has undertaken a systematic study of such historical complementary currencies. They have discovered many such currencies widely used locally in Europe from the 8th century to the 18th. Such currencies were circulating in parallel with centrally issued currency, some were even issued by central authorities, but they were not accepted for payment in

taxes by the central government (royal or imperial). See Luca Fantacci. *Storia della moneta immaginaria*. Marsilio Editore, 2004; Jacques Labrot. *Une histoire économique et populaire du Moyen-Age: les jetons et les méreaux*. Editions Errance, 1989.

12. The banking system partially resolves that problem by relending funds that people deposit with them. But, particularly from a regional viewpoint, there is no guarantee that the money will become available within the same community or area where it originated.

13. Ken Anderson. "Katahdin Time Dollar Exchange." *Magic City Morning Star*, May 18, 2005. [online]. [cited December 27, 2010]. magic-city-news .com/Community_5/Katahdin_Time_Dollar_Exchange_38833883 .shtml.

14. Barter Systems, Inc. *Success Stories*. [online]. [cited December 27, 2010]. bartersys.com/success.asp.

Index

About the Authors

GWENDOLYN HALLSMITH, The Director of Planning and Community Development for the City of Montpelier and founder and director of Global Community Initiatives, is author of *The Key to Sustainable Cities, Taking Action: the EarthCAT Guide to Community Development,* and *Local Action for Sustainable Economic Renewal,* has over 20 years of experience working with municipal, regional and state government in the United States and internationally. She has served as the Town Manager of Randolph, Vermont, the Regional Planning Director in Franklin County, MA, as a Senior Planner for the Massachusetts Executive Office of Energy Resources, as the Deputy Secretary of the Vermont Agency of Natural Resources and for over ten years as an international specialist on sustainable community development.

Her international experience has included work with the United Nations Environment Program, the United Nations Development Program, the Institute for Sustainable Communities, the International City/County Management Association and Earth Charter International. She has a Master's degree in Public Policy from Brown University and studied at the Andover Newton Theological School, exploring the links between our wisdom traditions, spirituality and work on the community level.

BERNARD LIETAER, the author of *The Future of Money: Beyond Greed and Scarcity* and the forthcoming *Of Human Wealth,* has been active in the realm of money systems in a wide variety of functions for close to 40 years. With the publication of his post-graduate thesis at MIT in 1971 (which included a description of *floating exchanges*) and the Nixon Shock of that same year which eradicated the Bretton Woods system by unhinging the US dollar value from its gold standard and inaugurated

the new era of universal floating exchanges (previous to that time the only floating exchanges involved some exotic currencies in Latin America), the fledgling management consultant suddenly found himself at the center of the financial world's attention.

The techniques that he had developed for those marginal Latin American currencies were overnight the only systematic research which could be used to deal with all of the major currencies of the world. A major US bank negotiated exclusive rights to Bernard's approach, which required that he begin another career. While at the central bank in Belgium (National Bank of Belgium) he implemented the convergence mechanism (ECU) to the single European currency system. During that period, he also served as President of Belgium's Electronic Payment System. His experience as a consultant in monetary matters on four continents ranges from multinational corporations to developing countries.

Bernard co-founded one of the largest and most successful currency management firms, GaiaCorp, and managed an offshore currency fund (Gaia Hedge II) which was the world's top-performing managed currency fund during the period (1987–1991) he ran it. *Business Week* magazine named him "the world's top currency trader" in 1992.

If you have enjoyed *Creating Wealth,*
you might also enjoy other

BOOKS TO BUILD A NEW SOCIETY

Our books provide positive solutions for people who want to
make a difference. We specialize in:

Sustainable Living • Green Building • Peak Oil
Renewable Energy • Environment & Economy
Natural Building & Appropriate Technology
Progressive Leadership • Resistance and Community
Educational & Parenting Resources

New Society Publishers

ENVIRONMENTAL BENEFITS STATEMENT

New Society Publishers has chosen to produce this book on recycled paper made
with **100% post consumer waste,** processed chlorine free, and old growth free.
For every 5,000 books printed, New Society saves the following resources:[1]

29	Trees
2604	Pounds of Solid Waste
2,865	Gallons of Water
3,737	Kilowatt Hours of Electricity
4,734	Pounds of Greenhouse Gases
20	Pounds of HAPs, VOCs, and AOX Combined
7	Cubic Yards of Landfill Space

[1]Environmental benefits are calculated based on research done by the Environmental Defense
Fund and other members of the Paper Task Force who study the environmental impacts of the
paper industry.

For a full list of NSP's titles, please call 1-800-567-6772 *or check out our website* at:

www.newsociety.com

NEW SOCIETY PUBLISHERS